CULTURE, POLITICS, AND NATIONAL IDENTITY IN MEXICAN LITERATURE AND FILM, 1929–1952

Currents in Comparative Romance Languages and Literatures

Tamara Alvarez-Detrell and Michael G. Paulson
General Editors

Vol. 96

PETER LANG
New York • Washington, D.C./Baltimore • Boston • Bern
Frankfurt am Main • Berlin • Brussels • Vienna • Oxford

Anne T. Doremus

CULTURE, POLITICS, AND NATIONAL IDENTITY IN MEXICAN LITERATURE AND FILM, 1929–1952

PETER LANG
New York • Washington, D.C./Baltimore • Boston • Bern
Frankfurt am Main • Berlin • Brussels • Vienna • Oxford

Library of Congress Cataloging-in-Publication Data

Doremus, Anne T.
Culture, politics, and national identity in Mexican literature
and film, 1929–1952 / Anne T. Doremus.
p. cm. — (Currents in comparative Romance languages and literatures; vol. 96)
Includes bibliographical references.
1. Mexican literature—20th century—History and criticism. 2. National
characteristics, Mexican, in literature. 3. Motion pictures—Mexico.
4. National characteristics, Mexican, in motion pictures.
5. Mexico—In motion pictures. I. Title. II. Series.
PQ7155.D67   860.9′358—dc21   99-053210
ISBN 0-8204-4939-3
ISSN 0893-5963

Die Deutsche Bibliothek-CIP-Einheitsaufnahme

Doremus, Anne T.:
Culture, politics, and national identity in Mexican literature
and film, 1929–1952 / Anne T. Doremus.
–New York; Washington, D.C./Baltimore; Boston; Bern;
Frankfurt am Main; Berlin; Brussels; Vienna; Oxford: Lang.
(Currents in comparative Romance languages and literatures; Vol. 96)
ISBN 0-8204-4939-3

The paper in this book meets the guidelines for permanence and durability
of the Committee on Production Guidelines for Book Longevity
of the Council of Library Resources.

© 2001 Peter Lang Publishing, Inc., New York

All rights reserved.
Reprint or reproduction, even partially, in all forms such as microfilm,
xerography, microfiche, microcard, and offset strictly prohibited.

Printed in the United States of America

To my parents
Jeanne and Burton Doremus

and to my husband
Trishul Chilimbi

Table of Contents

Acknowledgments..ix
Note on Translations..xi
Introduction..1

CHAPTER 1
Mexican Culture in the 1920s...18

CHAPTER 2
The Revolutionary and State Consolidation................................30

CHAPTER 3
The Alienation of the Indian and the Integration Process.............56

CHAPTER 4
Nationalism, the Pelado and the Myth of Authenticity................80

CHAPTER 5
The Psyche of the Provincial Mexican.....................................104

CHAPTER 6
Indigenism, Mestizaje and National Identity............................131

CHAPTER 7
The Construction of the Modern Mexican...............................156

Conclusion..182
Glossary...185
Works Cited..187
Index...200

Acknowledgments

I would like to express my deepest gratitude to the following people for their invaluable help and support: Professor Rubén Medina, from the University of Wisconsin at Madison, who read through numerous drafts and offered insightful comments; Professor Guido Podestá, also from the University of Wisconsin at Madison, who provided me with very useful suggestions; my parents, Burton and Jeanne Doremus, who were a constant source of encouragement and support; and above all my husband, Trishul Chilimbi, who spent hours proofreading and editing, and who boosted my morale countless times. Thank you all for your generosity. It was indispensable to the completion of this project.

Note on Translations

All translations of literary works published exclusively in Spanish are mine, including both primary and secondary sources. I used translations of the following works: *Cartucho* and *Las manos de mamá* (*Cartucho* and *My Mother's Hands*), by Nellie Campobello; "La cultura francesa en México" ("French culture in Mexico"), by Jorge Cuesta; *El Indio* (*El indio*) by Gregorio López y Fuentes; *El resplandor* (*Sunburst*), by Mauricio Magdaleno; *Nayar* (*Nayar*), by Miguel Angel Menéndez; *El laberinto de la soledad* (*The Labyrinth of Solitude: Life and Thought in Mexico*), by Octavio Paz; *El perfil del hombre y la cultura en México* (*The Profile of Man and Culture in Mexico*), by Samuel Ramos; *El luto humano* (*Human Mourning*), by José Revueltas; and *Al filo del agua* (*The Edge of the Storm*), by Agustín Yáñez

I am also responsible for all translations of film dialogue.

Introduction

In the decades following the Revolution, specifically from 1929 to 1952, Mexico underwent a period of intense nationalism as the newly emerging state sought to legitimize itself, consolidate its institutions and promote economic growth. As a direct and indirect consequence of this nationalism, these years witnessed an intense search for national self-awareness in the cultural sphere. Responding in part to the identity crisis triggered by the Revolution, many artists and intellectuals set out to define what it meant to be Mexican. They constructed new articulations of national identity that sought both to satisfy the demands of many Mexicans, and to help the state attain the social control it needed to consolidate itself and implement its economic policies. Among the ways they did this was by 1) stressing the notion of a shared or collective identity; 2) compensating for social and economic inequalities and containing social tensions (above all by glorifying the lower classes as the most virtuous and authentic Mexicans); 3) emphasizing character traits important to preparing Mexicans for modernity;[1] and 4) urging Mexicans to gain self-awareness (to avoid losing their identity as a result of cultural incursions from abroad, particularly from the United States).

Mexican society experienced enormous change in 1929. The presidential elections signaled the beginning of a new era in which the state would focus on creating political and economic stability through institution-building. This year also witnessed the complex transformation of caudillismo into the National Revolutionary Party (later renamed the Institutional Revolutionary Party), which has governed the country to this day. It further marked the onset of the Great Depression, which would prompt the Mexican government to direct even greater attention to its unstable economy, and provide a conjuncture for Mexican nationalism. This period would come to a close around 1952, which corresponds to the end of the Miguel Alemán presidency. By then, Mexico's most important institutions had been established, political stability was assured, and economic development, tied to U.S. capitalism, was fully underway. Due to the "developmentalist" focus of the Camacho and Alemán regimes, the economy was also booming. Nationalism subsequently declined, along with studies of "Mexicanness", which had appeared to fulfill their purpose.

Although the search for a national essence peaked from about 1929–1952, its initial impetus was the Revolution (1910–1921), a cataclysmic event that impacted all levels of Mexican society. Amid the economic and political chaos left in the Revolution's wake, the state confronted the problem of having to invent or reconstruct the nation's identity. The political theorist, Lucien Pye, has observed "identity crises arise in all communities when what was once accepted as the collective self is no longer applicable in the face of new historic conditions." (110–111) Constructions of national identity under Porfirio Díaz, which had privileged wealthier Mexicans of primarily Spanish descent, were invalid following the Revolution. Most Mexicans were no longer content with an image of themselves as inferior to and dependent on the wealthy and Europe. They demanded new articulations of national identity that celebrated the rural poor, the Revolution, and those traditions considered authentically Mexican. The state responded by promoting the creation of nationalist myths primarily in the arts—painting, music, film, dance, and literature. The muralist movement, which took shape in the 1920s, became one of the most successful expressions of these efforts. It appealed to the masses by simplifying the armed movement and depicting the peasant and Indian as national heroes or as important actors in the historical process.

Myths of a national identity are crucial in constructing the idea of nation. According to Benedict Anderson, they are what make the "imagined community" possible.[2] Anthony Smith explains that these myths provide "a powerful means of defining and locating individual selves in the world... It is through a shared, unique culture that we are enabled to know 'who we are' in the world. By rediscovering that culture, we 'rediscover' ourselves." (17) Smith adds that national identity enables people to feel they have transcended death by providing a "community of history and destiny", thereby saving them from personal oblivion; it offers personal dignity to those deprived of power by promising a status reversal whereby the last becomes the first; and it provides fraternity by making individuals part of a community or "family." (161–162) Myths in general have enormous appeal because, according to Roland Barthes, they simplify complex human acts, giving them the "simplicity of essences". In his words, myths organize "a world which is without contradictions because it is without depth." (143)

The political elite often uses myths of national identity to maintain social control. Irene O'Malley points out that mythification has played a central role in the official ideology of the Mexican regime and the political culture that supports and is supported by it. (5) Two of the artistic mediums that played major roles in constructing a national consciousness and identity from 1929–1952 were literature—particularly the novel and the essay—and film. The central purpose of this study is to explore the distinct functions that constructions of "Mexicanness" in film and literature served within the nationalist project and the country's modernization during this period. As I will demonstrate, although the dominant articulations of "Mexicanness" in literature and film appeared diametrically opposed to each other, they were actually complementary within the framework of nationalism. Each attempted to influence a distinct sector of Mexican society, but they both ultimately privileged bourgeoisie interests. Together they worked as a sort of two-pronged nationalist strategy, which wasn't devised by the state but rather occurred spontaneously as artists and intellectuals sought to appeal to specific social classes.

Literature did not enjoy a mass audience, as few Mexicans were even literate. Nonetheless, it reached an influential audience consisting of intellectuals and other members of the political and social elite. Constructions of national identity in many literary works reflected and shaped this group's attitudes and behaviors. Above all, they expressed their audience's desire for Mexico to become a modern nation. In accordance with a tradition in which writers have been considered experts on the national problems, they analyzed the Mexican character in order to reveal its flaws. They hoped to bring about the self-awareness and change they believed was necessary for the nation to defend itself against cultural imperialism (especially from the United States) and to compete economically and intellectually with the modern world.

These writers also wished to preserve the privileged status of intellectuals and the socio-economic elite, which was unstable in the Revolution's aftermath. They placated their audience by portraying middle-class and educated Mexicans as the most self-aware and authentic citizens. At the same time, they provided an emotional outlet for their audience's fears and resentments of the poor by portraying underprivileged Mexicans as embodying the most troublesome aspects of the national character. Furthermore, by emphasizing a national identity crisis, and by portraying educated Mexicans as the most capable of tackling it, they stressed intellectuals' importance in the nation-building process.

Literature and other forms of "high" culture also served as sources of national pride and identity, as they were widely perceived as being of high artistic quality.

In contrast, many films and other forms of popular culture attempted to appease the popular classes, and to mold their attitudes and behaviors. They sought to compensate the poor for the lack of true popular representation[3] and the growing economic disparities.[4] Recognizing cinema's enormous potential as an instrument of social control, the state subsidized the film industry once sound was introduced. According to Charles Ramírez Berg, "from 1931 to 1970 the state had subsidized the film industry in one form or another. The state's direct involvement gave it a stake and a say in the nation's cinema and in turn made the industry sensitive to governmental policies and goals." (6) Many films promoted nationalism by instilling a sense of pride, identity and unity in the masses, whom they idealized. They channeled social discontent by offering a number of compensations for social and economic injustices, and by providing catharsis. And they prepared Mexicans for modernity by providing models of conduct.

One of the main ways cinema compensated the poor for their hardships was by comparing them favorably to the wealthy. Film often extolled the lower classes as the most virtuous and authentic Mexicans, while it portrayed the rich as morally and spiritually corrupt. It further portrayed poor Mexicans as more emotionally fulfilled than the wealthy because they cultivate strong familial and community ties. It represented the rich, on the other hand, as incapable of establishing and maintaining such bonds because of their greed and selfishness. As Carlos Monsiváis explains, by repeatedly reinforcing the message that "the poor are always better than the rich," film and other popular art forms ridded the masses "of any vindictive conscience, of any show of just violence." ("Cultura urbana..." 16–17) It defused class tensions and focused attention away from the real economic and political injustices.

Cinema further sought to achieve social containment by providing catharsis. The two major cinematic genres during this period—the melodrama and the comedy—were enormously popular with the audiences, and aided the nationalistic cause by providing an emotional relief from individual and collective anxieties. The melodrama elicited audience approval by appealing to the emotions, which it usually exaggerated, and by simplifying complex social issues so that they appeared easily intelligible. Melodramatic plots usually involved the triumph of good over evil, and the characters, who lacked psychological complexity, were clearly defined as being either heroic or villainous. The heroic characters were frequently symbolic of the "pueblo"—the Mexican masses—, and their struggle against evil forces often connoted social issues of significance to the popular classes. In the family melodrama these issues included "the clash between old (feudal, Porfirian) values and modern (industrialized, urban) life, the crisis of male identity that emerges as a result of this clash, and the instability of female identity that at once guarantees and threatens the passage from the old to the new." (López 153) The epic melodrama dealt almost exclusively with the Revolution. It glorified revolutionary ideals and the masses' participation in the combat, and tried to give meaning to and make sense of the Revolution. The urban melodrama, which arose in the late 1940s, helped to explain to Mexicans the societal changes resulting from modernization, and offered models of conduct to deal with those changes.

The melodrama emphasized social stability and the status quo, dissuading its audience from seeking radical social and economic change. Carlos Monsiváis sustains that the melodrama's sentimentality helped to unify the nation by providing the masses with a sense of belonging. He explains:

> Cinema is a crucial element in the process of national integration. Its importance increases because of its status as intermediary between a victorious state and the masses who, lacking any democratic tradition, find in their sentimental education their most visible source of unity. If political life is denied them, let the laughter ring out and the tears flow instead. If Good Society excludes us, let film, radio, comic books forge a society that will accept us. ("Landscape I've Got the Drop on You!" 239)

Thus while it could be argued that the melodrama humanized the masses and made them feel part of a community, it was also an instrument for their oppression.

While the melodrama elicited tears, the burlesque comedy evoked humor and used parody as a means to defuse social tensions. This type of comedy became immensely popular with the appearance of two comics: Mario Moreno "Cantinflas," whose popularity began in the late 1930's, and Tin Tan, who began appearing in movies in the late 1940's. Both these comics grew out of the popular theatre and represented lower class figures. As a "pelado", Cantinflas exemplified the lower class immigrant to Mexico City, while Tin Tan, a "pachuco," personified the poor Mexicans residing temporarily in the large cities of the Southwestern United States. Cantinflas entertained the audiences with his unusual attire, his parodies of the rich, and his imaginative and nonsensical use of language. Tin Tan arose as a response to growing migration to the United States and the increasing Americanisation of Mexican life. Unlike Cantinflas, he dressed stylishly in a "zoot-suit", and was an expert at dancing and the "pachuco" language (a Spanish/English mix). He aspired to social mobility. Both these figures poked fun at the sources of lower class discontent, without ever threatening the existing socioeconomic order.

As the process of modernization and industrialization gained impetus (particularly in the 1940s), myths of national identity also became increasingly aimed at resolving social tensions produced by swift economic and social transformations. Political theorists concur that the constructs of nation and national identity are critical in a modern era of capitalism, as they create the social cohesion necessary to counteract the fragmentation and disintegration resulting from rapid industrial change. This study aims to underline the critical role that many films played in preparing the masses for modernity. First of all, it will show how cinema helped the masses deal with societal changes by providing them with idealized images of the past. Marshall Bermann observes that people experiencing modernity for the first time may feel that they are the first and only ones to be doing so, and that "this feeling has engendered numerous nostalgic myths of pre-modern Paradise Lost." (15) In particular, the "comedia ranchera", which idealized pre-revolutionary (Porfirian) agrarian Mexico, appears to have fulfilled this function. It dominated not only the Mexican film industry but also the Latin American one in the 1930's and 1940's. The "comedia ranchera" and other films served as an escape valve for many Mexicans who were confused and threatened by the modernization process. These films also reassured their audiences that many of their traditions and values would remain, and taught them which ones these were. They further constructed new codes of behavior that would be crucial in providing a sense of collective identity and ties, in stemming the social decay that can result from rapid modernization, and in facilitating economic growth. Among the characteristics film reinforced were devotion to work and the family, ingenuity, determination, honesty and integrity. Finally, film helped the masses make sense of the societal changes going on around them. Carlos Monsiváis explains:

> In the cinema they learned some of the keys to modern life. The modernization presented in films was superficial, but what was seen helped the audience to understand the changes that affected them; the destruction or abandonment of agricultural life, the decline of customs once considered eternal, the oppressions that come with industrialization. ("Of Myths & Demystifications" 143)

Discourses of national identity in both literature and film were often expressed through recourse to archetypes of the most disaffected members of Mexican society, including the campesino, the urban poor and the Indian. Archetypes are "recurrent patterns in art, literature, film, songs and other artistic endeavors." (Herrera Sobek xiii) They are extremely compelling because they appeal to what the celebrated psychoanalyst, Carl Jung, argued already exists in the psyche. María Herrera Sobek, employing what she terms "feminist archetypal criticism," takes issue with Jung's notion that archetypes are solidified images in the psyche. She argues instead that archetypes are malleable, "depending on historical, political and social forces for their formation." (xiii) My study supports Herrera Sobek's argument by showing how many Mexican artists and intellectuals from 1929 to 1952 constructed archetypes of the poor in order to convey particular ideas about the national identity. These archetypes reflected the values, biases, fears and desires of their creators and promoters, and were used to control and repress the underprivileged while empowering both the state and the privileged classes.

It is important to point out that film included archetypes of the female, which were not nearly as prevalent in literature. In both literature and film, it is almost always the male who embodies "Mexicanness." However, while in literature the female presence is often noticeably lacking, in film she is "represented as a terrain to be traversed in the quest for male identity." (López 152) Many critics have pointed out that Mexican society during this time attempted to limit the female's roles to just two: that of object of desire for the male, and that of mother. These roles corresponded to the figures of "la Malinche," the

Indian woman who supposedly betrayed the nation by submitting to Hernán Cortés, and the "Virgin of Guadalupe", mother and patron saint of Mexico. In other words, film reaffirmed the patriarchal order by exalting machismo and subordinating women to the roles of mother and wife.

In *The Cage of Melancholy* Roger Bartra conducts a similar study to the one undertaken here. However, Bartra views "Mexicanness" as forming part of a long Western tradition in which the construction of a national consciousness has played a major role in securing the hegemony of the dominant political culture. Bartra maintains that the Mexican system has managed to enjoy great political stability while avoiding modern democracy, largely because of the deployment of the nationalist myth. He contends that the myth's power derives from its ability to link the political elite with the masses through the idea of melancholy and metamorphosis. Bartra explains that national culture has created the idea that the Mexican reacts with melancholy to the constant changing or metamorphosis to which society is subjected as a result of mankind's modern need to progress. This idea, which is Western in origin, can be expressed in both "high" culture and "low" culture, and provides a bridge between the elite and the masses: "It is a complex of imaginary networks capable of crossing the frontiers between social classes without giving up its essential attributes." (170) He adds that the melancholy/metamorphosis duality "finds expression in different—very often contradictory—ideological guises, reappearing in a succession of oppositions that belong to different discourses." (170) These oppositions include barbarism versus civilization, countryside versus city, stagnation versus progress, underdevelopment versus development, and so on. "The duality is a powerful solvent of social contradictions as well as a unifying force with a strong adhesive capacity. Its decisive presence is observed in the formulation of national cultures and in the unification of modern states." (170)

While Bartra's observations are extraordinarily insightful, I believe that in his effort to place the construction of a Mexican national consciousness within a larger Western tradition, he ends up focusing almost exclusively on what these constructions have in common, glossing over the differences. Thus he doesn't explain the often very marked differences between articulations of "Mexicanness" in the "high" and the "low" arts, in terms of their possible implications for the nationalist project. Rather, he maintains that it is impossible to separate "popular" culture from "high" culture in analyses of the national identity. Bartra also tends to privilege literature's contribution to the creation of a national identity by maintaining that popular culture recycles the myths created by the "elite" culture. Thus he does not analyze constructions of national identity in popular culture nearly as much as he does those in "high" culture. In other words, he underestimates the enormous contribution film and other forms of "pop" culture made to the construction of a national identity.

I would like to take issue with these assumptions and suggest that from 1929 to 1952 articulations of national identity in the "high" and the "low" arts were usually dissimilar. As I explained earlier, this was a result of the distinct audiences towards which they were directed, and their disparate nationalistic functions. Additionally, despite "high" culture's disparagement of "pop" culture, film has constituted, since its inception, "without a doubt, the most profound influence on the culture of Latin America as a whole, beginning in the 1930s." (Monsiváis "Pop Culture and Literature in Latin America" 10) The film industry thrived between the early 1930s and the early 1950s, experiencing what has been termed a Golden Age. It became the leading film market in Latin America after Hollywood, and one of Mexico's most important industries.[5] Thus despite writers/intellectuals efforts to construct national identity and define Mexican modernity, film impacted a much larger segment of Mexican society. It is essential to study both mediums in order to obtain a holistic understanding of the articulations and functions of national identity during this period.

Organization

Knowledge of Mexican culture during the 1920's is critical to understanding Mexican culture during the succeeding decades. Chapter one is thus devoted to an analysis of the Mexican cultural milieu of the 1920s, including José Vasconcelos's cultural nationalism, the debate between the cultural nationalists and the universalists, writers' and filmmakers' relationship with the state, intellectuals' roles and concerns in Mexican society, and literary and cinematic trends. The following six chapters are divided evenly into two parts, the first of which deals with the period 1929–1940, and the second with the period 1941–1952. This division highlights the distinct purposes articulations of national identity served during those periods. In the 1930s, they were related to the general need to establish unity and order in the aftermath of the

Revolution, while in the 1940s they were increasingly directed towards the goal of modernization. Each of the three chapters within these two parts contrasts articulations of national identity in literature and film as they relate to a specific segment of the population, which the artists often summed up in an archetype. These archetypes include the rural Mexican, the Indian, and the poor urban dweller or "pelado". The goal of each chapter is to reveal the distinct functions that literary works and films fulfilled in the nation-building project.

Chapter two analyzes constructions of the Mexican revolutionary in three novels: *La sombra del caudillo* (1929), by Martín Luis Guzmán, *Vámonos con Pancho Villa* (1931), by Rafael Muñoz, and *Cartucho* (1931), by Nellie Campobello. It also includes the films *Vámonos con Pancho Villa* (1935) and *El compadre Mendoza* (1933), both directed by Fernando de Fuentes. Guzmán and Muñoz depict the Revolutionary peasant in a largely negative light as macho, violent and ignorant. Both writers were appalled at the barbarity of the war, threatened by the masses' increased access to power, and alarmed by the Revolution's implications for the nation's progress. Their works reaffirm the need for intellectuals in the nation-building project. In contrast, Nellie Campobello's *Cartucho* offered a more positive portrayal of the Revolution and the revolutionary fighter. As a woman, Campobello was virtually excluded from participation in the highest levels of politics. While her novel did not receive wide attention during the 1930s, its uniqueness underscores the political interests and motives underlying the other authors' articulations of the war and its combatants.

Contrary to Guzmán's and Muñoz's novels, Fernando de Fuentes's *Vámonos con Pancho Villa* and *El compadre Mendoza* glorify the peasant revolutionary as a somewhat flawed but nevertheless heroic figure who embodies the true revolutionary spirit. By idealizing this figure, these films sought to instill a sense of national community, identity and pride in the rural poor, and to provide models of conduct. They also attempted to give a sense of purpose and meaning to the Revolution, and to rekindle revolutionary ideals. This was essential to ensuring social harmony during a politically unstable time when many revolutionary promises were going unfulfilled.

Chapter three analyzes articulations of the Indian in two novels: *El resplandor* (1937), by Mauricio Magdaleno and *El indio* (1935), by Gregorio López y Fuentes. It also includes the films *Janitzio* (1934), directed by Carlos Navarro, and *El indio* (1938), directed by Armando

Vargas de la Maza. The novels emphasize the Revolution's destructive impact on the native population. For this reason, they are widely considered as forming part of the repertory of novels on the Revolution. Since its inception during the 1930s, the Mexican indigenist novel has supported the government's integrationist politics. In *El indio* and *El resplandor*, Magdaleno and López y Fuentes pinpoint the barriers to the native people's integration into mainstream life. They conclude that the Revolution has not benefited the Indians, despite the native people's participation in the fighting. In their view, corrupt politicians, landowners and the Church conspire to exploit Indian labor, while the mestizo population at large verbally mistreats this group and invades their lands. As a consequence, the Indians are becoming increasingly alienated from mainstream society, and pose a physical threat. López y Fuentes and Magdaleno emphasize the need for a new national consciousness based on respect for the indigenous people.

Only a few films on the Indian were produced during the 1930s, and none achieved wide success. Film romanticized the Indian as a noble being whose peaceful coexistence with nature is shattered by outsiders who attempt to exploit him. By implicitly associating the experiences and qualities of the Indians with those of the lower classes, it attempted to bridge racial divisions and foster pride in the Indian. However, cinema misrepresented the causes of the Indian's marginalization, attributing them to the abuses of a few individuals rather than to widespread racism and governmental neglect. Constructions of the Indian in these films may have promoted nationalism, but they probably did little to help combat the real problems facing the Indians.

Chapter four analyzes articulations of the urban poor (summed up in the archetype of the "pelado," the poor urban immigrant), and discusses the general debate between cultural nationalists and universalists about articulations of the national character. It includes Samuel Ramos's *El perfil del hombre y la cultura en México* (1934), various essays by Jorge Cuesta, Rodolfo Usigli's play *El gesticulador* (1937) and Arcady Boytler's film *Allí Está el Detalle* (1937). The writers set about identifying obstructions to the nation's progress towards modernity, and focused on "inauthenticity" as the main problem. Ramos, whose work significantly influenced others on "Mexicanness" to follow, employed the archetype of the "pelado" in order to point out the most severe national psychoses, including an inferiority complex. Cuesta and Usigli were more concerned with "inauthenticity" as it manifested itself in politics. They portrayed politicians as hypocritical, immoral and ignorant, and denounced them for promoting cultural nationalism. Cuesta argued that cultural nationalism led to works of inferior artistic value, a result of making art a function of politics. All these writers' agreed that by romanticizing the national character, cultural nationalism provided Mexicans with a mask they could use to hide from their real selves.

Contrary to these works, film in general continued to idealize the lower class Mexican. During the 1930's, cinema also tended to avoid dealing with urban life directly. Nonetheless, in 1940 the film *Allí está el detalle* marked Mario Moreno's ("Cantinflas") rise to fame. This and other "Cantinflas" films were to offer an image of the pelado that was very different from that of the literary works. They depicted him as likable, funny and harmless. The "Cantinflas" films were important not because they taught Mexicans lessons about urban life. Rather, they aimed primarily at the containment of social tensions by allowing the poor to parody the rich, who are often depicted as lascivious, greedy, selfish and hypocritical.

Chapters five through seven reexamine the archetypes analyzed in chapters two through four, but in the context of the 1940s. With respect to literary changes, the novel in the 1940's turned away from the outward manifestations of the national character to examine more closely the Mexican psychology. This may have been a result of changing times; the Revolution was fading into the past, and Mexico had entered into a period of political and economic stability with the Camacho and Alemán presidencies. Furthermore, beginning in 1937, articles began to appear in Mexican magazines that reproached the Mexican novel for not going beyond the surface, the anecdotal or the picturesque. They blamed novelists for either practicing a "false nationalism" or for lacking creativity. (Dessau 447) Writers were also probably responding to post World War II existentialism, and Ramos's famous essay, *El perfil del hombre y la cultura en México*. The new focus on the Mexican ontology is reflected in the point of view, which became primarily first person rather than third, and the extensive use of interior monologue and stream of consciousness.

Film likewise responded to societal changes. In the 1930's, the predominant film genres were the revolutionary and family melodramas and, above all, the "comedia ranchera". They all reinforced traditional Mexican values, including patriarchy, capitalism, "machismo", heterosexuality and Catholicism. In fact, the "comedia ranchera", which not only dominated the film market in Mexico but all over Latin America as well, idealized ranch life during Porfirian times. While these films continued to enjoy huge popularity in the 1940s, this decade also witnessed the rise of numerous films dealing with urban life, a response to mass migration to the capital. These included the immensely popular comedies based on the figure of the "pelado" Cantinflas and the "pachuco" Tin Tan, the cabaretera films, which focused on the prostitute and night-life, and a host of others.

Chapter five deals with constructions of the rural inhabitant in the novels *Al filo del agua* (1947), by Agustín Yáñez, and *El luto humano* (1943), by José Revueltas. It also includes the films *Los tres García* (1946), directed by Ismael Rodríguez, and *Enamorada* (1947), directed by Emilio Fernández. *Al filo del agua* studies the repressed mentality of the inhabitants of a small village in Jalisco, and the Revolution's impact on it. Yáñez views the Revolution favorably as ushering in a new era of progress. His interpretation of the Revolution reflects his interest in forging a modern Mexico. José Revueltas's *El luto humano* (1943) likewise attempts to uncover the destructive forces at work in the Mexican psyche by penetrating the thoughts and actions of a small group of campesinos destined to die in a flood. However, contrary to Yañez, Revueltas opposed the state, and wished to emphasize in this work capitalism's ravaging psychological and social effects. His novel depicts socialism as the best solution to poverty and despair. Interestingly, in his efforts to debunk capitalism and promote socialism, he engages in the same sort of myth making of the national character that Yáñez does. Both these novels reveal the ways in which some prominent writers constructed myths of the national character in their literary works as a means of supporting and promoting their political views.

In contrast to Yañez's and Revueltas's novels, *Los tres García*, a "comedia ranchera," and *Enamorada*, a revolutionary melodrama, idealize rural life. Besides constituting an escape from urban life, the popularity of *Los tres García* and the "comedia ranchera" in general seemed to reflect Mexicans' concerns about the loss of traditions and values resulting from modernization and industrialization. By glorifying many of those traditions and values, and making them inherent to national identity, they both reassured Mexicans and reinforced national unity. Furthermore, although they dealt with rural life in the late 1800s, these films conveyed the values and codes of behavior that would be important in a modern society. These included respect and obedience to authority, the importance of the family and the Church, and the primacy of the patriarchal order. *Enamorada* also inspired hope for social equality and justice, and sought to create class alliances by showing a new generation of wealthy Mexicans to be sympathetic to the revolutionary cause.

Chapter six focuses on articulations of the Indian and the mestizo in essays by Agustín Yáñez, Héctor Pérez Martínez and Luis Villoro, in the novel *Nayar* (1941), by Miguel Angel Menéndez, and in the movie *María Candelaria* (1943), directed by Emilio Fernández. The 1940s initiated a new direction in indigenism, in which priority was placed on mestizaje. While anthropologists such as Manuel Gamio and Alfonso Caso took concrete measures to mesticize the Indian, other artists and intellectuals set about trying to understand the reasons for the mestizo's denigration of the Indian. They identified the mestizo's mixed Spanish/Indian heritage as the root cause. They argued that these two heritages were at war within the mestizo psyche, and that the former was winning. By providing the mestizo with self-awareness, and by pointing out some positive aspects of indigenous culture, they hoped to prompt the mestizo's appreciation and acceptance of the Indian. They also hoped to make the mestizo more psychologically stable and secure.

Like the 1930's films on the Indian, *María Candelaria* attempted to inspire respect for native Mexicans by idealizing the film's protagonists as the most authentic and morally upright Mexicans. It further sought to identify the audience with the Indian by stressing shared characteristics and experiences. Some of the same traits that the film ascribes to its Indian protagonists were those that other nationalistic films had attributed to the popular classes. These included integrity, loyalty and dignity. The audience could also identify with the protagonists' victimization by the more powerful. However, in some ways the film undermined its objectives of inspiring pride in and identification with the Indian, and also failed to examine the real reasons for the Indian's isolation and poverty.

Chapter seven focuses on the attempts of some essayists and filmmakers to construct a modern national subject. This chapter examines works by Emilio Uranga and Leopoldo Zea, Octavio Paz's *El laberinto de la soledad* (1950), and the films *Nosotros los pobres* (1947), directed by Ismael Rodríguez, and *Los olvidados* (1950), directed by Luis Buñuel. The essayists inspired themselves in Ramos's work, trying to arrive at a definition of the Mexican and save the philosopher's work from being trivialized: "Samuel Ramos's ideas became vulgarized, converting themselves into the common place, into the insistences of the mass media." (Monsiváis *Historia general de México* 407) The essayists were eager to assert Mexico as a modern nation that could compete with and defend itself against other nations (particularly the United States). Thus like their predecessors of the 1930's (Ramos, Cuesta and Usigli), they were concerned with identifying traits they believed would be detrimental to the construction of a modern nation. However, unlike their predecessors, they viewed certain so called traits of the Mexican positively, including his solitary, reflective nature. In fact, against what they considered to be the increasing dehumanization of the modern world caused by technology, they believed that the Mexican offered a model from which to develop a new universal humanism.

In contrast to literature, many films in the 1940s focused on the poor urban masses, attempting to instill in them a sense of pride and honor and teach them how to behave in a modern society and cope with rapid societal changes. One of the most popular films of this type was *Nosotros los pobres*. This film romanticized the poor as morally superior to and ultimately more content than the wealthy. It also provided a model of conduct through the hero, "Pepe el toro" (played by a famous and charismatic singer-actor, Pedro Infante), portrayed as a prototypical urban male inhabitant. In stark contrast to *Nosotros los pobres*, *Los olvidados* took a hard look at the realities of poverty. Devoid of melodrama and critical of the modernization process and the state, this film was unpopular with the Mexican audience during its time (although it achieved international fame), and only gained wide recognition much later. It's unpopularity owed itself to the melodrama's huge influence. Film viewers as a whole rejected unpleasant images of themselves and their lives in cinema, preferring the romanticized ones that most filmmakers were eagerly providing.

Repeatedly throughout the period 1929 to 1952, many literary works constructed images of national identity that sharply contrasted with those being projected in numerous films. While contradictory in and of themselves, these opposing images made sense within the context of nationalism. They reflected and shaped the interests and desires of the political and social elite in much of literature, and the interests and desires of the popular classes in much of film. However, film ultimately thwarted the authors' goals of constructing a modern Mexico. While many writers/intellectuals called for Mexicans (especially poorer ones) to recognize their character deficiencies in order to thereby change, film idealized the lower classes. Frustrated, many writers/intellectuals spoke out against what they viewed as the false and simplistic notions of national identity that were being disseminated in the popular arts, and above all in film. Nevertheless, film was to reach a much wider audience and exert a much greater influence over most Mexicans as compared to literature. Despite literature's pretensions, film and the masses of Mexicans in general constructed the predominant view of national identity and modernity.

Notes

1. "Modernity" refers to the experience of living in a society characterized by rapid change. It is brought about by "modernization", the process that includes the industrialization of production, technological and scientific discoveries and urbanization. "Modernity", however, is a hotly contested term. For varying points of view, see Marshall Bermann's *All That is Solid Melts into Air: the Experience of Modernity* (New York: Simon and Schuster, 1982) and Perry Anderson's "Modernity and Revolution" (*New Left Review* 144 (1984): 96–113).
2. Anderson sustains in *Imagined Communities* that the nation is an imagined construct because "the smallest nation will never know most of their fellow-members, meet them, or even hear of them, yet in the minds of each lives the image of their communion." (6)
3. Since the Revolution, Mexico has had a one-party political system. In order to help avert political unrest, the government has organized potentially disruptive elements of the population (i.e. workers and campesinos) into such groups as the Confederation of Mexican Workers and the National Campesino Confederation, which it controls.
4. The distribution of wealth became increasingly uneven beginning in 1940, the year that is widely considered to mark the beginning of what has been termed the Mexican economic "miracle." Roger D. Hansen states in *The Politics of Mexican Development* that "during the 1940s income distribution in Mexico was characterized by (1) rapidly rising entrepreneurial incomes, (2) slowly rising *per capita* wage and salary earnings, and (3) a fall in real wage rates. The result was an increasingly unequal distribution of income accompanied by a slow rise in the general standard of living." (72)
5. According to John King, in 1938 the film industry was the country's second largest after oil. (47)

Chapter One

Mexican Culture in the 1920s

Many of the patterns of cultural life in the 1930s and the 1940s had their roots in the 1920s and before. For example, it was during the 1920s that art, under José Vasconcelos, began to play a primary role in nationalism. This provoked a controversy among artists, as some reacted against the use of art for political and social purposes. Thus began the debate between the "cultural nationalists," who favored art's use as a pedagogical and aesthetic tool directed at the masses, and the "universalists" who opposed it. This debate prevailed through the 1930s and the 1940s. Notwithstanding their disagreements, both the cultural nationalists and the universalists were highly involved in politics during the 1920s, whether through their art or other means, and most supported the state. This trend continued through the 1930s and the 1940s and, as we will see, could largely be attributed to such factors as economic necessity, a long tradition of close involvement with politics and the state (particularly in the case of the writers), and the state's intolerance for opposition.

The concepts of national identity that developed in literature and film during the 1930s and the 1940s also had their roots in the 1920s and before. National identity was a major topic for writers during the 1920s. Intellectual giants such as José Vasconcelos, Antonio Caso and Alfonso Reyes directed much of their writing towards understanding the national character and problems, considerably influencing writers in the decades to follow. The film industry was weak in the 1920s as a result of fierce competition from Hollywood. However, the main elements of what was to become a flourishing industry in the 1930s and 1940s also existed by 1920. These included the predominance of the melodrama and the comedy, the two genres that became particularly influential in constructing a concept of national identity for the masses.

Vasconcelos and Cultural Nationalism

The 1920s were dominated by José Vasconcelos who, as Secretary of Public Education under Álvaro Obregón from 1920 to 1924, led the government's efforts to assimilate the disenfranchised into national life by launching a massive campaign (known as cultural nationalism) to educate the rural poor. With Obregón's financial support, Vasconcelos vastly improved Mexico's educational system by building schools, hiring more teachers and raising their salaries, opening libraries and publishing newspapers and books. Between 1921 and 1923 he increased by almost 50% the number of buildings, teachers and students of official primary schools. (Blanco 91) Furthermore, he began a cultural renaissance by promoting the arts. Vasconcelos envisioned artists and writers as performing a messianic function. He thus lent financial support to artists who incorporated nationalistic themes in their works, and sponsored visits from foreign artists, particularly those from Latin America. For example, Gabriela Mistral, who served as a role model for female elementary school teachers, helped to give women a function in the nation's political and social life for the first time.

One of Vasconcelos's greatest successes was the promotion of muralism. He provided muralists (such as Diego Rivera, David Alfaro Siqueiros and José Clemente Orozco) with materials, the walls of public buildings, and subjects. Muralism became hugely successful both within and outside of Mexico. Its success was due in large part to the fact that it was accessible to the masses. Its themes—the Revolution, agrarian reform, Yankee imperialism, indigenous and popular culture—also appealed to the poor. The artists, who in 1923 became known as the "Mexican School", firmly believed that art should fulfill a social function. They perceived their own role as that of educating the public and of instilling a sense of ethnic and national pride. Hence they not only used exclusively national themes, but also turned to the forms and colors of pre-Columbian artwork for their inspiration. The scenes that emerged were larger than life, attributing heroic, mythological qualities to Mexicans and their past. For example, on the walls surrounding the stairwell of the Palacio Nacional, Diego Rivera, Mexico's most renowned muralist, painted a vast epic of Mexican history that glorified the country's Aztec heritage.

Despite its enormous success, muralism was not without its critics, and in fact a new group of painters arose in the late 1920's that reacted against the narrowly nationalistic perspective of muralism. The most famous of these artists, Rufino Tamayo, firmly rejected the social realism of the muralist movement and sought to create a 'pure' art, one that was free from ideology. Strongly influenced by modernist European art, Tamayo's art appealed to the poetic, subjective and personal experience. However, he infused his art with elements taken from modern Mexican artists, the folk arts and pre-Colombian sculpture. In particular, his use of indigenous elements of form make his art uniquely Mexican.

The muralists' nationalistic fervor was matched in music by works by Silvestre Revueltas and, most notably, Carlos Chávez. While their works were clearly original, and while they also brought in the new North American and European music to Mexico, these musicians borrowed melodies, themes and even instruments from Mexican popular and folk music. Like the muralists, they sought to evoke the true essence of Mexico in their work, although according to Otto Mayer-Serra, in different ways. Revueltas "was attracted to the present day Mexico of the festive markets, the burlesque and sad atmosphere of the 'carpas', the tumultuous sounds of the street crowds, the lively and loud colors, the people and the landscape, and the songs and music of the current generations." To him, "'lo mexicano' manifested itself as authentically in the vestiges of the primitive cultures... as in the surprising outcomes of the mixture of distinct races and civilizations." Chávez, on the other hand, was inspired by indigenous music and hoped to "reconstruct musically this atmosphere of primitive purity, hoping to find in it the 'true' Mexican character." (165) Revueltas and Chávez worked together at the Orquesta Sinfónica de México (OSM), the former as assistant conductor and the latter as conductor, hoping to bring about a renaissance in Mexican music. The creation of the OSM itself, in 1928, was particularly important in the musical life of Mexico. This organization, along with Carlos Chávez, played an essential role in the diffusion of art music from its birth to about 1950, actually setting the pattern of music life during this period. (Malmstrom 95)

Cultural Nationalism and Universalism

Not all artists were supportive of Vasconcelos's cultural nationalism. Beginning in the 1920s, and extending into the following decades, a polemic arose between the "cultural nationalists" and the "universalists." It centered on the articulation of national identity and the role of politics in art. The "cultural nationalists" tended to exalt the virtues of the lower classes, portraying this group as national heroes and symbols of national identity. They attacked the "universalists" for either excluding political and social concerns from their works altogether, or for failing to present the Mexican national character in a favorable light. The "universalists," on the other hand, opposed the cultural nationalists' use of art as political propaganda, and/or rejected that group's idealistic portrayal of national identity. They contended that the cultural nationalists were obstructing the process of self-awareness by idealizing the national character. They argued that cultural nationalism led to works of inferior artistic quality, and also promoted a false nationalism.

The universalists believed that any genuine philosophy reflects universal values and not strictly national ones. However, their emphasis on the universal also expressed their desire for Mexico to compete culturally and intellectually with modern nations such as Europe, whose philosophies transcended national boundaries. They believed that in order for Mexico to compete with Europe, it must create a philosophy that held meaning for all of mankind, and not just for Mexicans.

Importantly, neither the cultural nationalists nor the universalists objected to nationalism as a state project. Rather, the controversy centered on the forms (if any) it would take in the "high" arts. While many of the "universalists" wished "high" art to remain free from politics, they did not hesitate to promote cultural nationalism in other ways. The most important example of such artists were the Contemporáneos, a group of poets who in the 1920's practiced a modernist form of art. The Contemporáneos were instrumental in Vasconcelos's educational campaigns, and became well-known precisely through state patronage (principally through José de Vasconcelos, Bernardo Gastélum and Genaro Estrada). It is important to understand their relationship with the state, as it was modeled by many of Mexico's most renowned writers of the following decades.

Most of these poets were born between 1899 and 1904 and attended the Escuela Preparatoria (Preparatory School) together while Vasconcelos was director. Vasconcelos later recruited them when he became Minister of Education:

> Vasconcelos...continued the largest editorial campaign in the continent's history. That meant work for writers, translators, editors. Furthermore, he decided to found (in April of 1921) the first literary-technical-pedagogical-

> humanist review of long print-run: *El Maestro*... Against the 300 copies of *México Moderno*, Vasconcelos's review copied 75,000... The members of the new Ateneo, in spite of everything, decided to climb onto this editorial train. (Sheridan 102)

Because of their participation in *El maestro*, as well as their work on *México moderno* and *El universal ilustrado*, by the middle of 1921 the Contemporáneos had been drawn into the public eye and known as "the men in charge of the distribution of cultural power." (Sheridan 103) But they were affiliated with the state in many other ways as well. Besides financing their publications, the state employed them in numerous capacities. For example, Pellicer participated in Vasconcelos's literacy campaign, and both he and Julio Torri were employed as Vasconcelos's private secretaries. Through Torri the Contemporáneos collaborated on a number of publications.[1] Ortiz de Montellano became the librarian of SEP (Secretariat of Public Education) minister Estrada, while Torres Bodet and Gorostiza entered into diplomatic careers in Europe. Their collaboration with the state, in particular through Vasconcelos:

> was the best way of earning a living and gaining prestige. These jobs permitted an extraordinary capacity for movement, trips and dispensations; they enabled the efficient establishment of contact with artists, writers and editors; they cultivated advantageous influences with the institutions of superior education and, of course, permitted them to earn a decent living. (Sheridan 126)

Besides helping to advance government-sponsored educational programs, the Contemporáneos performed other important functions for the state. For example, they were highly gifted writers in whose works Mexicans could take pride. Even more importantly, they enabled wealthier and more educated Mexicans to feel they were leading a "modern" life-style. In other words, they appeased a small but influential group of Mexicans who resented the overwhelming importance placed on the return to a purely native culture, and who wished to experience European culture. The Contemporáneos kept current with European (particularly French) artistic and philosophical tendencies by reading the major reviews (including *Revista de occidente*, founded in Spain in 1923 by Ortega y Gasset) and traveling extensively through Europe. They also "give life to avant-garde reviews, grant great social value to criticism, do experimental theater, found film clubs, circulate post-impressionist European painting, support art galleries, believe compulsively in 'lo moderno.'" (Monsiváis, "No con un sollozo..." 722) In other words, they helped enable the Mexican elite to feel that they were on an intellectual and cultural par with Europeans.

Writers, Filmmakers and the State

As evident in the case of the Contemporáneos, writers benefited from their close relationship with the state. They gained an income they would not have been able to had they tried to survive on their art alone, given the small reading public at the time. They also gained access to political positions. The majority of Mexico's most renowned authors during the first part of this century were deeply involved in politics, and many held positions of substantial political power. Filmmakers, on the other hand, became linked to the nationalist project primarily through state subsidization.

Despite the tradition of intellectual involvement in politics, the status of writers/intellectuals in the Revolution's chaotic aftermath was precarious. Under Porfirio Díaz, writers and other intellectuals had enjoyed unprecedented esteem and privilege, occupying the highest political posts. The Revolution, a popular uprising that witnessed the lower classes' rise to power, threatened to displace them. Much of the literature of "Mexicanness" in the 1930's seems directed at least in part at assuring intellectuals a place within the newly forming state. By emphasizing the many problems with the national character, they were at the same time underscoring Mexico's need for educated men like themselves. During the 1940's, their situation was less precarious, as disciplines within the social sciences became institutionalized.

Another major reason why many writers and filmmakers promoted nationalism was that it favored the political and economic interests of the middle-class. Most of these artists were of middle-class background, and supported the interests of that socioeconomic group. Nationalism benefited the middle-class by helping to produce the political stability and support necessary for the state to implement economic policies designed to set the nation on the course of (more or less) classical capitalism. Frantz Fanon observes in *The Wretched of the Earth* that the bourgeoisie in underdeveloped countries often manipulates the national consciousness. Alienated from the masses, this group perceives its mission not as transforming the nation but rather "of being the transmission line between the nation and a capitalism, rampant though camouflaged, which today puts on the mask of neo-colonialism." (152–

153) Applied to Mexico during the 1920s through the 1950s, Fanon's observations help to explain why the state apparatus that emerged in the wake of the Revolution—a colossal *popular* uprising—ultimately privileged *bourgeoisie* interests.

Besides sharing similar socioeconomic backgrounds, intellectuals tended to be educated in the same institutions, and to reside in Mexico City. This helps to further explain their similar goals and interests. In his study on intellectuals and the state in Mexico, Roderic Camp found that almost all intellectuals in Mexico during the twentieth century (at least up to 1985 when his study was concluded) have come from the middle and upper socioeconomic classes. "Almost no intellectuals who come from lower socioeconomic backgrounds reach a recognized position in the intellectual community." (86) Furthermore, prominent Mexican intellectuals were overwhelmingly educated in two places: the National Preparatory School and the National University, both located in Mexico City. Here friendship networks could be developed that might prove useful to the advancement of political careers, and recruiting could be done for positions within the government. Finally, intellectuals tended to reside in Mexico City, where the federal government was based. (Camp 79–92) Intellectual activity thus continued to be centralized in the nation's capital.

This of course does not mean that all Mexican writers and other intellectuals allied themselves with the state, nor that those who did never expressed dismay at state policies with which they disagreed. However, the state took measures to keep dissent in check. One notable intellectual who strongly opposed the state, the Marxist writer José Revueltas, was jailed three times, tortured, and threatened with death. To his immense credit, he continued to pursue his political activities and his writing, which was not recognized until much later in his life. The case of José Vasconcelos provided another ominous example of what could happen if intellectuals pursued a course contrary to the state's interest. The former Secretary of Public Education was the only opposition candidate for the 1929 presidential elections who was initially tolerated by the forces in power. However, his accusations of political corruption and the perversion of the Revolution, along with his widespread support, primarily from young intellectuals and the urban middle classes, proved to be too big a threat. "His triumphal tour took on the glamour of a plebiscite and was so successful that the authorities resorted to all available means against him." (Meyer 169) Following his defeat in the elections, Vasconcelos and his followers accused the government of fraud, and made an appeal to arms. However, the army was solidly behind the government, and Vasconcelos was forced to escape abroad. He subsequently fell into obscurity.

As I will attempt to make clear in this work, an analysis of constructions of "Mexicanness" as they appear in many novels and essays from 1929–1952 reveals the large extent to which the majority of intellectuals aligned themselves with the state. Since the period of independence, the Latin American intellectual has fulfilled an important function for the state. Casting himself as the "maestro," or voice of authority, he has expounded on the most serious national problems, principally through the novel and the essay. He has concerned himself above all with specifying the nation's uniqueness in the face of the overwhelming presence of Europe and the United States, and with forging a modern national character that could rival those powers.

"Mexicanness" in Literature

It is important to point out that writer/intellectual activity in the 1920s established the model for subsequent decades, both in terms of writers' relationship to the state and their approach to the topic of national identity. Literature, in particular the essay, constituted a major medium for advancing ideas on nationalism and national identity during this decade. Among the most highly regarded authors of "Mexicanness" were José Vasconcelos, Antonio Caso and Alfonso Reyes, all of whom formed part of "a new breed of intellectuals, public men who rose to prominence through their creative abilities and government service." (Schmidt 117) Their dual role as writers and public servants would be emulated by many writer/intellectuals of subsequent generations. Their philosophical and critical approach to the question of national identity, and several of their ideas on this topic, also inspired many writers of "Mexicanness" to follow.

Vasconcelos, Caso and Reyes deviated from many artists of the period by taking a critical stance towards the national character. They stressed the urgency of gaining self-awareness as a means of counteracting foreign invasions of Mexican culture. Their concern was thus not so much on fomenting national unity through an idealization of the masses (although Vasconcelos also did this through his promotion of cultural nationalism), but rather on constructing a national character that could withstand cultural imperialism. They were particularly concerned with the United States, whose looming presence and expanding power were viewed as threats to Mexico's cultural independence.

To these three intellectuals, gaining self-awareness required that Mexicans become more aware of their own internal conditions. In their opinion, this entailed a rejection of imported models, which they maintained had alienated the Mexican from his "true" self and, in Reyes' view (presaging Samuel Ramos), caused an inferiority complex. However, they did not exalt Mexicans' indigenous inheritance as the most "authentic", but rather viewed the national character as a product of both internal and external factors.

These writers endeavored to help the Mexicans become self-aware by pointing up character defects. However, while they were often critical of the national character, they tended to view the future of Mexican man positively. For example, in *La raza cósmica* (1925), Vasconcelos (who related his concept of "Mexicanness" to the more general one of Latin American identity) envisioned Latin America as the birthplace of a fifth race, constituted from racial mingling, which would substitute a decaying Europe as world leader. His focus on mestizaje, and his idea of a "new humanism" originating in Latin America, would greatly influence future essayists of "Mexicanness."

Cinema

Unlike other art forms, cinema did not play a significant role in the promotion of cultural nationalism during the 1920s. Although the state promoted films through the Ministries of War and Marines, Education and Agriculture and Development, Vasconcelos "neither sponsored nor stimulated producers to develop narrative films." (De los Reyes 76–77) This might seem odd considering film's enormous potential as a propaganda tool. Carl Mora explains that the state, which was focused on combating widespread illiteracy and raising Mexicans' self-esteem, did not perceive a role for cinema in these enterprises. He adds that it would have been extremely difficult for the state to subsidize film anyway, given its limited budget. (25)

Cinema, which had its start in 1896 with the first public film screening, enjoyed success up until about 1920, when it began to languish. Film production declined from 14 films in 1919 to two films in 1923 and none in 1924. (Mora 22) This dismal performance continued throughout the rest of the 1920s. Although producers blamed the state for its lack of support, the real reason for cinema's decline was its inability to compete with Hollywood, which by the 1920s had established an enormous industry with international influence. A sign of Hollywood's huge presence in Mexico was the 1919 establishment of several U.S. production companies in Mexico City, including International Films, Fox Film and Universal Film.

US dominance in cinema went unchallenged in Mexico until the late 1920s, when sound was introduced. At this time, Hollywood began to produce low-quality Hispanic films for the Latin American market that proved unsuccessful because they failed to address the linguistic and cultural specificities of the Latin American audience. Providing what these Hollywood films lacked, the first sound film produced in Mexico—*Santa* (1931)—, met with surprising success. The Mexican film industry subsequently boomed.

Despite cinema's poor performance during the 1920s, the cinematic genres and themes that appeared repeatedly throughout the 1930s and 1940s had already been established by 1920. Perhaps most importantly, fiction films replaced the documentary films that predominated during the early years of cinema. This was a consequence of moral and political censorship during the Adolfo de la Huerta regime, which ended filmmakers' goals of documenting reality and informing the public. Film thenceforth avoided dealing with social and political issues, including those related to the Revolution, agrarian reform, poverty and illiteracy. Instead, it focused on producing melodramas. The theme of impossible love was the most popular, and religious and historical melodramas also predominated. (De los Reyes 71–72)

The seeds of what blossomed into the very popular comedy films of the late 1930s and the 1940s were present in theatre rather than cinema prior to 1920. Following the onset of the Revolution, the *género chico* began to gain popularity among the lower classes. These short plays were performed in *carpas*, or tent shows, and featured popular themes and characters, including "gendarmes with hanging mustaches, pulque parlor drunks, unrequited lovers, clownish ranchers, Spanish tavern owners, *peladitos*, Indians from Xochimilco, 'outsiders.'" (Mora 12–13) The *carpas* poked fun at Mexican authorities and at the lower classes, enabling the audiences to laugh at themselves and at those in power. Mario Moreno "Cantinflas," a "pelado" (poor, urban dweller of indigenous descent) from the Mexico City slums, was among those performers who attained tremendous success in cinema. "Cantinflas" easily survived the transfer from theatre to film, perhaps because film in many ways assumed the social function that the *carpas* had previously fulfilled—that of catharsis for societal tensions.

In conclusion, many filmmakers and writers of the 1930s and the 1940s continued the work on national identity begun by their predecessors of the 1920s. On the one hand, many writers of the 1930s and the 1940s, particularly novelists and essayists, patterned their work after the intellectual giants of the 1920s—Vasconcelos, Reyes and Caso—by analyzing the problems with the national character. They continued to concern themselves with constructing a national identity that could withstand foreign cultural incursions into Mexico. On the other hand, many films in the 1930s and the 1940s idealized the Mexican identity, reflecting the work of the cultural nationalists. These films promoted national unity and pride among the masses. They assumed the additional function of providing an outlet for social discontent, and of channeling that discontent in ways that were non-threatening to the social and political order. However, in contrast to the 1920s, the 1930s and the 1940s posed new challenges to writers and filmmakers concerned with national identity. In particular, as national unity and political stability became more secure, the state increasingly focused on promoting economic growth through industrialization. Writers and filmmakers throughout the 1930s and the 1940s increasingly reflected the state's interest in constructing a national character suitable to a more modern, urban Mexico.

Notes

1. José Gorostiza collaborated on the review *El maestro*, Torres Bodet directed *El libro y el pueblo*, and Novo, Villaurrutia and Ortiz de Montellano worked on the two volumes of *Lectures classiques pour l'enfant*. As the Secretary of Public Education (SEP), Ortiz de Montellano founded *La falange. revista de cultura latina* (1922–1923), Novo published the art review *Forma*, Villaurrutia and Novo directed *Ulises* (financed by Gastelum in 1927), and Torres Bodet founded and directed *Contemporáneos* (also financed by Gastelum in 1928 and later by Estrada).

Chapter Two

The Revolutionary and State Consolidation

With the Revolution still looming in the recent past, national identity during the Maximato (1929–1935) continued to be expressed through the archetype of the revolutionary. In novels such as Martín Luis Guzmán's *La sombra del caudillo* (*In the Shadow of the Caudillo*) and Rafael Muñoz's *Vámonos con Pancho Villa* (*Let's Go with Pancho Villa*), the revolutionary fighter is violent, immoral and ignorant. Such a depiction had predominated in novels of this type since Mariano Azuela's *Los de abajo* (1915), widely considered a founding work. One exception to this articulation was Nellie Campobellos's *Cartucho*, which portrayed the Revolution and the revolutionary fighter in a much more positive light. However, this work was not widely read during the period. Guzmán's and Muñoz's novels appeased many intellectuals and wealthier Mexicans, who were unable to relate to the violence and chaos of the Revolution, and who feared the masses' increased access to power following the war. Moreover, by underscoring the ignorance of the masses (as embodied by the revolutionary), and the troubled state of the national soul, these writers were establishing the need for educated men like themselves in the nation-building process.

In contrast, films such as *El compadre Mendoza* and *Vámonos con Pancho Villa*, both of which were directed by Fernando de Fuentes, paint a much more favorable picture of the revolutionary, despite being influenced to some degree by the novel. Partially funded by the state, this medium sought to attain audience identification with the revolutionary, a heroic figure who embodied the Mexican "pueblo". Through the revolutionary, film sought to fortify Mexicans' sense of national identity, pride and belonging to a community, to establish models of conduct that would help to ensure social harmony, and to compensate for unfulfilled revolutionary ideals (above all by depicting the peasant as a national hero). It also rekindled hopes for social equality and justice.

The Barbaric Revolutionary

In literature, the genre that dealt most with the national ego during this period was the novel, specifically the novel of the Mexican Revolution, which was considered "a model in the description of the national problems." (Dessau 11) The late 1920's and 1930's witnessed an outburst of these works, and constitutes this literature's apex. Critics disagree about which works begin and end the novel of the Revolution. They almost unanimously agree on *Los de abajo* (1915) as the first major work of this type, but are at great variance with respect to the last. For example, Max Aub argues that *Pedro Páramo* (1955), by Juan Rulfo, concludes the novel of the Revolution, while Adalbert Dessau identifies *Al filo del agua* (1947) by Agustín Yáñez and *Esa sangre* (1956) by Mariano Azuela as the last of such novels. Categorization also varies greatly. Some critics divide this novel in terms of its focus: life prior to the outbreak of violence, the armed struggle and way of life of the revolutionaries, the fight for land by the campesinos and Indians, the Cristero wars, etc... Others opt for a more general breakdown, grouping the novels according to periods. Marta Portal divides these novels into two periods: from 1928 to 1940, when authors focused on relating the experiences in the Revolution, and post-1940 when they concerned themselves with the ontology of the Mexican being. Dessau discerns three periods: 1920 to 1928, which constitutes the gradual union of literature with the revolutionary movement; 1928–1938, when literature participated in the class struggle; and 1938–1947, which marks the esthetic and social neutralization of the literature of the Revolution. In order to encompass the wide variety of novels of this type, I would argue for dividing these works into three broad groups: those focusing on the period of armed conflict, those dealing with the period of reconstruction, and those that reevaluate the Revolution and its impact on Mexican society. It is very difficult to place these groups within particular time periods, although in general novels on the armed conflict tended to precede those dealing with reconstruction, which in turn preceded those that reevaluated the Revolution. It is possible that a novel of the Revolution be written in the future, and therefore it is erroneous to speak of the conclusion of this particular genre.

The disagreements over dates and categories arise from the novels' tremendous variety of styles and themes. Indeed, controversy has always existed over what constitutes literature on the Revolution. The most cited definition is that of Antonio Castro Leal, in his introduction to an anthology on this literature:

> By novel of the Mexican Revolution one must understand the group of narrative works, of a length that is greater than a simple long story, inspired in the military and popular actions, as well as in the political and social changes that the diverse movements of the Revolution (pacific and violent) brought with it. (xvii)

Others point to common elements, including a focus on what it means to be Mexican, disillusionment with the Revolution and its outcome, and the incorporation of social realism, epic dimensions and autobiography. Still other critics, such as Jorge Von Ziegler, argue that the only characteristic truly uniting this genre is the general theme of the Revolution. I would agree with Von Ziegler that it is impossible to provide a definition that would take into account the tremendous variety of works on the Revolution. The only truly common element of all these novels is a central focus on the topic of the Revolution.

Despite the considerable differences between the novels of the Revolution, one characteristic appears repeatedly throughout them: an unfavorable assessment of the Revolution and its participants. As Dessau puts it, practically all of the novelists "were distant and even hostile to the Revolution." He adds "the majority, believing that Mexico was threatened by the ghost of the popular uprising and 'chaos,' placed themselves on the side of 'order.'" (104) These novelists insisted on depicting the war as irrational and barbaric, and the revolutionary as violent, machistic, insensitive and ignorant of revolutionary ideals.

Some critics attribute such uniform articulations of the revolutionary to the fact that these novels were written by authors from the privileged classes who were unable to relate to the war's brutality, and who feared the masses and their potential rise to power. For example, Sara Sefkovich states:

> The novels were written by a middle class who believed in the Revolution and in "the hope of a more just life"...but who were frightened by the violence and the barbarity, the disorder and the facility of death that didn't fit within their values. The criticism was petit bourgeoisie and liberal, made from

individualism, the love for private property and the fear of the masses. (97)

Sefkovich further explains that many writers were disillusioned by the change in social relations the Revolution incurred. The traditional elite was no longer the sole political spokesperson and beneficiary, but rather the masses began to play a much more integral role in the nation's political life. Many writers reacted negatively to this change in social status, and thus to the Revolution. (97)

I would add that the precarious status of intellectuals during the Revolution and its aftermath further influenced writers to portray the Revolution and its participants in a negative light. Daniel Cosío Villegas explains that the revolutionary leaders almost never allied themselves with intellectuals (with the exception of Vasconcelos and Martín Luis Guzmán), and were themselves usually poorly educated (most with no more than a primary school education) and anti-intellectual.[1] (11–13) Thus intellectuals felt compelled to legitimize themselves to the state. They did this by casting themselves as experts on the national character and problems. They were not just trying "to explain to themselves the events in which they participated," as Sefkovich asserts (97), but rather they also wished to reestablish the privileged position in Mexican society they had enjoyed prior to the Revolution.

It is partly because these intellectuals did not consider themselves primary participants in the Revolution, and did not fully comprehend it, that the narrators in their works establish a distance between themselves and what is narrated, attempting to make sense of the turmoil. This distancing technique enabled the novelists to both give the appearance of being objective about what they were narrating, and gain favor with their audience, whose sentiments they were reflecting. Their articulations of the politician as corrupt and uneducated, and the masses as ignorant and submissive fulfilled a cathartic function for these intellectuals and their economically and socially privileged audience. At the same time, the writers sought to persuade their audience that they understood better than anyone else Mexico's ills and how to remedy them.

La sombra del caudillo

During the Maximato, two novels were written that have long been considered among the most representative works on the Revolution: *La sombra del caudillo* (*In the Shadow of the Caudillo*) (1929), by Martín Luis Guzmán, and *Vámonos con Pancho Villa* (*Let's Go with Pancho*

Villa) (1931), by Rafael Muñoz. Of the two authors, Guzmán is more widely known, particularly for his treatment of the national subject and political power in the emerging state. Both *El águila y la serpiente* (*The Eagle and the Serpent*) (1928) and *La sombra del caudillo,* the two novels of the Revolution for which he is most famous, put into fictional format the ideas on Mexican national identity and politics he had outlined earlier in *La querella de México* (*The case of Mexico*) (1915) and other essays.

In *La querella de México* Guzmán traces Mexico's political and economic problems to a spiritual void that has manifested itself in a host of character deficiencies, including a lack of patriotism, greed, injustice, apathy, and brutality. He attributes this problem to the fact that "Mexicans have had to edify a country before conceiving it purely as an ideal and feeling it as a generous impulse; that is, before deserving it." (21) He adds that: "We were born prematurely, and the consequence of that was a spiritual poverty that weakens our best efforts, always shaky and disoriented." (22) Guzmán makes a distinction between the character faults of the indigenous population and those of the Creoles and mestizos. He argues that since precortesian times "the Indian is there, prostrate and submissive, indifferent to good and evil, without a conscience." (18) Since the Indian is incapable of saving himself, the mestizos and Creoles must perform this task for him:

> The Indian neither demands nor provokes anything; in the totality of Mexican social life he has no more influence than that of a geographical accident; he should be considered as integrated in the physical medium. The day in which the creole and mestizo classes, socially determined, resolve to pull him away from there, he will come off easily and let himself be carried until his own wings begin to serve him. (20)

Guzmán criticizes the Creoles and the mestizos for being unethical. He contends that, as the classes holding power, they could institute democratic forms of government, but instead they pander to corrupt politicians in return for special favors. They thereby permit injustice and brutality to pervade Mexican politics. He expands on this argument in *A orillas del Hudson* (*On the Shores of the Hudson*) (1920), another collection of essays. Here he argues that Mexican politics remain in a constant state of upheaval because the educated classes allow uneducated men to wield power:

> There prevails among the most educated classes the theory that politics, at least Mexican politics, deserves only adventurous or inferior spirits and those who seek quick power or wealth. And such an attitude favors the continuation of the regime of violence. Because if these classes, from whom talented politicians could emerge…, politicians capable of utilizing language and writing, abstain from all public activity, there is no alternative to stop the reign of those who understand only violence, nor is there moral justification for those who lament that this occurs. (51)

La sombra del caudillo plays out these arguments in fictional form. In it, Guzmán emphasizes the nation's need for intellectuals (like himself) who understand the country's most deep-seated problems. To underscore this point, it is important to take into account the author's intellectual formation and involvement in the Revolution and the post-revolutionary state. Since his youth, Guzmán had concerned himself deeply with the nation's cultural and political affairs. Just before the beginning of the war in 1909 he began to participate in the Ateneo de la Juventud, a group of young intellectuals (founded in 1909) that also included Antonio Caso, José Vasconcelos, Pedro Henríquez Ureña, and Alfonso Reyes, and played a prominent role in the nation's political and cultural life both during and after the Revolution. This group was inspired by Justo Sierra, in particular his ideas on Mexico's spiritual and political renewal, education, and "lo mexicano." The group's main characteristics included: 1) an admiration for classical art ; 2) a concern for "lo mexicano"; 3) the promotion of cultural nationalism; 4) an interest in Mexico's indigenous population; 5) a strong belief in the education of the masses as a means of creating a more just society; and 6) a rejection of their positivist upbringing. The ateneístas immersed themselves in the country's cultural and political life, believing it was their civic duty to play the role of moral leader.

Two years after Guzmán joined the Ateneo, his father, a coronel in the Revolution, died as a result of wounds incurred during the fighting. While in bed, he told his son that although he had defended the government, the rebels were faultless. Shortly thereafter, Guzmán joined Pancho Villa's forces in the northern part of the country. Because Carranza prevailed during much of the fighting, the author spent most of the next ten years, first in jail for a short time in Mexico City, and then from 1915 to 1920 in exile in the United States (*El águila y la serpiente*, published in 1928, is based on these experiences). Following Carranza's death in 1920, Guzmán returned to Mexico City, where he became a congressional representative and founded and directed the newspaper *El Mundo*. He was forced to leave the country again in 1923 after de la Huerta, whom he supported for presidency over Obregón and Calles, was defeated. For a year Guzmán resided in the United States, then moved to Madrid where he remained until 1936.

La sombra del caudillo, written and published in exile, is a deconstruction of power and a denunciation of the caudillismo of the 1920's. This was a politically unstable decade as the state, not yet institutionalized, was forced to contend with local political bosses, or strong men, as well as tend to the nation's economic, political and cultural needs. This instability led to a form of enlightened despotism, where the state imposed its will on the populace in the name of getting things done. Some of the more negative consequences were violence (the state tolerated no opposition) and political corruption, both of which Guzmán condemns in his novel.

La sombra del caudillo is a fictionalized and allegorical account of two actual events: the rebellions of Adolfo de la Huerta in 1923, and Francisco R. Serrano and Arnulfo R. Gómez in 1927. De la Huerta rebelled when Alvaro Obregón appointed Calles rather than himself as his successor. Resolving the crisis required that Obregón ratify the treaty of Bucareli, which would assure him of U.S. political and military support. He accomplished this in part by buying off some senators and terrorizing others through the assassination of their most outspoken member, Senator Field Jurado. With U.S. aid, Obregón succeeded in crushing the rebellion in a matter of weeks. Serrano and Gómez rose up in arms against Calles upon declaring their candidacies for the presidency. Both were captured and shot dead (including a group of Serrano's supporters who were accompanying him).

All the main characters in the novel also represent real-life figures. As Guzmán explains himself in an interview with Emmanuel Carballo:

> The Caudillo is Obregón, who is described physically. Ignacio Aguirre—Minister of War—is the sum of Adolfo de la Huerta and general Francisco R. Serrano; externally his figure does not correspond to either of the two. Hilario Jiménez—Minister of the Interior—is Plutarco Elías Calles. General Protasio Leyva—named by the Caudillo, following the resignation of Aguirre, chief of operations in Mexico City, and supporter of Jiménez—is general Arnulfo Gómez. (66)

Importantly, Guzmán fails to mention one critical character in the novel, Axkaná González, whom I will later argue represents the author himself.

Calles was so incensed by the novel that he wanted to prevent it from circulating in Mexico City. He was deterred, and instead:

> The government and the representatives of Espasa-Calpe (the publishing company that published the book), who had been threatened with having their agency closed in Mexico, made a deal: the representatives of the Spanish publishing company would not be expelled from the country, but Espasa-Calpe agreed not to publish, later, any book of mine that dealt with the period after 1910. (Carballo 67)

La sombra del caudillo probes deeply into the political structure that emerged following the Revolution, uncovering immorality and ignorance on the part of its leaders. Through the Caudillo, a shadowy figure lurking in the background, and a host of pandering politicians he controls like puppets, Guzmán aims sharp criticism at the Revolution's political outcomes, including the use of violence to maintain power, corruption, and the predominance of self-interested and uneducated leaders. Guzmán's particular attention to the poor education of Mexico's leaders points to his disdain for politicians who gained power not because of their intellect but rather because of their military prowess during the Revolution. For example, the presidential candidate and Minister of War, Aguirre, "had a certain looseness of manners that remedied, with simpleness and facility, the deficiencies of his incomplete education." (739) Another military figure, Encarnación Reyes, "had never been in school, didn't know how to write, nor could he count on any other spiritual baggage other than his military intuitions, to which he owed his career as a politician." (757) He reserves his most acerbic attacks for General Catarino Ibáñez, governor of the State of Mexico, whom he emphasizes used to be only a milkman: "He was one of the many soldiers of the Revolution, converted, as if by magic, into governors or ministers: illiterate, patently uncultured, in public seats of the highest responsibilities." (799)

Guzmán also denounces the elite for their aloofness and lack of patriotism. For example, during a political rally the wealthy disdain the lower class Mexicans who are marching, describing them as "a grotesque procession of painted clowns and savage beasts escaped from their cages." (810) Guzmán blames them for the sad state of Mexican politics:

> Look well,— Axkaná said to Mijares—; Look at the smile of "the decent

people." They lack a feeling of citizenship to such an extent, that they don't even realize that it is their fault, not ours, that Mexican politics is what it is. I don't know which is greater, their foolishness or their pusillanimity. (810)

The author completes his picture of Mexican society with the poor masses, who hardly appear at all, except briefly during the political rally, where they demonstrate docility, submissiveness and ignorance: "They stuck with mechanical enthusiasm to the cheers and booing that had been prescribed to them beforehand by their bosses." (808)

Only one character in the novel sets himself apart from all the others, Axkaná, political adviser to Aguirre. Educated, astute, and sincere, Axkaná represents Guzmán's only hope for Mexico's redemption. He not only understands the inner workings of politics, but is also the one person in the novel who cares about and can communicate with the masses. During the political rally, his speech alone inspires a heartfelt reaction from the crowds:

> It was evident... that Axkaná's words, while simple, didn't reach the intelligence of the miserable multitudes that listened to him. Between the conception of his listener's and him there were abysses, abysses of time, class and culture. But it didn't matter... The ideological structure of his paragraphs was the scum that fell to the ground; the intuitive, irrational principle—generator of enthusiasm and fertilizer of hope—went straight to the heart. (813)

Axkaná's communication skills enable him to inspire the masses even though he has little in common with them. However, this talent is cut short by his collaboration with politicians much more powerful but much less educated than he. This is a key element of the novel. Axkaná symbolizes the unfortunate fate to which a Mexican intellectual (like Guzmán) could befall. Indeed, it is obvious that Guzmán related very closely to this fictional character, as Héctor Aguilar Camín points out:

> Axkaná González, multiple and normative conscience of the novel... is the only one who does not have any replica in reality. "Axkaná"—says the author—"represents in the novel the revolutionary conscience. He plays in it the function reserved in the tragedy for the Greek chorus: he tries to make the ideal world cure the wounds of the real world." But one thinks he can see in Axkaná another I of Guzmán, and thinks he can hear in the flow of his thoughts an echo of the young university student who, between tumbles and illuminations, lets us know *El águila y la serpiente*. Axkaná, like Guzmán in 1915 and in 1923, is the political survivor, the witness who guides the interpretative plot of the novel. A little made up and improved physically and

genealogically..., Axkaná is the young Guzmán. (108)

La sombra del caudillo plays on the privileged classes' fears of a government run by uneducated politicians, mostly from the lower classes, who hold power not because they are the most capable but because they rose through the revolutionary ranks. At the same time, it points to Mexico's tremendous need for both spiritual and political guidance, a task the intelligentsia is portrayed as the only one capable of undertaking. As the novel shows, the elite is self-interested, and the masses—particularly the Indian—lack the moral and intellectual fiber. In short, this novel constructs myths about the Mexican character in an attempt to promote a state apparatus firmly guided by the hand of the intellectual.

Vámonos con Pancho Villa

Rafael Muñoz did not enjoy as brilliant a political and literary career as Guzmán, but his life and work resembles that of his counterpart. Muñoz was born in 1899 in the northern state of Chihuahua and worked for many years as a journalist. Of particular impact on his work as a writer were his encounters with Pancho Villa. At the age of 16 he began traveling with Villa, whose exploits he wrote about for a newspaper based in Chihuahua. The presence of this revolutionary leader dominated Muñoz's novels and short stories.

Unlike *La sombra del caudillo*, published two years prior, *Vámonos con Pancho Villa* is set not following the Revolution but during it, and centers not on the elite but rather on the experiences of a campesino who joins Pancho Villa's forces. Nevertheless, these two novels share many characteristics. First of all, like Guzmán, who based his novel closely on a real event, Muñóz underscores the veracity of the events he recounts by telling us before we even begin the novel that "the events referred to here are true, one by one," and by explaining at the conclusion that his information is based on the words of a general who had accompanied Pancho Villa for thirteen years. (661) We are to believe, furthermore, that because the narrator did not participate directly in the action he is more objective about them. At the same time, this narrative device establishes a distance between the narrator, who is educated, and the ignorant revolutionary masses. In other words, like Axkaná in Guzmán's novel, the narrator is presented as an intellectual who thoroughly understands the Revolution and its protagonists.

As an intellectual authority in the vein of Axkaná González, the narrator in *Vámonos con Pancho Villa* articulates a similar image of the revolutionary Mexican. On the one hand, he conveys a paternalistic sympathy for the poor campesinos swept up by revolutionary ideals only to become disillusioned by the brutality and corruption of their own leaders. On the other hand, the revolutionaries are nothing more than animals ruled by their instincts rather than their intellects, who join the revolutionary forces "because of a vague intuition that they were going to fight for a cause that favored them. They themselves didn't know exactly what the Revolution meant, but each had his complaints and desires for a better situation." (668)

The revolutionary's most salient characteristic in this work is machismo. In *The Myth of the Revolution*, Irene O'Malley astutely points to machismo as one of the major cultural constructs to emanate from the Revolution. In her words:

> Foremost among the constructs that facilitated the mystification of the Revolution was patriarchy, one form of which is Mexico's famous machismo...What gives Mexican machismo its peculiar quality is its self-consciousness, its "officialness," its openly proclaimed status as part of the national identity. Even the casual observer of Mexican society will notice that nationalism and machismo are somehow related. (7)

However, O'Malley fails to distinguish between machismo as it appeared in "popular" culture, and machismo as it appeared in "elite" culture. As she shows in her study, the former heralded machismo, as witnessed by the hero cults of Francisco Madero, Emiliano Zapata, Venustiano Carranza, and Francisco Villa. Film also glorified machismo, as I will show later in this chapter. "Elite" culture, on the other hand, tended on the whole to cast a very different light on this so-called national trait. In such novels as *La sombra del caudillo* and *Vámonos con Pancho Villa*, for instance, machismo is the direct cause of the brutality unleashed by the Revolution.

Examples of machistic behavior permeate *Vámonos con Pancho Villa*, one of the most extreme being a game of Russian roulette among comrades who refuse to stop until one winds up dead. But even this example does not top many of the actions of Villa, the incarnation of machismo. Rand Morton aptly summarizes Muñoz's depictions of Villa:

> Villa, effectively, symbolizes... many aspects or elements that are Mexican. On

> the one hand, that of the soldier, whose development demonstrates amazing ability and ingenuity. On the other hand, that of the man, whose cruelty, illogic, uncontrolled reason, demonstrate a lack of maturity, childishness, that degenerates into a horrifying bestiality. Put in balance, the two parts do not achieve an equilibrium. Unfortunately, it is the second that weighs most... It could be said that for Muñoz Villa's personality resembles that of an animal... Taking, then, Villa as symbol, one must agree that the same characteristic exists in many other Mexicans. In Muñoz's short stories, it is almost always that class of men who appear as protagonist... For Muñoz the Revolution is completely animal-like, very rarely human. (146)

In Muñoz's own words, Villa "is cruel to the point of brutality, dominant to the point of absolute possession. His personality is like the bow of a ship; it divides the surge of passions: or one hates him, or one gives in to his will, to never recover it again." (668) Villa's influence is such that Tiburcio Maya, like a faithful dog, fights loyally for him, sacrificing his own life to save that of his leader, and watching his friends and others suffer painful deaths knowing they had sacrificed their lives senselessly. He does this even though Villa himself had insulted and betrayed him, is obviously never concerned about his welfare and, perhaps most shocking of all, shoots his wife and daughter dead before his very eyes (the son is spared). But even Tiburcio is an exception. The majority of the revolutionaries in this novel do not even share his redeeming quality of loyalty. They fight simply because they enjoy the slaughter.

Muñoz and Guzmán, in addition to a host of other novelists of the Revolution beginning with Mariano Azuela, coincide in their articulations of the revolutionary as unfeeling, ignorant and machistic. The critic Carlos Monsiváis insightfully points out that this conformity stems from an inherent sense of class superiority: "By not having at their disposal a purchasing power, suggestive language and refined culture, these characters lack the right to an individualized psychology, and become mere synonyms of Pueblo." ("De las relaciones entre..." 48) I would add that many of the authors of the Revolution were also playing upon the privileged classes' fear and contempt of the underclasses as a means of assuring their own position in society. In particular, *La sombra del caudillo* and *Vámonos con Pancho Villa* seem to emphasize that, because he is uneducated and unethical, the revolutionary campesino is unfit for participation in the nation's political life and could prove dangerous if not led in the right direction. In other words, these novels could be read as an attempt to prove the need for educated and civilized men like the authors in the nation-building process. Such a message is not surprising considering that both novels were written and published during a period of transition between caudillismo and the institutionalization of the modern Mexican state, when strongmen like Calles still held the reins of power.

Cartucho

It is important to point out that one novel published during this period, which has only recently been given wide acclaim, offers a very different articulation of the revolutionary and the revolutionary movement: *Cartucho* (1931), by Nellie Campobello. Campobello has often been compared with Guzmán and Muñoz (all three concentrated on the struggles in northern Mexico and on the figure of Villa), but her novel diverges from theirs in some very important respects. Most significantly, national identity, as embodied by the archetype of the revolutionary, is depicted in a much more favorable light. Campobello also grants the revolutionary much greater emotional complexity and variety than do the other two novelists, and includes the female as a protagonist in the Revolution.

Cartucho has a unique style and structure. It is told from the point of view of a young girl growing up amidst the Revolution, rather than a male participant in the fighting. The point of view is first person rather than third person, which creates a greater sense of intimacy with the war. And it actually resembles more a series of stories or sketches than a novel, lacking an epic dimension. Catherine Nickel suggests that the use of this structure might be a consequence of Campobello's gender, saying it "closely corresponds to the kind of writing often engaged in by women who in their letters, diaries, and other forms of discourse find themselves piecing together small narrative units to create an elaborately intertwined network of meaning." (126) *Cartucho* includes other stylistic elements that have traditionally been associated with women, including storytelling. Dennis Parle, for example, draws parallels between *Cartucho* and the corrido, the popular ballad of the Revolution, including its simple, colloquial language, repetition, variations in mood, the stark and graphic depiction of violence, and a narrator who functions as the voice of the people. (210–211)

I would agree that Campobello's gender influenced her writing style, and would extend that argument to include her articulation of the revolutionary and national identity. Writing was not considered a profession suitable for women at the time, a fact that Campobello was acutely aware of:

> With my intrinsically restless nature, and my love of truth and justice for all humanity, I found myself needing to write. I knew that the environment I lived in was not favorable for my desire. I knew that many of the people close to me would not approve of my attitude and would feel displeased when they saw me engrossed in a mission that would bring me no personal benefit. ("My Books" 203)

As a female, Campobello could never hope to form part of the elite literary circles, but she could assume an important role within Vasconcelos's cultural nationalism. As Jean Franco points out in *Plotting Women*, Vasconcelos granted women a vital function within his literacy campaigns and educational missions. However, as she explains, the messianic spirit he incarnated "transformed mere human beings into supermen and constituted a discourse that associated virility with social transformation in a way that marginalized women." (102) The rural school teachers were expected to remain unmarried and pure, and could never expect to rise within their professions. Nonetheless, the majority of Mexico's most renowned female artists of the period linked themselves to some degree to Vasconcelos's program, perhaps perceiving it as their only hope of contributing in any significant way to Mexico's cultural and political life. Besides Campobello, these included the painter, Frida Kahlo, the photographer, Tina Modotti, and the writer, Antonieta Rivas Mercado.

According to Dale Verlinger, cultural patriotism was "the principle characteristic of Nellie's life and work." (100) Campobello's main contributions to cultural nationalism involved dancing. Beginning in 1923 she traveled throughout Mexico with a group of young dancers on cultural missions sponsored by the Ministry of Education, then headed by Vasconcelos. Upon gaining proficiency in Mexico's native dances, she became professor of dance at the National University in 1932 and director of the National School of Dance in 1937.

Contributing to Campobello's positive articulation of the Revolution was her family's involvement in the Revolution. Born in 1900 in the state of Durango in northwestern Mexico, she witnessed the Revolution firsthand. Her father died in the fighting in 1914, one of her brothers served with the northern army under Pancho Villa, and her mother and other relatives helped the war effort as Villa supporters. Her own loyalty to Villa was such that, in an interview with Emmanuel Carballo in 1958, she revealed that *Cartucho* was written to avenge him: "The novels that were being written during that time, and that narrate the fighting, are replete with lies against the men of the Revolution, principally Pancho Villa. I wrote in this book the facts of villismo, not what has been told to me." (Carballo 385)

Despite being female, Campobello never directly challenges the myth that privileged men as the protagonists of historical and social change and relegated women to the role of motherhood. However, she did subvert it in some subtle ways. For example, Campobello feminizes the revolutionary hero to a degree not found in much of the other well-known literature on the Revolution, granting him much greater emotional complexity. He is not only capable of violence but also of compassion, not only indifference to suffering but sensitivity to it (even Villa cries). He expresses hatred of the enemy but also loyalty to and love of his comrades, is not entirely machistic but expresses fear and weakness as well. Furthermore, his existence is not so marked by poverty, oppression and violence that he is incapable of moments of great joy. In fact, throughout the novel the characters celebrate with each other. Similarly, Pancho Villa is depicted in a very positive light as just, loyal, brave, sensitive and completely devoted to the revolutionary cause.

Furthermore, although Campobello focuses on the male revolutionary, her novel is distinct from others in granting the female a presence. In fact, the mother assumes a central role in *Cartucho*, although she is rarely the protagonist. Campobello portrays her mother as independent, strong and brave, characteristics that were not usually associated with women at the time. Despite her dire circumstances (she is widowed with several children to raise), the mother manages to both provide for and protect her children, at times putting herself at risk to do so. She also rarely displays emotional weakness, shedding tears only when harm has been done to others.

Importantly, the mother is a staunch defender of the Revolution (in particular of Villa), and participates in it by nursing wounded soldiers. She is one of the only figures in all the literature of the Revolution who is recognized for her contributions to the revolutionary cause. Her character could be interpreted on a symbolic level as being that of mother of the "revolutionary family" or nation. She is the protector of revolutionary ideals and of those who fight for them—the poor masses. Thus in *Cartucho*, Campobello carves out a place for women in the nation-building project.

Cartucho is further unique in its use of a female narrator. Campobello says she used the voice of her childhood and its apparent naivete "to display what I knew to be essential: a sincere and direct way of speaking." ("My Books" 203) This device creates a greater sense of intimacy with the Revolution than do Guzmán's or Muñoz's novels. However, the narrator does not display much sentimentality, and in fact her emotional detachment from the brutality she observes often shocks the reader. Campobello thus subverts, as she had done with her mother, the traditional view of women as emotional. Take for instance the following scene, from *Cartucho*:

> Gudelio Uribe, Catarino's personal enemy, took him prisoner, mounted him on a mule, and paraded him through the streets of Parral. His ears had been cut off, strung together, and hung around his neck. Gudelio was a specialist in cutting people's ears off. Blood dripped from the many wounds in his ribs. Four soldiers on horseback surrounded him as he went along. Whenever they wanted the mule to move faster, they just poked Catarino in the ribs with a bayonet. (17)

The narrator not only fails to express dismay or horror at the atrocities she views, she often becomes fascinated by them. For example, when she and some others come across soldiers carrying a tray with a general's guts displayed on it, they react with curiosity: "When we heard 'they're guts,' we moved up close to see them. They were all rolled together, as if they had no end. 'Guts! How nice! Whose are they?' we said, our curiosity showing in our eyes." (35) Some critics have found such behavior by the narrator disturbing and unnatural, particularly for a female. Others, however, have lauded its originality. Through her narrator, Campobello was probably trying to draw attention to the Revolution's psychological impact on those who witnessed the violence on a regular basis. As Max Parra has noted, the narrator copes with the violence that surrounds her by familiarizing herself with it, and by dehumanizing the Revolution's victims (170).

In sum, Campobello reflects the basic image of the Revolution and the revolutionary promoted by Vasconcelos, but alters it in ways that seem likely to be attributable to her gender. Its articulation of the Revolution is inconsistent with that of most of the other novels at the time, a consequence of her allegiance to cultural nationalism. *Cartucho* is thus highly unique.

Cartucho was not widely recognized during its day, and thus did not play a fundamental role in the promotion of national identity. However, it is important to mention this work as a means of underscoring some significant points about the construction of national identity in the 1920's and 1930's. These include the marginalization of women, who barely appear in the novel and could not contribute through literature to the creation of national identity. A comparison of Cartucho with other novels of the revolution also reveals the large extent to which writers/intellectuals formed a unified group with similar class backgrounds and political aspirations. As pointed out earlier, their unfavorable articulations of the Revolution and the revolutionary were influenced by an urban, middle-class bias, and the desire to preserve the status of intellectuals. Campobello, on the other hand, was excluded from this group, and could only contribute to the nation's political and cultural life through cultural nationalism. That, added to her personal experiences with the Revolution and her gender, resulted in a very distinct articulation of the war and its combatants.

The Heroic Revolutionary

The Revolution constituted a major theme in cinema, as in literature, since the beginning of the war in 1910. However, contrary to literature the images of the Revolution that appeared on the screen became significantly modified over time as a result of state censorship. During the initial years of the Revolution, the Mexican film industry produced many revolutionary documentaries, as they proved popular with the audiences. These films attempted to objectively document the armed struggle. In Aurelio de los Reyes's words: "Mexican cinema at this time set out to inform. It had developed its own mode of representation and carefully documented, unhindered, the major national events with complete freedom." (69) In 1913, however, the de la Huerta regime began to impose both political and moral censorship on cinema, which led to the replacement of the documentary with the fiction film. "The exhibition of Revolutionary documentaries dwindled, and by 1916 they had disappeared from the theatres to reappear later only in exceptional circumstances." (de los Reyes 71)

During the 1920s cinema production was extremely weak as a result of intense competition from Hollywood. Thus film never played a major role in cultural nationalism during this period. However, this situation changed in the early 1930s with the introduction of sound, which enabled the Mexican film industry to flourish again. The Revolution made a strong reappearance in cinema during this time, but filmmakers did not resume making documentaries that sought to reveal the "truth" of reality. Rather, many of these films appear to support cultural nationalism by glorifying the revolutionary fighter and revolutionary ideals.

Two highly significant films on the Revolution were produced during the first part of the 1930's—*El compadre Mendoza* (*Godfather Mendoza*) (1933) and *Vámonos con Pancho Villa* (*Let's Go With Pancho Villa*) (1935). These two films formed part of a trilogy on the Revolution (the third movie was *Prisionero trece*), all of which were directed by Fernando de Fuentes. De Fuentes became one of the most famous directors in Mexican cinema in the 1930s and the 1940s. He gained fame not only for these films, considered "the most important fiction films about the Mexican Revolution," but for a wide variety of others as well. (García 158) His most acclaimed film was *Allá en el Rancho Grande* (*Over there on the Big Ranch*) (1935), a "comedia ranchera" (ranch comedy), which enabled the Mexican film industry to take off on an industrial scale. This genre, which celebrated ranch life prior to the Mexican Revolution, became enormously successful in the 1930's, not only in Mexico but also all over Latin America.

De Fuentes's trilogy on the Revolution, all of which preceded *Allá en el Rancho Grande*, were considered his most objective and realistic films. The director's balanced treatment of the Revolution, along with his technical skills, were highly praised by many of the most renowned film critics. Carl Mora, for instance, characterized *El compadre Mendoza* as "a film of rare sensitivity, insight, and dramatic power. It has and continues to draw praise from Mexican critics… who tend to be hypercritical of their country's cinema." (39–40) He likewise praised *Vámonos con Pancho Villa* as "a remarkable film" that "coldly demythologizes" the Revolution, revealing it for what it was. In his opinion, this movie constituted "the last Mexican motion picture to deal honestly with the country's recent past." (44–45)

On the surface, it would seem that these films lacked nationalistic impulses. In fact, their articulations of the revolutionary seem to reflect those in many novels, with cruelty, machismo and ignorance as central traits. In fact, both films were based on novels, the first one by Mauricio Magdaleno and the second by Muñoz. It is valid to say that literature on the novel influenced film to some degree. Like many novels on the

Revolution, these two movies, and in particular the second, reject an idealized depiction of the Revolution, despite the mass audience to which film appealed.

Such a seemingly unbiased assessment of the Revolution might seem peculiar considering the state's continued strong interest in the creation of idealized images of the Revolution (as witnessed in the muralist movement). This treatment of the war becomes even more perplexing considering the mass audience to which film appealed, and its strong power of persuasion, which together made it among the most powerful of the artistic mediums in terms of its ability to influence its public. But not only did the state support Fernández's reconstruction of the Revolution, it backed him up financially. Cinema in the early 1930's depended in part on state support. For instance, in 1934 the state granted a guaranteed loan to finance the construction of the first modern film studio in Mexico City, CLASA (cinematográfica Latino Americana, S.A.). CLASA Films, the production company, also received government support and, when it declared bankruptcy following the production of its first film, *Vámonos con Pancho Villa*, it was saved by a government subsidy. Besides the financial backing the state gave to this particular film, it also provided military equipment. (Mora 43)

But why would the state help finance films that were critical of the Revolution? The reason is that these films were actually quite nationalistic. They provided a sort of catharsis for those who were disappointed by unfulfilled revolutionary ideals. The revolutionary is also portrayed in a much more favorable light in the films than in the novels. The heroic peasant fighter is central in both of these films, symbolizing the true revolutionary spirit. Felipe Nieto, in *El compadre Mendoza*, and Tiburcio Maya, in *Vámonos con Pancho Villa*, distinguish themselves for their dedication to the revolutionary cause, their unwavering loyalty to their friends, comrades and leaders (Nieto to Zapata and Maya to Villa), and their bravery in fighting. Through these campesinos (symbols of the masses), the films recognize the lower classes as the genuine revolutionary heroes. They thus instill a sense of national pride and identity. At the same time, they construct codes of conduct aimed at maintaining the status quo. *El compadre Mendoza* additionally kept alive revolutionary ideals, including that of land reform and social equality.

El compadre Mendoza

El compadre Mendoza (*Godfather Mendoza*) centers on the efforts of a shrewd and opportunistic landowner, Rosalío Mendoza, to maintain his properties intact by extending a hearty welcome to the troops of all sides whenever they visit. He becomes particularly friendly to the zapatista general, Felipe Nieto, who saves his life. Despite their close relationship, however, Mendoza betrays his friend to a carrancista official, Colonel Bernáldez, in return for monetary gain.

El compadre Mendoza portrays the Revolution basically as a failed venture. Not only do depraved revolutionary leaders and corrupt businessmen gain the upper hand, but the Revolution also fails to realize one of its essential goals: the takeover and redistribution of large properties. Nonetheless, the film promotes the nationalistic cause in two important ways. First, it inspires admiration for the zapatistas and, by extension, poor Mexicans. The zapatistas not only embody the true revolutionary spirit, but they are also morally superior to and more emotionally fulfilled than the wealthy. Secondly, the film rekindles revolutionary ideals, including that of social equality.

El compadre Mendoza sympathizes with the zapatista fighters, comparing them favorably with the larger and more powerful forces of Huerta and Carranza, and with the nation's economic elite. As John Mraz has observed, the film champions the zapatistas' struggle for land ownership. In the opening shot we see a furrow that is being made in the earth by what appears to be a plow but turns out to be a rifle butt being dragged by a weary zapatista fighter. Thus the film immediately identifies the zapatistas with the land. It also makes positive references to the Plan de Ayala, Zapata's strategy for carrying out agrarian reform. (101–102) The film additionally praises various aspects of the zapatistas' character, such as their fortitude. It shows these fighters fatigued, hungry and wounded, yet persistent in their struggle, even when the odds are against them. It also highlights their camaraderie with each other. In one sequence, the film alternates between shots of Dolores and Mendoza's wedding reception, and a zapatista celebration, as if encouraging the audience to compare the two events. It emphasizes the more joyful atmosphere of the latter. Although elegant, the wedding is stiff and formal. Mendoza himself declares that it is like a funeral. By contrast, the zapatistas entertain themselves quite naturally with song, dance and conversation, despite their much less sumptuous surroundings and fare. The movie suggests that the poor are more content than the wealthy because they know how to enjoy life and to relate more intimately with each other.

Although overall *El compadre Mendoza* portrays the zapatistas positively, it shows a few individuals who lack scruples. However, their immoral conduct serves to highlight Nieto's heroism. One zapatista officer invades Mendoza's wedding ceremony, threatening to kill the groom along with a huertista general who is celebrating with him. Nieto arrives just in time to save Mendoza. He denounces the zapatista officer as bloodthirsty. Another zapatista suggests to Nieto that they burn down Mendoza's ranch and kill the owner so that the general can have Mendoza's wife, Dolores, to himself. Nieto angrily rejects the proposition.

El compadre Mendoza offers Nieto as a role model for Mexicans. It encourages its audience to revere and emulate his qualities and to reject the type of behavior displayed by his less admirable counterparts. It thus hoped to mitigate any persistent inclinations towards violence against the wealthy. Further emphasizing this objective, Dolores repeatedly states that she wishes all zapatistas were like Nieto. The film casts the general as a Christ-like figure, who struggles and dies on behalf of the poor. Nieto never renounces his ideals. He flatly refuses to engage in any unscrupulous conduct, or to quit fighting even when his forces are far outnumbered. He even dies like Christ, betrayed and hung at Mendoza's ranch entrance as if he were on a cross.

El compadre Mendoza contrasts Nieto's behavior not only with bloodthirsty revolutionaries, but also with Mendoza. Unlike Nieto, Mendoza places his self-preservation and enrichment above everything else, protecting those interests at all costs. He has no integrity whatsoever. Mendoza says and does whatever is necessary to placate the troops who visit him. He puts up a portrait of their revolutionary hero (carefully replacing that of the rival faction who previously visited). He feeds the troops, and seduces the leaders with fancy meals, cigars, and cognac. He even helps to conduct business for them, extracting a profit for himself in the process. For example, Mendoza sells guns from the huertistas to the zapatistas at a cost higher than their actual value. He is so adept at this maneuvering that he actually profits from the Revolution. Worst of all, Mendoza agrees to set up Nieto for murder by the carrancistas, even though Nieto saved his life. The general, by contrast, never considers betraying his friend, despite the many opportunities to do so. Mendoza treats his relationships with others like business deals. Only a day after meeting Dolores, he persuades her father to let him marry her, stating: "I'm an enemy of romanticisms. Things should be done quickly and well". He says the same to Colonel Bernáldez following Nieto's death, although with much less conviction.

Although *El compadre Mendoza* portrays Mendoza negatively, it is careful not to vilify him. Like many other films from the 1930s and the 1940s, it portrays the wealthy as flawed but not evil, most likely because it did not want to aggravate class tensions. Mendoza displays genuine warmth towards Nieto, a poor campesino. He only betrays his friend because he believes he has no other options for saving himself and his wife and son. Mendoza initially plans to flee to the capital with his family, as it is becoming increasingly dangerous to remain on the ranch. However, these hopes are crushed when the zapatistas blow up his entire harvest, which is headed for the capital by train. He no longer has the financial means to move. Mendoza is further prompted to betray Nieto by Colonel Bernáldez's assurances that he would be doing a favor for the country, and by the certainty that Nieto will be caught and killed soon anyway. Even then, he delays the decision to help Bernáldez, and is profoundly shaken when his friend is murdered. In the end, *El compadre Mendoza* inspires pity rather than anger for Mendoza, who will clearly suffer from the knowledge of his actions.

El compadre Mendoza further attempts to placate the poor by portraying the Revolution as an ongoing process, with social promises still to be fulfilled. Nieto, for instance, states "one day those of us who fight with ideals will have justice." Mendoza's deaf and mute servant, who symbolizes the "pueblo", also reminds the wealthy of their social obligations through her constant presence and watchful eye. Although she lacks a voice, like the masses, she reads lips and knows of Mendoza's underhanded dealings. The movie focuses on her eyes at key points during the movie, including when Bernáldez explains to Mendoza his plans to murder Nieto. As Mendoza paces outside the room where Nieto and Bernáldez are meeting, the movie does a close up of the woman's eyes boring into him. Her staring so upsets him that he orders her to leave the room. Through the servant's example, the masses understand that their very presence disturbs the conscience of those who exploit them, and that it is only a matter of time before justice is served.

Even more importantly, *El compadre Mendoza* suggests the possibility of an alliance between social classes. This is evident not only in Nieto and Mendoza's friendship, but also more significantly in Nieto's platonic love affair with Dolores. Dolores likewise appears to be attracted to Nieto. In fact, the movie implies that she is only wedded to Mendoza for financial security (her father, who owned a hacienda, was ruined by the Revolution). There is no possibility of a union between Nieto and Dolores (or, in another words, of the social classes), but the prospect is shown to be very appealing. Scenes picturing Dolores, Nieto and the son idealize them as the perfect family. Even more importantly, Dolores and Rosalío's son, named after Nieto, appears more loyal to Nieto than to his own father. He begs Nieto to visit, and he is fiercely loyal to the zapatistas. When the carrancistas visit the ranch, he shouts out on behalf of Nieto and the zapatistas, thereby embarrassing his father. He also takes an instant dislike to Colonel Bernáldez, telling him "I don't love you, you're bad". In other words, the son represents the possibility of a future generation of wealthy Mexicans who are sympathetic to the less privileged.

Vámonos con Pancho Villa

Vámonos con Pancho Villa (*Let's Go With Pancho Villa*), which focuses on the revolutionary experiences of six campesinos who join up with Pancho Villa, echoes *El compadre Mendoza* in its reliance on audience identification with the main characters. Like the other movie, the presence of a heroic campesino, Tiburcio Maya (the same actor who played Felipe Nieto), is central. Maya, like Nieto, stands for the true revolutionary ideals. But the other "Leones" (Lions—their nickname) are also key characters. Their good sense of humor, happy-go-lucky attitudes, bravery, faithfulness to and fondness of each other are appealing attributes. Although their obsession with proving their manliness borders on being absurd, it does not negatively affect the audience's opinion of them. Machismo even at times endears the characters to the audience.

Besides being likable figures, the audience could relate to "Los Leones" because in many ways they symbolized the typical Mexican campesino, who joined the Revolution enthusiastically but with vague notions of why, and who became increasingly disillusioned with it. "Los Leones" are at first in awe of Pancho Villa, whom they consider the model "macho" and whom they strive to emulate. Villa exudes charisma, bravery and leadership skills, and appears to champion the cause of the poor. "Los Leones" aspire to prove to Villa their skill and bravery in battle. Three of them survive to be inducted into Villa's elite calvary, the "Dorados" ("the Golden Ones"). However, two die ignominiously shortly thereafter, leaving only Tiburcio Maya, the main character in the movie. Tiburcio's admiration for Villa steadily wanes as he watches his friends die senselessly (in his opinion) and as he realizes that the revolutionary leader is not as macho as he at first seemed. Villa, for instance, is arbitrary in meting out justice. He is also cruel, as evidenced when he orders the execution of a band of federal musicians simply because he already has a band. He reveals cowardice as well when ordering that Tiburcio incinerate his friend, Miguel Angel, who is ill with smallpox, refusing to approach either of the two for fear of infection.

To an extent, *Vámonos con Pancho Villa* takes a hard, critical look at the Revolution, paying particular attention to Villa and the often negative influence he exerted over his followers. As Deborah Mistron notes, "Villa is shown in all his historical ambiguity—as an inspiring yet flawed leader who came to embody both the positive and negative aspects of the revolution." (7–8) Most outstanding about Villa is his code of machismo, which his followers strive to follow to the point of absurdity. A salient example is a game of Russian roulette that the participants argue will lead to the death of the most cowardly. Wounded, one of the Lions proves he is not the most cowardly by shooting himself while proclaiming "Mira como muere un León" ("Look at how a Lion dies"). The movie echoes literature in its emphasis on the machismo of the revolutionaries, and in bringing out many of the more gruesome aspects of the Revolution. However, it diverges in some very important respects. First, machismo is not judged, and it is not portrayed as an entirely negative trait. At times it almost endears the characters to the audience. Secondly, the main characters in the movie, as pointed out earlier, have many admirable qualities. Thus while the film doesn't idealize the Revolution, to an extent it glorifies the common, ordinary revolutionary, as symbolized by "Los Leones" and, in particular, Tiburcio.

Interestingly and importantly, the movie ends with Tiburcio's desertion from the army. In the novel, as noted earlier, Tiburcio is persuaded by Villa to rejoin the forces, and he dies defending him. The difference is crucial because in the movie the "pueblo" (symbolized by Tiburcio) exercises free will and rational choice, whereas in the novel it is ruled by a blind instinct (an articulation of the revolutionary that is repeated throughout literature on the Revolution beginning with Mariano Azuela's *Los de abajo*, published in 1915). Pancho Villa also emerges as a much more brutal leader in the novelistic ending. In addition to a more positive articulation of the "pueblo" and Pancho Villa, the ending is important in that it reflected a widespread feeling among Mexicans of the lower classes of having been betrayed by the Revolution. As such, it served as a catharsis for the injustices of the war. However, this was not the original ending. According to Ayala Blanco, the original version had continued for ten minutes more, but had been censored:

> The mysterious case of the mutilated end of the classic of all classics of revolutionary Mexican cinema reeks of censor and self-censor... It's possible that... under governmental pressure the producer, CLASA, elaborated up to three distinct versions of the end of the film, perhaps as a result of some censorious bureaucrat fearful of the brutal and almost inhuman image of the controversial hero, Pancho Villa. (27)

Eduardo de la Vega Alfaro maintains that Lázaro Cárdenas himself censored *Vámonos con Pancho Villa*, finding the ending (in which Tiburcio is murdered by another Villista) too cruel and bloody. (83)

Film emphasized the positive aspects of the revolutionary in order to pacify a mass audience disappointed in the Revolution's outcome. It not only depicted the lower classes as the true revolutionary heroes, but also conveyed the hope of social justice by portraying the Revolution as an ongoing process. At the same time, it established codes of conduct that would preserve the status quo. In film, the poor are content with their simple and humble lives, and they never challenge those who exploit them. They understand that it is better not to aspire to a higher social position anyway because the rich are morally flawed and have more problems than they do. In other words, these films told the poor that while they may have few economic resources, they enjoy many other benefits that the rich do not, including camaraderie and nobility of spirit. Through reaffirmation of the code of machismo, the male could also count on enjoying the added benefit of gender superiority. These messages were reiterated in film throughout the 1930's and 1940's.

Notes

1. After 1940, when Avila Camacho, a bureaucrat, replaced Lázaro Cárdenas (the last military president), and the Mexican state began to institutionalize itself, political leaders began to collaborate more closely with intellectuals.

Chapter Three

The Alienation of the Indian and the Integration Process

Since the time of conquest and colonization, and above all since independence from Spain, writers and intellectuals have sought to capture the essence of Latin America through an analysis of the indigenous peoples and cultures. Following independence, archetypes of the Indian were often employed to foster national identity and create social and political cohesion. In the wake of the Mexican Revolution, these archetypes proliferated as artists and intellectuals aspired to construct a national identity based not on European culture, as had been the case during the porfiriato, but rather on a uniquely Mexican one. Authentic "Mexicanness" was discovered in Mexico's Aztec heritage and glorified in the work of many artists, most famously that of the Mexican muralists.

During the 1930s idealized images of the Aztecs continued to prevail in the work of many intellectuals and artists. However, at the same time, some writers began to take a more critical look at Mexico's indigenous populations and to analyze the reasons for their continued isolation. In stark contrast to the muralists, the main indigenist novels of the 1930s, *El resplandor* (1937), by Mauricio Magdaleno, and *El Indio* (1935), by Gregorio López y Fuentes, find very little to redeem the Indian; he is apathetic, indifferent (even to death), meek, superstitious, fatalistic and prone to alcoholism and violence. The novelists attribute these characteristics to the Indian's long history of exploitation and abuse. They underscore the need for measures to improve the Indian's economic plight, emphasizing the dire consequences that failure to do so could have. They contend that besides obstructing economic progress, the Indian's continued exploitation by non-indigenous Mexicans could cause the Indian to become even more distrustful of mestizo and white Mexicans, making integration more difficult and causing the Indians to become dangerous.

In contrast to these novels, film dealt with the Indian in a more ambiguous fashion. Very few films were made during the 1930s that dealt exclusively with the Indian. Film often depicted the Indian in minor roles as the stereotypical dark villain or clown. A few movies portrayed him more positively as a noble savage who lives in harmony with nature and is innocent, pure, proud, dignified and strong. These films attempted to generate sympathy for the Indian as well as to identify the masses with the native Mexican by stressing shared experiences and characteristics. However, they were not highly successful. It was not until the 1940's, with the movie *María Candelaria*, that the Indian enjoyed a major presence in film (see chapter 5).

Indigenism as a movement didn't really get started in Mexico until 1940, with the celebration of the Primer Congreso Indigenista Interamericano (First Inter-American Indigenist Congress). This was much later than in other countries like Perú, Bolivia, and Ecuador. Nevertheless, important works existed on indigenism in Mexico much earlier. Perhaps most importantly, Manuel Gamio gained wide recognition for his treatment of the indigenous question (as well as other issues related to effective governance) in a book of essays, *Forjando patria* (*Forging Nation*) (1916). Gamio's views regarding how to integrate the Indian into mainstream society deserve some attention, as they profoundly influenced indigenist literature and governmental policies for many decades to follow.

Forjando patria is based on the need to attain unity from the nation's diverse elements (Gamio frequently compares the country to a family), a prerequisite to the transformation of an underdeveloped nation into a modern one. Gamio devotes most of the book to addressing the problem of how to integrate native Mexicans into mainstream society. He asserts that the key to this process consists of ridding the Indian of his fear of mestizo and white Mexicans. This requires that non-indigenous Mexicans stop viewing the Indians as inferior and begin to address the native people's concerns. Gamio believed that the Indians would participate wholeheartedly in national life were non-native Mexicans to respect and care about them: "If he stops being considered biologically inferior to the white, like he currently is, if his food, clothing, education and recreation are improved, the Indian will embrace contemporary culture just like any individual from any other race." (24) According to Gamio, Mexicans, and especially the nation's leadership, must begin acquainting themselves with the indigenous populations. He argues that without understanding these groups' characteristics and necessities, it is impossible to know how to integrate them. Gamio insists that once the Indians' needs are determined, the government immediately take measures to address them. However, he already lists a number of actions he believes are necessary. For instance, he demands that the Indians be guaranteed possession of their lands, and that properties taken from them be returned. He also calls for legal reforms so that laws reflect the needs of all citizens and the legislative body contains members belonging to diverse ethnic groups.

Gamio's ideas only really began to be implemented with the presidency of Lázaro Cárdenas (1934–1940), who did more for the Indian than any other previous government. In 1936, Cárdenas created the Departamento de Asuntos Indígenas (Department of Indigenous Affairs), whose main purpose was to study the problems facing Mexico's indigenous populations, and to propose measures to solve them. His efforts to improve the Indian's plight centered on economics and education. Economically, Cárdenas favored a model oriented toward agriculture rather than industry, one that would primarily benefit the campesino and Indian populations. He attempted to deviate from classical capitalism, hoping to avoid some of its enormous social costs by making industry subordinate to the creation of newly formed agrarian communities.[1] He stimulated agrarian reform, and ordered the creation of the Confederación Nacional de Campesinos (National Confederation of Campesinos) or CNC, whose ultimate goal was the socialization of agriculture. His agrarian reform program resulted in the beginning of the break up of the haciendas and the end of a rural form of life that dated back to colonial times. In 1930, ejidal properties constituted about 13% of the cultivable lands, while in 1940 they represented about 47% and almost half of the rural population depended on the cultivation of ejidal lands. (Meyer 169)

Cárdenas took other economic measures aimed solely at the indigenous peoples. For example, he organized indigenous cooperatives and trained Indians to manage them. He also provided funds to enable indigenous communities to purchase agricultural equipment and to construct schools.

With respect to education, Cárdenas supported a program that favored the group over the individual, that championed social programs such as agrarian reform, and that emphasized a technical education over a literary one. This program aimed to improve the Indian's social and economic status by teaching practical skills, and bolster self-esteem by including classes on prehispanic history. Native languages were also allowed as a first step to learning Spanish. Cárdenas established 30 vocational agricultural schools in areas where indigenous people predominated, which approximately 3,000 students attended. (Germán Parra 48) He also sent some 270 Indian students to the capital to continue their studies at various institutions. (Medin 177)

Indigenism reached far beyond economic and educational programs for the Indian, to larger Mexican society. Cárdenas and his supporters sustained that Mexico's authentic identity was grounded in its indigenous heritage, and also that the Indians had a vital role to play in the formation of a future Mexico. As such, they attempted to stimulate interest in indigenous customs, arts and languages, and held the Indian up as a symbol of national pride for all Mexicans.

Idealizing the Indian and Mexico's indigenous heritage served some important purposes. First of all, it was probably aimed in part at combating widespread racism against the Indian. This was important not just for the Indian himself, but also for the integration process. Secondly, while Cardenistas may have been genuinely interested in the Indians' welfare, indigenism also played an important role within nationalism by helping to establish what was unique about the nation. It promoted a sense of national identity and pride and, along with it, national unity.

Despite the glorification of the Indian, Cardenistas clearly did not wish to Indianize the Mexican. Rather, they wanted to Mexicanize the Indian. Importantly, they did not embrace contemporary indigenous culture as a whole. They exalted Mexico's indigenous past and a few aspects of contemporary indigenous culture, such as the arts. They also praised certain qualities of the so-called indigenous character, but only ones that would benefit a modern society, such as tenacity, dignity, respect for others, a sense of civic duty, community spirit, artistic abilities, work ethic, and so on.

The Savage and Exploited Indian: *El resplandor* and *El Indio*

A few artists and intellectuals countered the trend to idealize the Indian, and were also critical of the president's indigenist policies. These included Gregorio López y Fuentes and Mauricio Magdaleno, who were actually Cárdenas supporters. The novelists employed the archetype of the Indian in order to criticize the Revolution, the post-revolutionary leadership, and indigenist policies, as well as to enter into the debate on "lo mexicano". They contended that while the Revolution had made use of the services of the native population, including supplies and labor, it had excluded the Indians' concerns altogether. Most significantly, by colluding with the large landowners, political leaders neglected agrarian reform and perpetuated the system of exploitation of Indian labor. However, the mestizo population in general is also shown to be complicit in the abuse of the indigenous population. In fact, the novelists infer that one of the Revolution's major shortcomings was its inability to forge a new consciousness that would compel Mexicans to treat each other with respect and dignity, regardless of race or class. In an attempt to underscore this point, they depict the mestizo as exploitative, greedy, corrupt, ignorant, physically abusive, uncaring and unsympathetic towards the Indian's suffering. Indeed, they posit the mestizo, rather than the Indian (whom the authors imply is in no way representative of the average Mexican[2]), as the true symbol of national identity.[3]

According to the novelists, the continued mistreatment and neglect of the Indians has caused this group to become increasingly distrustful of mestizo society, and also hostile towards it. As a consequence, efforts to integrate the Indian into mainstream society have been frustrated, and the Indian has become a physical threat.

As was the case for the novelists, Martin Luis Guzmán and Rafael Muñoz, the criticisms leveled against the armed struggle partly aimed to appease wealthy and educated Mexicans, who were upset by the ravages of the war and the prospect of displacement by the underclasses. They were also a reaction against the displacement of intellectuals by what those intellectuals perceived as uneducated, immoral and ignorant men.[4] By condemning the Revolution and those in power, and by posing themselves as experts on the Indian, Magdaleno and López y Fuentes were substantiating the nation's need for intelligent and ethical men like themselves. For this reason, they fulfill a didactic function in their novels, explaining to their uninformed reader various aspects of the indigenous culture and mentality, and the reasons for the Indians' continued isolation.

The status of intellectuals had not improved since the time Guzmán and Muñóz wrote their novels, in the early 1930's. Cárdenas did more than any of his predecessors to improve higher education,[5] but given the extremely small reading public, it was still nearly impossible to make a decent living from literature alone. However, literature could be used as a means to eventually garner political positions. Indeed, that these novelists aspired to such positions was reflected not only in their literary works (although they were most known for their novels, Magdaleno also wrote plays, essays, and film scripts,[6] while López y Fuentes published poetry and a book of short stories), but also in their non-literary careers. Both were employed as journalists, a profession shared by many writers since it provided them with the opportunity to influence political leadership and public opinion. López y Fuentes, who was born in 1897 (Magdaleno was born later, in 1906), also participated in the Revolution. He joined the constitutionalist forces at the age of 17, and later fought with Carranza against Pancho Villa. Magdaleno aided Vasconcelos in his educational projects and in his presidential campaign, and held two elected positions, that of congressman and senator.

These writers also shared with their predecessors competition from the cultural nationalists, who were stronger and more numerous than ever. In 1934 a group of artists and intellectuals created the Liga de Escritores y Artistas Revolucionarios (League of Revolutionary Writers and Artists), or LEAR, many of whom were Marxist, members of Mexico's communist party, the PCM (Partido Comunista Mexicano), and Cárdenas supporters. This group included some of Mexico's most prominent artists and intellectuals, including the painters David Alfaro Siqueiros, Rufino Tamayo (later expelled for being a "purist"), María Izquierdo, and Carlos Mérida, the musician Silvestre Revueltas, and the engravers Leopoldo Méndez and Guadalupe Posada. It gained prominence through its concerted didactic efforts—the organization of theater, cinema and literature groups—and by voicing its opinions in major publications, including *Crisol* and *El Nacional*. Unifying itself around the slogan "socialist realism", which implied the rejection of all art that failed to serve a socialist cause, the LEAR provoked heated debate around the topic of cultural politics. In fact, in large part because of this group, intellectuals became polarized during the Cárdenas years around those who supported cultural nationalism and those who opposed it. (Lempériere 138–140)

In contrast to the cultural nationalists, *El resplandor* (*Sunburst*) and *El Indio* had practically nothing positive to say about the Indians, the country's leadership, or the mestizo population at large. Although they differ in structure and style, their plots are practically identical, relating the Indians' exploitation by a post-Revolutionary leadership purportedly trying to help them. In *El resplandor* history repeats itself as an hacienda, abandoned during the Revolution, is revived at the expense of cheap Indian labor. Assuring them that they will share in the profits, the new governor, an Indian who was born and raised in the region, convinces the Otomí Indians (Mexico's most impoverished indigenous group) to contribute free labor to put the hacienda (now called a "campo de experimentación") back into working order. However, the Indians' hopes are crushed as they watch a handful of the men in charge pocket all the farm's extensive earnings, and as the cruel overseer, Felipe Rendón, is increasingly more brutal in his treatment of them. Rendón runs the farm exactly as if it were an hacienda of Porfirian times; the Indians are treated like acasillados, receiving a pittance for their labor: a salary that is not enough to live on, pulque, and credit at the only local store, where items are so overpriced that the Indians are kept in constant debt. Like the landowners of pre-revolutionary Mexico, Rendón hunts down Indians who attempt to escape him, and metes out justice as he sees fit (usually hanging the accused). At the same time that the Indians are dying of starvation, Rendón is storing the farm's abundant harvests—originally promised to the Indians—until the prices are driven up in a nearby town. The Indians' anger and resentment finally explode as they kill Rendón and flee with the sacks of corn. Rendón is avenged by his brother, who hangs eight of the Indians and burns the village to the ground, killing women and children in the process. Rendón is replaced by Don Melquíades Esparza, less brutal but equally as ambitious. Esparza has a school built and brings in a teacher, but the teacher has very little success in persuading the Indians to attend regularly, as they are by now entirely distrustful of the government's intentions. Meanwhile, the farm continues to prosper, prompting immigration to the area. The newcomers, many of them campesinos, invade the Indians' land and treat the native population as if they were worse than animals.

As was the case in *El resplandor*, in *El Indio* the Indians' already arduous existence is worsened by the arrival of mestizo outsiders who attempt to profit at the expense of the native population. First, a mestizo outsider seeking gold with two others attacks a young Indian woman. Then, an Indian guide is crippled in his attempt to flee from these same men, who tried to torture him in order to extract information regarding the whereabouts of the gold mines. Outraged, the Indians attack the outsiders as they hastily leave the village, killing one of them. Fearing harsh reprisal, they go into hiding. The whole village is burned to the ground. However, a representative of the government assures the Indians that they will not be punished, and urges them to return to their homes. The reason for this uncharacteristic attitude is that the government needs Indian labor on the haciendas. Starving, the Indians readily agree to return, although they remain suspicious. Their lives return to normal for a short while, until the Revolution breaks out and they are obligated to contribute supplies and labor for the construction of a highway and a school. The highway, they are surprised to discover, will not even pass through their village, while the school benefits only the wealthier mestizo children (the teacher does not speak Spanish, the youngest Indian children cannot make the long hike to get there, and the older children are kept home to work). An Indian is eventually chosen as the school's teacher, and for a while he gives hope to the village by sincerely trying to improve the Indians' conditions, but his efforts prove futile. For example, he gets a head-tax abolished, but soon another tax is levied on each person to pay for the arms needed to defend the land that had belonged to the ranch owner and has now been broken up according to the new government's agrarian policy. Eventually, all the Indian's time is spent defending the lands and showing support for the new leaders, while their crops remain neglected and the lands that should have been divided up among the majority remain intact.

As both authors make overwhelmingly clear, the post-revolutionary political leadership is aggravating the already tense relationship between mestizos and Indians. Forcing the Indians to work the lands, to build roads and schools, to show support for politicians through attendance at political rallies, to pay taxes that do not benefit them, and to send their children to school, has only alienated this population more. The main problem, as both authors see it, is the Indians' extreme distrust of the mestizos, on the one hand, and the mistreatment and denigration of the Indians by non-Indians, on the other hand. They suggest that both Indians and mestizos would be better off were the mestizos to treat the indigenous people with respect. In the words of the teacher in *El Indio*:

> My theory rests on... restoring confidence. How? By kindness, because fortunately the Indian is appreciative. We should treat them in a different way, attract them by giving them some real help and not the sort of protection that has always been aimed at keeping them alive in order to sweat them as if they

> were work animals. And for all this, there is nothing like roads. But not those that go through the valley to connect the cities; link the ranches instead. Highways teach the language better than schools. Then bring the teacher. But he should be someone who knows the customs and feelings of the Indians, and should not try teaching them exactly as if they were whites. Given all this, they would work much better—either on the land they have or the land that would be given to them. (77)

The teacher in *El Resplandor* expresses this same idea, although not so much in words as in actions. He sympathizes with the Indians against their mestizo exploiters, protests the sycophantic actions of Esparza (changing the name of the village to "Villa Herrera"—the name of the governor—and forming a committee with the same name), and determines to help the Indians to one day become major landowners. But by refusing to go along with the local politicians, he is isolated and left defenseless. For example, when he adamantly rejects the offer to give a speech at a ceremony to change the village's name, the politicians denigrate him:

> Vargas thought he must surely be some sort of Communist, and felt that sooner or later they would all be sorry they had helped him. People of that sort, he said, should be isolated somewhere, so they could do no harm to society...So it was decided to have the formal speech delivered by someone else; and they chose Rogelio Oliva Arroyo, a pretty intellectual of Actopan, an opportunist and sponger, who would turn it out like a thousand marvels and consider the task an honor. (284)

Significantly, neither of the teachers in the two novels are able to effect the kinds of changes they believe are necessary to improve the Indians' conditions. Alone in their efforts, they are powerless to counter the greedy politicians and landowners.

Both novels also attempt to inform their readers of indigenous culture. *El resplandor* focuses on the Indians' social relations and dealings with the mestizos, while *El Indio* resembles a novel of customs. The latter makes constant reference to indigenous vocabulary, and describes in great detail Indian rituals and traditions. Since they want to present an overall picture of indigenous life, these novels tend not to give in-depth characterizations. It is striking that of the vast array of indigenous characters introduced in these novels, few stand out for their uniqueness or emotional complexity. Cornejo Polar notes that indigenist literature as a whole avoids complex characterizations of individuals:

"the characters of this novelistic system don't develop before the reader an individual adventure but rather a collective and symbolic history. This is without mentioning the many cases in which the characters are actually collective." (69) Daniele Musacchio points out that:

> The inhabitants of San Andrés (and those of San Felipe) constitute a collective being. Only a few individuals emerge, not because they are different from the others but rather because they play an eminently social role in the group, or because their destiny is a little more clearly drawn. Among the five thousand inhabitants of San Andrés, the reader can with difficulty pick out three whose symbolic function in the novel is evident. (379)

The three Musacchio refers to are Bonifacio, the wise elderly Indian whose authority is widely respected among the Otomí; Lugarda, the consummate mother figure who carries within her the grief of her race; and "Nieves el Colorado" the witch doctor who is feared and esteemed for his relationship with the occult. *El Indio* likewise stresses the importance of the elderly, the female and the witch doctor, but only one figure is a constant in the novel: the crippled guide, symbol of a race broken down by centuries of subjugation.

Besides emphasizing their knowledge of indigenous culture, the authors gain the reader's attention and backing by reinforcing their own prejudices against Mexico's native population. This is a clue that their motives for writing the novels include positioning themselves as mediators or interlocutors of Indian issues. In numerous ways the authors highlight the savage, uncivilized nature of Mexico's native population. For example, they reduce the Indian to his base instincts. In both novels, the Indians' lives revolve primarily around eating, drinking alcohol, procreating, working and defending themselves against intruders. The authors narrate very little else about them. Frequently they compare the Indian to wildlife, as in the following example from *El resplandor*:

> They are bronze faces, color of seasoned fodder, and impassive. The women's eyes gleam darkly, at times innocent as an animal's, at times ambushed and suspicious. The full-fleshed lips are cracked by the arid winds that rise in whorls on the gleaned fields... Their mops of hair glisten like the cactus blooms that ornament the bleak anguish of the highlands. (5–6)

López y Fuentes's analogies between the Indians and animals are even more frequent than those of Magdaleno. Here is one of his more outstanding ones:

> They passed and disappeared. Only thus, stealthily, can this race be seen at its full height. They are like all untamed animals. When they believe themselves alone, they draw up to their full size, but then at the slightest suggestion of danger, how they shrink! What timidity! Even the peccary is beautiful when it is free; the stag a sculpture in solitude. (95)

There is also an emphasis on the grotesque, which satiates the reader's thirst for the morbid, but again dehumanizes the Indians. Both authors stress the constant presence of death among the Indians, giving detailed descriptions of decomposing corpses. Magdaleno offers a particularly revealing description of the men who were hung by Rendón's brother:

> They were swollen and green like carrion, the faces bloated and partly gone. The dogs bunched together, howling... A flock of buzzards hung overhead, flapping about stubbornly. The ragged breeches of the dead men had come loose and fallen down over their legs, uncovering their knotty dirty bodies. Their arms hung stiff, swinging in rhythm with the bodies, the fists clenched in spasm. Clumps of flies beat on their faces, which gaped from ear to ear, the mouths horrible cavities that seemed to be vomiting their tongues (261).

Similarly, López y Fuentes describes the missing face of a volador who fell to his death, and the body of a drowned man whose flesh is being torn apart by vultures: "He was horribly swollen, and the minnows had chewed up his lips and eyelids." (196)

The authors further insist on the Indian's close relationship with the occult. On the one hand the authors point to the ignorance underlying superstition. On the other hand, they lend credence to the superstitions, thereby associating the Indians with what is mysterious, dangerous and evil. In both novels, the tremendous powers of the witch doctor are taken as a given. As already pointed out, Nieves el Colorado, the witch doctor in *El resplandor*, is one of the most feared and esteemed men in the village. As just one example of his powers, on the tree where he is hung (by Rendón's brother) a huge cross inexplicably appears which the Indians interpret as meaning that he will protect the village from the work of the devil. Similarly, *El Indio* narrates in minute detail the workings of two brujos pitted against each other by two families: that of the crippled man, angered by the elders' decision that he not be allowed to marry the woman to whom he was engaged (because he can no longer work productively), and that of the family of the woman's new suitor. The brujo helping the suitor's family discovers that the other brujo is actually a "nahual", particularly powerful because he can change forms. The brujo hence uses his own powers to kill the "nahual" when he is in one of his animal forms. The nahual is found in his bed, transformed back into a human, but with wounds all over his body as if he had been attacked by a pack of animals. Later, the suitor is attacked by a herd of wild boars when he's out hunting:

> Witchcraft was stirring a new uneasiness in them. Every person who saw the body of the hunter, covered with wounds, maintained that they were not made by peccary tusks at all, but were the marks of the *tlahuelilo*, the devil himself, which the spirit of the *nahual* now inhabited, and from whom they had all been expecting reprisals. (184)

By reinforcing these negative stereotypes, the authors instill in the reader an instinctive repulsion and fear of the indigenous population. I would argue that this is one of their intentions. On the one hand, they are making the point that the Indians' superstitious thinking prevents them from being agents for their own integration. They imply that the Indians must rely on others for this task. On the other hand, Magdaleno and López y Fuentes are underlining the urgency of finding ways of integrating, and hence taming, a segment of the population that could prove dangerous otherwise. That the Indian represents a threat is not just hinted at, but expressed outright. *El resplandor* highlights the Indians' savagery right from the beginning of the novel, where we learn that the inhabitants of two villages, San Felipe and San Andrés, are killing each other over access to the river that runs through the hacienda. The violence has become so severe that the local priest can no longer endure living there and leaves the region. In *El Indio*, the author points to the danger of giving the Indians any authority or weapons. When they are provided with arms to defend themselves against the ranch owners who are trying to regain their land, they behave like savages:

> Now they were men: that is what a gun and authority will do. They went along jauntily, and when they met whites on the highway they looked them in the eye... The troop, which included all the able-bodied men from the ranchería, was impressive. The Indians gave yells of pure savage joy. A few drinks at a roadside stand excited them more and more. (245)

Besides being potentially dangerous, the Indian is every bit as apt as the mestizo to misuse power in these novels. For this reason, the authors suggest that it does no good to entrust educated Indians with positions of authority. The Indian educated in mestizo society may feel sympathy for members of his own race, but he will ultimately put his own ambitions above them. This enhances the Indians' distrust of outsiders. In *El resplandor* the Indian who eventually becomes governor exploits the very people who raised him. El Coyote, whose parents were killed at an early age, is nurtured by Lugarda, who treats him as her own son. He leaves the village as an adolescent to study in a nearby village. Following the Revolution, he experiences a meteoric rise to power, exploiting his indigenous roots to gain support and win the elections. The Indians of San Felipe and San Andrés have high hopes that "El Coyote" (his nickname) will improve their lives, but they are sorely disappointed. Under him, the cycle of abuse of landowner against Indian is revived. Symbolically, he even marries the inheritor of the hacienda, giving birth to a son whose non-indigenous features he's immensely proud of. "El Coyote" quickly forgets the Indian girl (the daughter of his surrogate father) he impregnated, and her fiancé, whom he killed in order to eliminate any opposition to his affections for the girl.

Because "El Coyote's" non-indigenous education led him to betray his own people, the Indians become more wary of mestizo society. Thus when Herrera offers a scholarship to send a child to the city to study, all the Indians resist (although the child is sent anyway). By creating more distrust, Saturnino Herrera actually does greater damage to mestizo/Indian relations than a mestizo who had acted in a similar manner would have done.

Likewise, in *El Indio* the indigenous teacher who seems so intent on helping the Indians winds up putting his own political aspirations first. Because of his success in organizing the Indians to resist the landowners and to support the new politicians who supposedly have their interests in mind, the teacher is able to advance his political career (even though this wasn't his original intention). Eventually, he abandons the Indians to further his career in the city. Faced with attacks by the former landowners' armies, the Indians are more wary and distrustful of mestizos than ever before. In fact, the novel ends with a short chapter entitled "Distrust", which reads as follows:

> The cripple still spies from his hiding-place in the brambles. Distrust itself, as he looks out on the highway—civilization. High on the mountain, the sentinel waits for the signal. Like the rest of their people, all they know is that the *gente*

de razón want to attack them, that hatred snarls in packs in the valley and the sierra, and that, in the city, the leader is well taken care of. (256)

Interestingly, the authors further reinforce what they perceive as some of the Indians' main attributes through the narrative structure itself. For example, Denis Parle notes that Magdaleno offers two perspectives of time, one that is static and the other that is active. The former is identified with the Otomí Indians, the latter with the mestizos:

> In the first three chapters of the novel, the narrator evokes an atemporal reality that reflects the interior reality of the Otomí world. Although the narration begins with a concrete line of action, in the following chapters the narrator progressively erases the sensation of a concrete line of action and time. Consequently, the reader becomes disoriented and gets lost in an opaque and sinuous sphere of time in which the past and the present exist simultaneously. In other words, time doesn't exist for the Otomí; its reality is uniform and unalterable. ("Las funciones del tiempo..." 59)

As Parle further notes, the unchanging nature of the Indians' lives is reinforced by a lengthy flashback in time, in which the author recounts the hacienda's history. Magdaleno emphasizes that the hacienda's post-revolutionary operation closely resembles that of previous times, going all the way back to its foundation in the 1600's. The static nature of time for the Indians hence connotes primitiveness, while the linear nature of time for the mestizos signifies progress and civilization. In other words, through his manipulation of time, Magdaleno stresses a couple of major points: 1) the Indians have little in common with the rest of Mexican society (their temporal perspective is completely different); 2) they are uncivilized (they continue to live like savages); and 3) the Revolution has failed to bring progress to them. López y Fuentes employs narrative techniques in a similar way, although they are not nearly so complex. Like Magdaleno, he reinforces his main message—that nothing has changed for the Indian—by beginning and ending the novel in the same way: with the Indians' distrust of the mestizo. However, unlike Magdaleno, he employs highly simplistic language and sentence structures, which convey a paternalistic attitude towards the native people, who are viewed as child-like.

Despite the largely deprecatory view of the Indian, the mestizo actually fares much worse in these novels. The Indians have some positive qualities, the most notable being their physical prowess, and their sense of community, responsibility to each other and justice. The mestizo has virtually none. He is greedy, self-seeking, abusive, insensitive and corrupt. His treatment of the Indian is particularly odious. In both novels, it is not just the politicians and landowners who consider the Indians as less than human, but everyone else as well (with the exception of the teacher). In *El resplandor* the bourgeoisie from the city ridicule the Indians who come to show their support for their political candidate, and refuse to let their children have anything to do with them. The same occurs with the campesinos, who invade the Indians' land as they arrive to work on the hacienda. Even the priests, who connive with the landowners, denigrate and exploit the Indians. Likewise, in *El Indio* no one from outside the indigenous community, with the exception of the teacher, treats them with respect or cares about their welfare (the Church included). According to the authors, the mestizos' racist practices and attitudes are isolating the indigenous population like never before.

Further influencing these novelists' articulation of the indigenous community was the projection of their own personal experience and world-view onto the native population they were attempting to describe. Magdaleno and López y Fuentes grew up in the provinces, but they moved to Mexico City at an early age to receive their educations, and remained there permanently. They had little contact with the indigenous people, and their writings reveal a bias towards the city, which they viewed as representative of civilization and progress, in contrast to the country, which to them connoted backwardness. This is evident, as pointed out earlier, in their articulations of the Indian. In addition to the city bias, the authors' choice of the novel as the medium through which to construct the indigenous experience is prejudiced towards a westernized literary system. In fact, the use of the written word itself went contrary to indigenous preferences for oral forms of narrative. The novel, in other words, was best suited to convey the novelists' concerns, but was completely alien to the Indians, who expressed their experiences orally. The novel "is the genre most consistently tied to the bourgeois and its privileged space—the city—and in the same measure appears profoundly detached from the referent that indigenism is intending to clarify." (Cornejo Polar 59–60)

According to Antonio Cornejo Polar, the inherent contradictions in most indigenist literature result from social and cultural heterogeneity, or the lack of correspondence between the socio-cultural milieu to which the authors belong and that which they are describing. Social heterogeneity refers to the disparities between a modern, urban capitalist system and a less developed, precapitalist, agrarian society. Cultural heterogeneity pertains to the dissimilarities between a western culture that is based on values, attitudes and procedures dominated by rationalism, and a native culture that, in spite of modifications, remains distinct from the western one. Cornejo Polar states:

> In both cases the definitive note is the heterogeneity of the components that form indigenism, product of a society and a culture that mobilizes its resources to reveal the nature of another society and culture with which one national space is shared. Indigenism is a pluriculture and plurisocial movement. (26–27)

Some critics have argued that Magdaleno's and López y Fuentes's novels were supportive of Cárdenas, who was obviously devoted to the improvement of the conditions of Indian life. Donald Schmidt, for example, contends that the indigenous novels of the 1930s portray the Indian largely in terms of the abuses he suffers because the novelists had been angered by the frustration of Cardenas's programs. (654) Cynthia Steele likewise maintains "if we turn specifically to the conditions of production of the Mexican *indigenista* novel during the 1930s and 1940s, we find a coalition between the progressive Cárdenas government and liberal and radical intellectuals." (78) Steele concedes, however, that in spite of the editorial espousal of official policy by the rural school teacher in *El Indio*, "several aspects of character and plot tend to undermine the very theories that the author endorses on an explicit level." (78) In particular, she explains that "the explicit espousal of Indian integration into mestizo society is undermined by characterization that implicitly argues for the Indian's continued isolation from the decadence and evil of urban, industrial civilization." (78) The plot is also contradictory in the sense that "the leader", or school teacher, who conforms to the ideal of the bilingual teacher (depicted as a national hero during the Cárdenas regime), allows himself to be coopted by the mestizo leadership. According to these novels, the solution to the Indian's oppression does not lie in such teachers, but rather elsewhere.

It is important to note that, although the authors may have supported Cárdenas, and although their novels were supposedly based on the period when Calles dominated the nation's leadership, their works are nonetheless critical of this president's political and social policies, indigenism among them. Joseph Sommer argues the same in his analysis of *El resplandor*, in which he finds a "genuinely critical challenge with respect to the social politics of Cardenist Mexico." (29) First of all, had the novelists really been supportive of Cárdenas's indigenist initiatives, it would likely have been reflected in their novels. Yet, in spite of this President's many efforts to improve the Indians' situation, no mention is made of them. Most importantly, there is no allusion to the large-scale nature of agrarian reform under Cárdenas's presidency. Rather, the authors appear intent on portraying the agricultural milieu of pre-Cárdenas Mexico, when the nation's cultivable lands still remained in the hands of the large landowners, with whom many politicians and military leaders made illicit deals in return for financial profit. Even more telling, while the novels actually do allude to some changes that occurred most dramatically during the Cárdenas presidency, including the formation of agrarian organizations and cooperatives and the construction of highways and irrigation systems, they view none of them favorably. The authors depict these changes not only as new twists on an old system that remains entrenched, but also as worsening the Indian's already deplorable condition. They stress that Indian labor is being exploited like never before, and new immigrants to the area are disparaging the Indians and invading their lands. Finally, the authors' opposition to Cárdenas's indigenist policy is apparent in their depictions of the Indian. Magdaleno and López y Fuentes emphasized the negative aspects of the Indian character, and portrayed rural education and social programs as having been a failure.

The novelists, in other words, expressed criticism of Cárdenas without directly attacking him. They were, after all, Cardenistas themselves. For this reason they concentrate on pre-Cárdenas Mexico and on the Indian's repression not by the government itself but by corrupt politicians, the Church, and the general population. Their critical stance, along with their self-portrayal as experts on indigenous culture, aimed at least in part at carving out a niche for themselves in Mexican politics.

To their credit, Magdaleno and López y Fuentes put their fingers on some of the principal reasons for the government's failure to integrate the Indian, most importantly of which was the Indian's profound distrust of mainstream Mexico, exacerbated by continued injustices committed against him. However, their implied solutions to the problem—creating infrastructure that directly benefits the Indians, condemning the Church as well as immoral politicians and landowners, and teaching the mestizo population to respect the indigenous population—were not new (Gamio had suggested them much earlier). They also required the loss of indigenous cultural identity. Ironically, by assuming that the Indian should adapt to Western society, Magdaleno and López y Fuentes were complicit in the very diminishment of the indigenous people that they denounce others for. By privileging Western culture, through the use of non-indigenous literary devices and the portrayal of the Indian as savage, they imply that the native population is inferior to the rest of Mexican society. Both indigenist writers and the state failed either to notice or to address the contradictions implicit in the indigenist theories of their times, and consequently the Indian's integration remained an unrealized goal.

The Noble Savage: Film

Indigenism also influenced cinema in the 1930s, but not nearly to the extent that it did literature, muralism, and other artistic mediums. Only six films on the Indian were produced during this decade: *Janitzio* (1934), directed by Carlos Navarro, *El indio* (1938), by Armando Vargas de la Maza, *La india bonita* (1938), by Antonio Helú, *Rosa de Xochimilco* (1938), by Carlos Véjar, *La noche de los mayas* (1939), by Chano Urueta, and *El signo de la muerte* (1939), also by Chano Urueta. None of these films achieved wide success. It wasn't until the 1940s, with Emilio Fernández's *María Candelaria* (1943) that a film focusing on the Indians became popular. Evidently film lacked an audience interested in Mexico's indigenous population.

Most of these films were highly nationalistic, both in style and content. Stylistically, many of the filmmakers were influenced by the work of Sergei Eisenstein, a Soviet director who worked in Mexico during the late 1930s and developed an aesthetic of nationalism. Eisenstein traveled throughout Mexico while working on the film *¡Que viva México!*, paying close attention to the land, the people, and post-revolutionary culture. He left the country before finishing the film, which was nevertheless released without his authorization. According to Carl Mora, this film "was to have an important influence, even if indirect, on subsequent Mexican filmmakers who were to develop a 'national' style of cinema." (37) Among the techniques that Eisenstein developed, and that were to be copied by Mexican filmmakers, were "low-angle long shots in silhouette that emphasize the stark landscape and sky and the smallness of the human figures before them; the close-ups of Indian faces and shrouded women; and the 'dead tree framing' in which long shots are composed between the gnarled branches of a dried-up tree." (Mora 79–80) Eisenstein and his followers attempted to evoke Mexico's essence through shots of the landscape and native people. Directors of indigenous films further exalted "Mexicanness" by portraying indigenous customs and practices, local dances and nationalistic music (often by Silvestre Revueltas). The result was a sort of tourist image of Mexico.

With respect to content, these films tended to glorify native Mexicans, attributing to them such characteristics as dignity, honesty, moral purity, courage and physical strength. By doing this, they were attempting to foment respect for the Indian. They were also promoting a sense of national identity and pride, and attempting to identify the masses with the Indians by stressing shared characteristics and experiences. Many of the same traits ascribed to the Indians were also those applied to non-indigenous Mexicans in other films. The masses could further relate to the Indians' exploitation by the wealthy and powerful, their struggle to earn a living, and their desire to fulfill such basic human needs as finding love.

Most of the indigenist films in the 1930s were melodramas. Generally they portray the Indian as a noble savage who lives in harmony with nature but is exploited by outsiders or a local non-indigenous authority. For example, in *Janitzio* the Indian, Zirahuén,[7] who fishes for a living, is jailed for complaining about an outsider, Manuel, who is fixing the prices at which fish are sold. Manuel promises Eréndira (Zirahuén's girlfriend) to free Zirahuén if she spends time with him in Pátzcuaro. She agrees. Upon being freed from jail, Zirahuén discovers what happened and kills Manuel. He must return to the island of Janitizio with Eréndira, who is to be stoned to death according to custom, which forbids women from the community from sleeping with outsiders. However, on the boat ride back, Zirahuén decides to choose love over his social obligations and heads back to Pátzcuaro. However, his action fails to save Eréndira.

This movie is somewhat ambiguous in its depiction of the Indian. On the one hand, the Indians are innocent victims of the outsiders who exploit them. On the other hand, the film appears to reproach the rigidity of indigenous customs that, for example, demand the brutal death of a woman who acted selflessly on behalf of the man she loved. It also appears to blame not just exploitative outsiders for the Indians' seclusion, but also indigenous culture itself, which resists contact with the outside world (as emphasized by the fact that the community resides on an island). The film is equally ambiguous regarding the Indians' integration. It seems to react against the outside world that tries to exploit the indigenous community, but at the same time depicts the Indians' isolation as undesirable. These same ambiguities would appear later in *María Candelaria*, which was loosely based on *Janitzio*.

Ironically, one of the most nationalistic of the indigenous films was *El indio*, based on the novel by Gregorio López y Fuentes. The novel suffered significant changes in its adaptation to film. For example, while López y Fuentes underscores the Revolution's negative impact on the native population, the movie's prologue boasts that the Revolution redeemed the Indian. Even more significantly, the movie idealizes the native hero, in stark contrast to the novel, which emphasizes many negative aspects of the indigenous character and life. In addition, the movie focuses (in the spirit of the melodrama) on the conflict that arises between two Indians, Julián and Felipe, who desire the same woman, María. In the novel this conflict is a subplot, not part of the main plot. Moreover, the movie significantly modifies this love triangle for dramatic purposes. The Spanish boss, Gonzalo, attempts to take advantage of María, only to be promptly killed by one of her other two suitors. Another very important change to the film involves the ending. In contrast to the novel, which stresses the Indians' powerlessness, the movie ends happily with an indigenous rebellion and the union of María with Felipe, her true love.

Another important difference between the indigenous novels and films of this period involves the portrayal of the mestizo. In their novels, Magdaleno and López y Fuentes condemn the mestizo's mistreatment of the Indian, blaming him for the Indian's continued isolation. In the films, those who abuse the native people are stereotypical villains who do not represent the mestizo and white population at large. To the contrary, the films attempt to identify the mostly mestizo audiences with the Indian, invoking sympathy for these downtrodden but proud people. The film audiences could thus go home guilt-free.

Through their constructions of the Indian, the filmmakers, like the novelists, discoursed about the native people without ever including their voices. They also used the archetype of the Indian for reasons having little to do with the Indians themselves, including most importantly the promotion of nationalism. Unlike the novels, cinema did not focus on many of the real problems facing the native Mexicans, including widespread racism. In fact, in some senses the films contradicted the novels. Just as the novelists were trying to bring attention to the mestizo's implication in the Indian's plight, the films (which actually reached this audience) were sending the masses home with a guiltless conscious. Unlike the novels, the films also sent contradictory messages regarding the Indian's integration, appearing to at once champion and reject it. Thus while films on the Indian may have advanced nationalism, they probably did little to combat racism or to promote the integration process.

Notes

1. While Cárdenas undertook numerous measures to achieve a "Mexican socialism", including agrarian reform, the organization of popular organizations, and the implementation of a socialist education, he proved unsuccessful. Economic development after 1938 was for the most part modeled after orthodox capitalism. External and internal pressures prevented Cárdenas from deviating from the capitalist model. These pressures grew following his 1938 decision to expropriate the petroleum industry, a move that precipitated an economic and political crisis. On the one hand, Cárdenas was faced with severe economic and political reprisals from the United States, which demanded compensation. On the other hand, the crisis strengthened the position of anticardenist forces, among whom included important members of the military, who objected in particular to Lombardo Toledano and the CTM, whose growing power they considered a threat to their own. In addition, the struggle over who was to succeed Cárdenas had begun, and with it the debate over whether to continue with the Cardenist program during the next presidential period. According to Lorenzo Meyer, the crisis in part led Cárdenas to choose Ávila Camacho as his successor. Camacho did not have the support of the campesino sector, but was the candidate of choice of the governors and legislators. The campesinos and workers lacked the independence to effectively oppose these developments, as they were organized into institutions directed from the top down. Among these institutions were the Confederation of National Workers (Confederación de Trabajadores), or CTM, and the National Campesino Confederation (Confederación Nacional Campesina), or CNN, both of which supported the new official party, called the Party of the Mexican Revolution (el Partido de la Revolución Mexicana). (Meyer 161–166)
2. Interestingly, although in these novels the Indian character was not intended to emblematize the national character as a whole, in later works many of its main aspects would reappear as symptomatic of the national soul. Most notably, the Indians' alleged indifference

towards death, their solitary and melancholic natures, stoicism and proclivity towards violence (especially when drunk) would be posed as inherent to the Mexican character in such works as *El laberinto de la soledad*, by Octavio Paz.

3. Depictions of the Indian actually aid in the delineation of mestizo character traits. On the one hand, the Indian's alterity provided a contrast by which to more clearly define the mestizo. On the other hand, since the mestizo shaped the Indian (according to the authors), the Indian's deplorable state served to underscore some of his abuser's particularly despicable qualities.

4. In an interview with Emmanuel Carballo, Magdaleno stated outright that he had supported Vasconcelos because "he (Vasconcelos) wanted to regenerate the country. And the country was in the hands of murderers and thieves." (357) Furthermore, when asked whether he had sympathized with Pancho Villa, he replied: "he was a bandit like everyone who participated in the Revolution. Well, not everyone, the Revolution had a handful of idealists." (361)

5. Under Cárdenas, the financing of the University of Mexico (Universidad de México) was resumed, and several important institutes of higher education were created, including the National Polytechnic Institute (Instituto Politécnico Nacional), the National Institute of History and Anthropology (Instituto Nacional de Historia y Antropología), and the College of Mexico (Colegio de México).

6. Interestingly, Magdaleno wrote film scripts for movies in the 1940's dealing with the province and the Indian (*Flor Silvestre*, *María Candelaria*, *Bugambilia*, *Río Escondido*, *Maclovia* , *Pueblerina*), in which his depictions of the native population often differed drastically from that of his novel, *El resplandor*. For instance, *María Candelaria*, one of the most popular films of the 1940's, offers a bucolic portrait of Indian life. Why Magdaleno would contradict his view of the Indian character and life as portrayed in his novel is not completely clear. His motives could have been purely financial. Magdaleno stated in an interview with Emmanuel Carballo that he made most of his living from the film industry. (362) He also revealed that he often couldn't choose the topics. For example, the director, Emilio Fernández (nicknamed "El Indio"), imposed the topic of *María Candelaria* on him. (Carballo 371) It is also possible that he did not object to compromising his views in film because he did not consider film to be the appropriate medium through which to

express the political messages of *El resplandor*. It is more probable, however, that those views would not have been accepted for cinema, as they were highly critical of the government and Mexican society as a whole.
7. Emilio "El Indio" Fernández (who was of partial indigenous descent) played Zirahuén. Fernández later directed *María Candelaria*, along with a host of other popular films.

Chapter Four

Nationalism, the Pelado and the Myth of Authenticity

By the middle of the 1930s a period of incipient industrialization had begun that attracted increasing numbers of Mexicans to the urban areas, particularly to Mexico City.[1] Reflecting these changes, some authors began to focus on the urban milieu and on what it meant to be a modern Mexican. Film was more hesitant to deal with the urban environment, and instead concentrated on Mexico's countryside. Nevertheless, it was responding to the changes brought about by the modernization process and Lázaro Cardenas's (1934–1940) agrarian policies. Film's idealization of ranch life in porfirian Mexico expressed nostalgia for times past, and a rejection of Cárdenas's agricultural policies, which called for the breakup of the large haciendas. It reinforced traditional values that many Mexicans felt were being threatened. Nonetheless, in the late 1930s one urban figure began to appear in cinema who became tremendously popular during the next decade: the comic Mario Moreno "Cantinflas", a pelado (poor urban immigrant, of partial indigenous descent) from the Mexico City slums.

The pelado was also employed in literature, usually as an archetype through which to analyze the Mexican character. However, constructions of the pelado in literature were usually quite different from those in film. Often they embodied the worst national character traits, those that were maintaining the nation in a state of economic backwardness. Reflecting and promoting the interest of the educated elite and the economically privileged, many authors of "Mexicanness" sought to identify Mexicans' pre-modern characteristics in the hope of forging a more modern Mexican. The essayists, Samuel Ramos and Jorge Cuesta, and the playwright, Rodolfo Usigli, focused in particular on Mexicans' inauthenticity, arguing that it constituted the root cause of a number of other character deficiencies. They attributed inauthenticity not just to the pelado, but also to the nation's cultural and political leadership, which they wished to discredit. Ramos, Cuesta and Usigli, as well as many other intellectuals of the period, felt threatened by the cultural nationalists, who grew in influence during Cárdenas's presidency. They maintained that by glorifying the masses, the cultural nationalists were aggravating Mexicans' most serious problem. In their view, the cultural nationalists were providing the Mexican with another mask he could employ to evade coming to terms with his real self. As a consequence, they were obstructing the process of modernization, maintaining the country in a state of cultural and political backwardness and fragmentation.

Many filmmakers of this period, who relied on the masses for its financial survival and also partially on the state, took a different course. Most never attempted to point up Mexicans' character defects. To the contrary, they glorified the national character, in particular through the *charro* (cowboy or ranch owner), who embodied what film considered some of the best and most authentic Mexican traits. These traits included dignity, pride, benevolence, bravery and physical prowess. Through the *charro,* the "comedia ranchera" exalted machismo and reinforced the patriarchal structure. As such, it appeared to reaffirm the permanence of traditional Mexican values in the face of rapid social and economic change.

Like the essayists, the Cantinflas films highlighted inauthenticity as one of Mexicans' main character traits, but ascribed this trait not to the poor but rather to the wealthy. These films consistently portrayed the upper class as hypocritical, corrupt, affected and arrogant. In contrast, the pelado Cantinflas is portrayed as being highly authentic. To some extent his authenticity was degrading, as his appearance and behavior were often unappealing. However, he was not meant to symbolize the urban poor, although some Mexicans may have related to aspects of his demeanor and personality. Rather, he was a caricature, just as the wealthy in the movie are also caricatures.

One of the major purposes of the Cantinflas films was to enable the poor and the rich to laugh at each other. Through humor, the Cantinflas films defuse social tensions without ever threatening the existing socioeconomic order. The laughter the film provokes is never derisive, nor is it reserved solely for the rich. All members of Mexican society are made fun of, and in fact Cantinflas himself is the primary source of entertainment. The wealthy, moreover, are ultimately shown to be good at heart. Indeed, once the communication barrier is overcome (Cantinflas becomes tongue-tied and spouts nonsensical chatter—"cantinflismos"—when communicating with the rich), everyone gets along just fine.

The Inauthenticity of the Mexican Character

Some of the major writers of the early to mid 1930's, including the essayists Samuel Ramos and Jorge Cuesta, and the playwright Rodolfo Usigli, analyzed Mexicans' character defects in even greater depth than the novelists, stopping not just at an identification of their countrymen's aberrant behavior, but carefully examining as well its causes and effects. All three stress inauthenticity as Mexicans' gravest problem, but approach the problem from different angles. Ramos searches for its historical causes and its current manifestations, studying the "pelado" as the most representative archetype of the Mexican character. Cuesta and Usigli, reacting against cultural nationalism, apply Ramos's concept of inauthenticity to examine Mexican politics.

These writers' ideas were taken very seriously at the time, and generated wide debate. This reception was not solely the result of the controversial nature of their works, but of the history of the essay in Latin America and the nature of essay itself. Ramos and Cuesta were participating in a long essayistic tradition of dedication to the subject of the nation. The essay has held a preeminent place in the intellectual development of Latin America, beginning with such founding works as José Enrique Rodó's *Ariel*, one of the first texts to propose a Latin American identity. José Miguel Oviedo points out that "the founders of the continent's cultural and literary conscience are its essayists. And the intellectual impact of certain works of critical thought in the imagination of poets and novelists may still be seen in our days." (22) The importance given to the essay is a result of the genre itself. More inclined towards exploring ideas than in developing a story line, it is generally considered more objective than other genres. The historical referent is also usually more obvious in essay than in film. As a consequence, the ideas expressed in essay are generally taken more seriously than those expressed in fiction.

The most important factor contributing to the strong reaction the authors' works received was its timing, as nationalism was in full swing by the end of the Maximato and the beginning of the Cárdenas presidency. Intellectuals who opposed the concept of "Mexicanness" forged by José Vasconcelos faced intense opposition. The Contemporáneos,[2] of whom Cuesta and Ramos formed a part (Cuesta, the only essayist, was considered the group's main spokesperson, while Ramos has often been cited as its philosopher), formed the main targets of opposition for the cultural nationalists. This group refused to mix art and politics, flatly rejecting the use of literature as a means to advance a nationalistic agenda. As such, the concept of "Mexicanness" hardly enters into their works.[3] To the contrary, the Contemporáneos practiced a modernist form of art that excluded politics and celebrated the decadent. As a consequence, they were attacked as being elitist, aristocratic and unpatriotic.

Cuesta and Ramos defended the anti-nationalistic stance by arguing universalism was actually more Mexican than the "false" nativism of the nationalists. The Contemporáneos believed that European culture was far superior to any native one. It is partially for this reason that Ramos, making an implicit comparison with the more "mature" European culture, insists Mexico is at the adolescent stage of development, and also argues that the Creoles (Mexicans born in colonial times of Spanish parents) are the most "genuine" Mexicans. In other words, it was natural for many intellectuals, formed in the European tradition, to react against a cultural movement that rejected Europeanism altogether. The Contemporáneos also reflected the belief, widespread among the elite, that Mexico was culturally inferior to Europe, and they perceived their role as rectifying that situation. They believed that in order to compete culturally with Europe, Mexican art should reflect universal values rather than solely national ones, as European art did. They argued that only by being meaningful to mankind in general could Mexican art attain the status of that of European art.

The Contemporáneos were not uniform in the degrees to which they opposed cultural nationalism. Ramos, for example, was much more conciliatory and moderate in his criticism than Cuesta was. In fact, he argued against both proponents of either a purely nationalist or a purely Europeanist school of thought (the latter to which the Contemporáneos belonged). This difference became apparent in 1932 when an ongoing polemic between the Contemporáneos and the *Crisol* writers came to a head. Just when the magazine *Contemporáneos* could no longer be published due to a lack of funds, and the writers were divided about what direction to take, an article in the newspaper El *Universal* raised a question—Is the avant-garde in crisis?—that sparked a heated debate. Both Ramos and Cuesta responded, but in surprisingly distinct manners. Ramos, along with Gorostiza, adapted a conciliatory approach toward the nationalists by proposing a return to Mexican values or "lo mexicano." Cuesta, on the other hand, took the opportunity to praise the critical spirit of the Contemporáneos and condemn the compromised one of *Crisol* writers. These different degrees of anti-nationalist sentiments between the authors could owe itself in part to the fact that Ramos was less interested in modernist art than Cuesta, and maintained closer ties to the state. He held several high public positions (at the National Preparatory School and the Autonomous National University of Mexico). Cuesta, to the contrary, was never directly employed by the state.

That both Ramos and Cuesta concentrated on the inauthentic nature of the Mexican was crucial to their goal of debunking nationalism and bolstering their own position within Mexican society. In other words, their focus on "inauthenticity" formed part of a power struggle over who defined the "genuine" Mexican character. Labeling "inauthentic" a movement that searched for and exalted the so-called authentic Mexican soul was about the strongest criticism that could be made of that movement. At the same time, arguing that intellectuals formed the most "authentic" segment of the Mexican population constituted a means of according themselves greater authority. In other words, contending that cultural nationalism was a manifestation of Mexican's tendency toward inauthenticity enabled these intellectuals to at once discredit that movement and lend credence to their own arguments. Their authority on the subject was fortified by a long tradition (not only in Mexico but in all of Latin America as well) of preoccupation with inauthenticity. Within this tradition it has been intellectuals who have been entrusted with the task of defining what and what does not constitute a "genuine" national character.

Although neither Ramos nor Cuesta clearly define what makes up the "genuine" Mexican character, that both endorsed an acceptance of European values as a means of regaining authenticity was telling. On the one hand, it constituted a sort of self-defense of their own intellectual and social backgrounds, inspired in the European tradition. Also, as pointed out earlier, portraying themselves as the most authentic segment of the population constituted a means of attaining respect. On the other hand, maintaining that European values were central components of the Mexican character and culture actually masked a desire to return to a tradition (for Ramos humanism and for Cuesta classicism) that valued intellectuals. It betrayed a feeling of insecurity during an era when intellectuals were no longer granted the respect they had enjoyed prior to the Revolution. As Henry Schmidt puts it:

> While the Revolution contributed to the dismantling of positivism it also generated a conflict between social values and a humanism that masked the resurgence of the ego threatened by the leveling tendencies of the masses. This partially explains why Ortega, the elitist philosopher par excellence, was a guiding spirit at this time. Thus in a sense Ramos and his group were creating a new aristocracy of thought. (161)

As Schmidt notes, Cuesta's and Ramos's (as well as many other Mexican authors') obvious debt to the ideas of the Spanish philosopher Ortega y Gassett betrays a feeling of insecurity in the face of the increasing power wielded by the largely uneducated masses. Ortega y Gasset believed in the existence of select minorities ("minorías selectas" or "hombre excelente"), who constituted the authentic segment of the population, versus the inauthentic and much more numerous masses ("hombre masa"). In the face of growing communist movements in Europe, he was concerned by the power held by the masses, whom he believed were incapable of leading nations, a task that should be left to the "minorías selectas." It is not surprising that Ramos and Cuesta would be influenced by Ortega y Gassett, as parallels could be drawn between Europe and Mexico. Not only had the Revolution empowered the masses and enabled some of their members to attain positions of great power, but the presidency of Lázaro Cárdenas, during which Cuesta and Ramos wrote their essays, also had a distinct socialist ring.

El perfil del hombre y la cultura en México
Ramos, who enjoyed a privileged and happy upbringing, began from an early age to attend some of the most prestigious Mexican schools. His literary and journalistic talents became evident when he was young, and at the age of 13 he began publishing. Despite his obvious writing talents he studied medicine, but changed course after attending lectures by Antonio Caso.[4] In 1918 and 1919 he studied philosophy at the Universidad Nacional de México. Among his colleagues were Vicente Lombardo Toledano, Alfonso Caso, Daniel Cosío Villegas, and Manuel

Gómez Morín, who later became some of Mexico's most prominent cultural and political leaders. In 1920, when Vasconcelos became Secretary of Public Education (SEP), Ramos was among those intellectuals asked to collaborate on his national education projects. He also aided him with the review *La antorcha*, founded by Vasconcelos after he left the SEP. When the former Secretary of Public Education went abroad to live, he handed over the direction of the review to Ramos. Ramos was deeply influenced by Vasconcelos's *La raza cósmica* and *Indología*, which sparked his interest in creating a philosophy of the Mexican culture, a pursuit to which he dedicated most of the rest of his career as an educator[5] and writer for numerous literary and philosophical reviews. (Hernández Luna xi)

Without a doubt, Ramos's *El perfil del hombre y la cultura en Mexico (Profile of Man and Culture in Mexico)* constitutes his most renowned work. It represents the first attempt at an in-depth analysis of the Mexican character, and decisively influenced all works of the same nature to follow. In this work, Ramos applied psychoanalysis to diagnose Mexicans' inferiority complex, which he believed leads Mexicans to hide their authentic selves behind masks: "This character is lent, and we wear it like a mask to cover our authentic beings." (50) Ramos argued that only by removing these masks could Mexicans combat their inferiority complex. In order to do this, however, Ramos argued that Mexicans needed to first acquire self-awareness. Hence he began an extensive analysis of what it means to be Mexican, believing that only by making Mexicans aware of themselves could they change.

Ramos likens Mexico's growth as a nation to that of a human being. Mexicans, in his opinion, are at the childhood or adolescent phase, which he contends is the stage when character is being formed and an inferiority complex appears. By making such an analogy, and by playing the role of psychologist, he sets himself up as an authority figure. He emphasizes this role further by constructing an hierarchical ladder of "authenticity" in which his own social class occupies the highest rung. Interestingly, the lowest rung is dominated by the "pelado," the poor urban dweller, who epitomizes all that is wrong with the Mexican character. The pelado displays Mexicans' worst characteristics. Ramos considers the pelado, and with him the lower classes in general, as the most inauthentic Mexicans. In his view, the pelado is little more than an animal. As he puts it: "The *pelado* belongs to a most vile category of social fauna; he is a form of human rubbish from the great city. He is an animal whose ferocious pantomimes are designed to terrify others." (58–59) Ramos characterizes the pelado as resentful, hostile, intellectually primitive, physically and verbally abusive, extremely sensitive to criticism and very easily provoked. The pelado, he says, exalts his virility in order to compensate for his sense of inferiority and his downtrodden ego.

Notably, Ramos stresses that the pelado is someone to be feared, mainly because of his proclivity towards abrupt, violent outbursts. In other words, he reinforces a common stereotype of the poor as irrational and extremely physical. Even if his description were true, it is highly suspect that he fails to place the pelado's behavior within a proper social perspective. That is, he doesn't explain how difficult social and economic conditions (i.e. unemployment, poor working and living conditions, discrimination, etc.) may have contributed to the behaviors he mentions. He probably does not because this would have entailed a critique of the socioeconomic system of the time, which he wished to promote, and implicated his middle-class audience, whose favor he wished to garner.

The urban Mexican, and especially the middle-class Mexican fare much better than the pelado.[6] In the author's opinion, the city inhabitant demonstrates the following character weaknesses: he is distrustful, suspicious, sensitive, nervous, almost always in a bad humor, often irate and violent, passionate, aggressive and warlike. He lives for the day rather than planning for the future, and functions through instinct rather than intelligent reflection. From the middle-class come the majority of the nation's most intelligent and cultivated men. Nonetheless, they are still plagued by an inferiority complex, whose origin is not economic, intellectual or social in nature but rather related to the mere fact of being Mexican. Middle-class Mexicans understand how to conceal their inferiority complex, though, because they have more intellectual gifts and resources than the proletarian. In fact, they are so adept at concealing their true ego that it becomes indistinguishable from their fictitious one. Mexicans are introverts, says Ramos, because they must direct constant attention towards themselves in order to form a self-image that makes them feel superior rather than inferior. However, they do this subconsciously, and are hence unaware of the fact that they are living a lie. Mexican society further reinforces this false self-concept because, without the acceptance of others, Mexicans would be forced to confront their real selves. As a consequence of this self-deception, they put off all attempts at effective betterment (they are satisfied with their own image of themselves). Moreover, they are indifferent to collective interests, and extraordinarily sensitive to criticism. Mexicans are always ready to convince themselves that others are inferior.

According to Ramos, one of the manifestations of Mexicans' mistaken self-concept is nationalism. In his opinion, it is impossible to shed all vestiges of European influence on Mexican culture and attempt to invent a pure Mexicanism. In fact, he asserts that the middle class, "whose whole existence evolves in conformity with European modes of living," "constitutes the real nucleus of Mexican life."[7] (75) Creoles have endowed Mexico with its only tradition of high culture:

> Due to their quality as *men* (Ramos' italics) they have reached the highest level to which a Hispanic American can aspire. Their spiritual growth would have been impossible without the nourishment of European culture, which in giving them a more profound consciousness of life has bound their ideal interests to their native soil. Almost all have had a relatively significant social impact as educators, guiding forces, and even exemplary personalities. From time to time their elevated consciences have acted as lightning flashes in the obscure destinies of Hispanic America. Up to the present time, the development of these men in the New World's rarefied atmosphere has been impossible to explain; they have been considered simply as the fruits of a remote European influence. (76–77)

Ramos clearly believed that from the middle-class—his own social group—came the genuine representatives of Creole culture, educated men who made a significant impact on Mexican society.

Upon concluding his analysis of Mexicans' character flaws, Ramos discusses how his countrymen might go about gaining self-awareness, a necessary step towards the eradication of these flaws. Identifying a humanistic education as vital to this process, he begins by elucidating the problems with Mexico's educational system. Ramos complains that since 1920 respect for higher education and for intellectuals has waned considerably, leading to the "abandonment of culture" in Mexico. He further laments that the intellectuals of the day, who were divided into two schools—the "nationalists" and the "europeanizers"—did not truly understood the Mexican soul. In particular, the "radical nationalists…are usually poorly educated men with no culture whatsoever. They see things superficially, through a narrow provincialism which makes them believe that the Mexican essence is local color." (111–112) What is really needed, according to Ramos, is a "universal culture made over into *our own,"* one that accepts the European contributions to a Mexican culture but is not a "false Europeanism." (108) Ramos makes clear that what is required to "set our course amidst the chaos" are men like him, "great intellectuals... gifted with a clear awareness of our unique historical destiny." (114)

He concludes, however, that a universal culture will be difficult to achieve because utilitarianism has begun to prevail. Interestingly, although Ramos denounces nationalism, he resorts to nationalistic tactics to rally support for his ideas. To replace the hostility directed towards European culture, he identifies U.S. culture as the real threat to the process of self-awareness and the creation of a uniquely Mexican culture. He laments that "the North American ideal of life has been rapidly replacing the European norms that once prevailed. Practicality, money, machines and speed are the thing that provoke the greatest enthusiasm in modern men." (98) He adds, "when instinct inspires material civilization, it sacrifices the authentic life of man for a false one, composed of automatism and mechanization." (100) This is not to say, however, that Mexico should refuse to modernize. Ramos is able to have it both ways, that is criticize the infiltration of U.S. culture (hence diverting criticism away from Europe) and at the same time champion the cause for modernization (which would benefit the middle class, to which he belonged) by sustaining that:

> Mexico at present is vulnerable to the threat of the white man, who, if we are not careful, may overcome the country by the pacific means of finance and technology. We refer, clearly enough, to the Yankees. It is imperative that we, as men of color, take advantage of the 'betrayal of technology' by assimilating modern civilization in this country—even if it is not completely compatible with our spirit—so as to avoid becoming, in the future, slaves of foreign interests. (123)

Ramos is concerned here with forging a modern national subject that could defend itself against foreign encroachments. Essayists in the 1940s would express this same concern.

Jorge Cuesta: Essays

While Ramos employed the archetype of the pelado as a means of probing the causes of Mexico's economic and cultural backwardness, Jorge Cuesta and Rodolfo Usigli targeted the politician as the most serious impediment to the nation's progress. Both Cuesta and Usigli depend heavily on Ramos's findings to support their views, focusing in particular on inauthenticity as politicians' major defect.

Cuesta reached the peak of his career between 1930 and 1937 (a decisive period in the search for national identity) with the publication of 83 articles, many of which focus on nationalism in the arts. In them, he agrees with Ramos that Mexican life "has acquired an illicit and clandestine character" because of its imitation of Europe. (138) Fervently anti nationalistic, he argues that nationalist works are nothing but a servile imitation of European nationalism, and that they promote a false image of the Mexican. "The most falsely Mexican that has been produced in our art and literature are the nationalist works," he states. (140)

As an intellectual formed in the European tradition, Cuesta (like Ramos and Yáñez) contends that while Mexico should not blindly imitate Europe, European values and traditions are integral to its character. Specifically, he advocates a classicism based on the French model. As opposed to native traditions, Cuesta maintains that universality, the main value underpinning classicism, constitutes the true mark of an authentic Mexican culture. He bases his argument on Hegel's theory that an authentic culture is one that is able to let go ("desprenderse"). That is, in Hegel's (and Cuesta's) view, only by going outside of itself is a culture able to encounter its genuine self. Cuesta uses Hegel's theory to argue that the return to native traditions, the intent of the cultural nationalists, is false, and that were Mexico to detach itself ("desprenderse") rather than clinging to such inauthentic traditions, it would find that many of its best and most authentic characteristics have European (in particular French) roots:

> The influence of French culture has been so constant and profound in Mexico that anyone feeling a repugnance towards it runs the risk of repudiating the most personal part of his own life. Mexico already is a country that is French in all orders of its culture, and has been so since its birth as an independent nation, from the first evidence of a will that was free and conscious of itself... The influence of France has not been an accidental or capricious factor in our national development, but a determining or inseparable part of it, and still more is this so with regard to her personal character, distinction, and quality. Take away this factor and hardly any sense is left to our national existence, and nothing remains of our literature or politics, our society, or our moral concepts. For more than a century now all our cultural life has found its sustenance in France... ("French Culture in Mexico" 339)

Cuesta contends that Mexico will never discover its authentic self so long as politicians continue to promote a fictitious idea of the nation. He asserts that the politician has no expertise in art at all, and should stay out of it: "Some young Marxists come to public office and, since they ignore what the ends and effects of the Revolution have been, they think that being Marxist and occupying these offices gives them sufficient ability to 'direct art.'" (*Ensayos políticos* 146) He contends that politicians' promotion of nationalism as a whole has had ruinous consequences for Mexico, not only morally and psychologically, as Ramos pointed out, but politically and economically as well. For example, he says that the idea of a national economy has proved particularly ruinous, "creating barriers to the importation of capitals that is cheaper than the 'national' capital; closing doors to immigration, and forcing us to consume, as 'national' falsified articles." (*Ensayos políticos* 140)

The crux of the problem, according to Cuesta, has been the access to power of politicians who are uneducated, uncultured and immoral. The inauthenticity that pervades all areas of Mexican life is a direct result of politicians who are inauthentic themselves. The politician "lacks personality, becomes nationalist, fascist, socialist, it doesn't matter what; he affiliates himself to a school; he obeys a fashion; he copies somebody; he becomes false." (*Ensayos políticos* 49) Cuesta argues further that the politician has taken advantage of his position to "improvise and satisfy his vanity. To the proud and sincere revolutionary intuition corresponded later a false, vain, and fatuous action, more inclined to take advantage of the Revolution's triumph than to make himself worthy of it." (*Ensayos políticos* 112)

Cuesta argues in his essays for the replacement of the politician by the intellectual. To make his point, he contrasts the arts with politics, finding the former to be overwhelmingly superior:

> Art, science and philosophy are the product of select minorities, laboriously cultivated. Politics, on the other hand, is the product of improvisation, fatuity, and violence, and from here its intellectual inferiority; from here its dogmatic and sufficient character; from here its repugnance for liberty; and from here its fear that the future manifests its incapacity and discards its unsolid constructions; from here its fever to "control," to "plan," to "rationalize," to "strengthen," that is... the buildings it raises would, if abandoned to themselves, inevitably fall to the ground, due to its lack of roots in society's conscience. (*Ensayos políticos* 110–111)

Most importantly, he sustains that the intellectual has endowed modern society with "its propriety, its character, its distinction, its personality, its authentic culture". He adds that this has all been sacrificed by the reactionary nature of the politics of the day, which "aspires to remove from modern society an intellectual attitude." (*Ensayos políticos* 57)

Cuesta, in sum, employs the discourse of authenticity to make the point that intellectuals, rather than men with very little education at all, should be in charge of the nation's affairs. In his view, politicians hinder the nation's progress by corrupting political life and promoting a false sense of nation. By returning to a tradition whereby intellectuals were esteemed, Mexico could discover its authenticity and become a modern nation. Ultimately, his intentions were the same as those of Ramos: to reaffirm the value of the intellectual by emphasizing his role in the attainment of modernity.

El gesticulador

The concept of inauthenticity developed by Ramos and Cuesta was played out later in other literary genres and in film. One of the most notable examples was the play written by Rodolfo Usigli, *El gesticulador* (*The Gesticulator*), which gained considerable prestige, albeit some time after 1937, the year it was written. *El gesticulador* was not published until 1943 and premiered even later, in 1947. Even at this late date, the play was not permitted to show beyond two weeks. This is not surprising considering its subject matter. A political satire, the play denounced hypocrisy and immorality in politics, just as Cuesta's essays had done.

Usigli initiated his work as a dramatist with the "Contemporáneos," but less inclined towards experimentation than they, he set out in his own direction. Most of his plays are written in the realistic mode and center on social and political issues in Mexico. Besides writing plays, Usigli was a professor of theater history and technique at the Escuela de Verano (Summer School) and the Universidad Nacional Autónoma de México (National Autonomous University). Between 1938 and 1939 he was chief of the Bellas Artes Theater Section, a branch of the Public Education Secretariat, and in 1940 he created the Teatro de Media Noche (Midnight Theater). Between 1944 and 1973 he periodically held diplomatic posts in Britain and France, as well as ambassadorships in Norway, Lebanon, and Belgium.

El gesticulador focuses on how the political system helps shape the national character. It highlights Mexicans' tendency towards falseness, and explores its implications in politics and personal life. Usigli himself states in the play's introduction that the idea for the play came about as a result of his interest in the Mexican psychology. That the playwright had read and been influenced by Samuel Ramos's *The Profile of Man and Culture in Mexico* is obvious in his frequent mention of the philosopher throughout his writings, and in the fact that *El gesticulador* in many senses fictionalizes Ramos's findings. In particular, the play emphasizes the inauthenticity of its main character, César Rubio, who assumes the identity of a famous revolutionary general of the same name who disappeared mysteriously during the Revolution.

Formerly a poorly paid professor at the National Autonomous University of Mexico, Rubio has just moved back to his hometown in northern Mexico in the hopes of providing himself and his family with a better life. He is depending on his knowledge of the Revolution and on information he had obtained about certain politicians to gain himself a position in politics or education. However, he spots a quick and easy means of financial gain in the naive Harvard professor Oliver Bolton, who knocks on his door after his car breaks down near Rubio's house. Bolton, eager to find information on the revolutionary hero César Rubio, agrees to pay Rubio ten thousand dollars for his knowledge, and accepts his assertion that he himself is that general. However, contrary to César's wishes, Bolton publishes his findings, and suddenly César finds himself inextricably enmeshed in local politics. After deciding that he indeed is the general, representatives of the revolutionary party recruit him as the party's candidate for governor, realizing that he would easily appeal to the masses, who would (and indeed do) idealize him as a revolutionary hero. César makes a weak effort to protest, but is attracted by the prospect of fame, wealth and respect, especially since he feels that he has failed to provide his family with a comfortable living. Surprisingly convincing in his role as General Rubio, he gains huge popularity. César, however, does not entirely realize the type of people with whom he's dealing, and on his way to the elections the opposition candidate Navarro kills him. Navarro manages to convince the angry crowds that the assassin was a radical Catholic.

On one level, *El gesticulador* is a harsh indictment of Mexican politics during the time. Usigli condemns politicians as false, hypocritical and violent, uninterested in anything but their own self-aggrandizement. He reinforces this message in the play's epilogue, a long essay that outlines the history and manifestations of the Mexican's tendency towards falseness and hypocrisy. Ironically, out of all the politicians in the play, Rubio is the most honorable, as he is genuinely concerned about the nation's welfare. Rubio incarnates the ideal of the Mexican revolutionary hero, but he is false and could never hope to survive rival interests. On another, more personal level, the play sets out to probe the Mexican psychology, concentrating (mainly through César) on Mexican's proclivity towards inauthenticity. Here Usigli is more sympathetic. In concordance with Ramos's *The Profile of Man and Culture in Mexico*, he links César's behavior to an inferiority complex. Furthermore, he implicitly blames Mexico's leaders for creating an atmosphere of inauthenticity that permeates all levels of society. As Rubio himself puts it, he's not doing anything worse than Mexico's most respected men, and in fact he is much more honorable than they:

> Everybody here lives by appearances, by gestures. I have said that I am the other César Rubio... Who does this harm? Look at those who wear the eagle of a general without having fought in a battle; at those who say they are friends of the people and rob them; at the demagogues who stir up the workers and call them comrades without having ever worked with their hands; at the professors who don't know how to teach, at the students who don't study. Look at Navarro, the precandidate... I know that he is nothing but a bandit, and of that I have proof, and he's taken as a hero, a great national man. Those people are harmful and live off their lies. I'm better than many of them. (47)

Usigli explores the effects of inauthenticity on a national level, showing how inauthenticity in politics has led to the corruption of revolutionary ideals. More important, however, is the attention he directs towards the family. César's actions split the family apart: His son Miguel, who has a childish, unrealistic obsession with the truth, is at constant odds with his father; Julia, easily swayed by appearances (her main concern is the fact that she's ugly), is enthralled by her father's newfound aura of power and influence and criticizes her brother for opposing him; And Elena, the mother (the only genuine character in the play), strives unsuccessfully to maintain peace in the family and to persuade her husband to desist in his actions, which she instinctively (and correctly) knows will have ruinous consequences.

It is not specifically the Rubio family itself, however, that is important in the play, but rather the symbolic function it assumes. The conflicts within this family to some extent mirror those outside of it. As Mabel Moraña puts it: "the family appears as a microcosm in which the contradictions of the social medium are reproduced." (1266) More specifically, the tensions within the Rubio family reflect Mexican society's conflict between traditional and modern values and ways of life, a result of rapid social change. Notably, the Rubio family moves from Mexico City, where the modernization process is most rapid, to the countryside, where traditional ways of life persist. "The familiar problematic which has César Rubio as its axis arises from the coexistence of 'traditional' values and forms of social conduct with expectations and behaviors that are activated as a result of the modernization process." (Moraña 1266)

That César's attempt to revisit the past ends in disaster is indicative of Usigli's rejection of a return to so-called traditional Mexican values. In particular, the Mexican political system is viewed as outmoded and corrupt. Usigli is especially critical of the concentration of power in the hands of a few political leaders. He is equally critical of the masses, whom he repeatedly depicts as gullible and blindly instinctual in its support of political leaders. As César puts it on more than one occasion, the people do not need proof that he is the real César Rubio because "they have their instinct and that's enough." (54) The masses are mere pawns in a political game controlled by men who do not have their interests in mind. In a telling analogy, César likens the political system to a wheel whose axis is occupied by the politician: "The politician is the axis of the wheel; when it breaks or is damaged, the wheel, which is the people, falls to pieces." (75)

Usigli's play, in sum, builds to a large extent on Ramos and Cuesta's ideas. Above all, his focus on the Mexican's inauthenticity constitutes a means of entering into the identity debate from the point of view of the anti-nationalists. This anti-nationalist stance is further supported by his satirical depictions of politicians, the masses and the political process. Furthermore, that Usigli, like Ramos and Cuesta, laments the lack of qualified men in politics is evident in two ways; first, he conveys no respect whatsoever for politicians. To the contrary, men like Navarro, who attain positions of great power such as governor, not only lack credentials but are immoral. As César puts it to Navarro:

> César Rubio made you a tenant because you knew how to rob horses; but that's it. The old caudillo, you know which one, made you a division chief because you helped kill all the Catholics they were apprehending. Not only that... you got him women... That's your page of services... Every night you drank an entire bottle of coñac in order to be able to personally kill those detained in

inspection. And if it hadn't just been coñac... (82)

Second, it is ironically César, an educated university professor with extensive knowledge of the revolution, who governs with the greatest moral convictions and effectiveness. But César wouldn't have been there had it not been for Bolton's naiveté. Moreover, Usigli makes a point to underline the lack of regard paid to educated men in Mexico. As a university professor, César barely eked out a living. He also received very little respect, including from his son, Miguel, who opposed him in student protests. Finally, Usigli (like Ramos and Cuesta) stresses Mexico's need for learned and morally upright leaders in his articulation of the masses who, in the Orteguian spirit, are viewed as completely irrational.

Usigli was not alone in assuming that the masses lack the capacity to make rational decisions. This attitude was reflected as well in Ramos and Cuesta's works. These authors were unconcerned with the lack of popular representation in Mexican politics. To the contrary, emphasizing the ignorance of the masses only enhanced the importance of the intellectual. These works reflect a power struggle at the higher levels of politics and culture, where the voice of the popular classes was virtually excluded. They helped to advance the agendas of some of the most privileged members of Mexican society, who had little if no contact with the subjects about whom they write. In the case of the authors studied here, this agenda included the reinforcement of the status of the intellectual, of the primacy of European culture, and of the modernization process.

The Glorious Charro

In stark contrast to the essayists, most films during the 1930s avoided a critical analysis of either the national character or Mexico's modernization process. They fled from the grim social, political and economic realities so tirelessly depicted in literature, finding refuge in family and an idealized provincial life. Marshall Bermann seems to be describing many Mexicans at this time when he says that those experiencing modernity for the first time yearn for a pre-modern Paradise Lost. (15) The "comedia ranchera" appeared to fulfill that need. These films returned to an idealized past, that of porfirian Mexico, when the large haciendas flourished. Far from being the source of abuse and social injustice, the hacienda in the "comedia ranchera" is a tranquil and happy place. The owner is usually fair, generous and upright. Poverty and hard work are nonexistent. Peace and order prevail. In the 1930s and the 1940s, the "comedia ranchera" enjoyed enormous success, more so than any other film genre in Mexico. In fact, it became popular all over Latin America during this time, dominating the film market.

Besides offering viewers a refuge from the threats posed by an urban life in the process of rapid transformation, the "comedia ranchera" also reacted against Cárdenas's agrarian reform policy. García Riera writes that *Allá en el Rancho Grande* (*Over on the Big* Ranch), the first film of this kind:

> attempts to flee from the Pancho Villas, from the compadres Mendoza, from the Revolution entirely, and at the same time a moment—cardenismo—is giving the country a disquieting orientation. This escape signifies the recovery of a happy and idyllic universe that the urban bourgeoisie liked to suppose existed: the bucolic Arcady whose myth the Revolution destroyed without second thought. But if it is already known that the Mexican countryside is no longer as such, that in 1936 the Agrarian Reform is a real fact, the myth of the happy hacienda is zealously maintained by a cinema whose class content advises the rejection of reality. (130–131)

The "comedia ranchera" enabled viewers to take pride and comfort in their national identity. On the one hand, it constantly affirms and exalts "Mexicanness" through the breathtaking shots of the landscape, traditional dance, music and costume, and the feats of the "charro". On the other hand, it defines national identity as part of a social order based on respect for family and church (the two pillars of moral authority) and, above all, the supremacy of the male. The "comedia ranchera" is a paean to paternalism and machismo. The film critic, Charles Ramírez-Berg, discerns a trade-off between the male and the state in film of the period: "the male receives a secure identity and the state receives his allegiance; the male gains a favored place in the patriarchal system while the state accumulates political might." (23)

Comic Relief and the Subversion of Authority: *Allí está el detalle*

Alongside the comedia ranchera and the family melodrama, another genre began to gain popularity in the latter part of the 1930's—the comedy, given a uniquely Mexican twist with the figure of Cantinflas, a pelado, played by Mario Moreno. The Cantinflas films became enormously popular all over Latin America, and stayed so until well into the 1960s. By the time Cantinflas produced his last film in 1981, *El Barrendero* (*The Garbageman*), he had starred in some 47 films, all of which were huge box office hits. (Stavans 42)

Cantinflas embodied some of the characteristics of the pelado described in Ramos's works: he represented the lower-class immigrant to the city, of partial indigenous descent. He always held typically lower class jobs such as bellman, newspaper delivery man and taco vendor. He was poor, unkempt and unmotivated, except when it came to food, alcohol and women. Most notably, he had a language of his own, but not one characterized by abusive epithets. Cantinflas manipulated language in comic ways to extricate himself from difficult and embarrassing situations. Mostly, he talked on and on without ever saying anything meaningful, a language usage that inspired the creation of the verb "cantinflear." Harmless and very funny, Cantinflas was far from the morally abhorrent character described by Ramos.

Cantinflas's language, ragamuffin attire and physical appearance and comportment were all designed to provoke laughter. He wore a dirty, long-sleeved t-shirt, baggy pants that were barely held up by a rope, floppy shoes and a battered felt hat that was too small for his head. His physical features included undeveloped muscles, a slightly bulging stomach, slumping shoulders, and prominent facial features such as a distinctly wide nose, thick lips, wide-spread eyes, exaggeratedly dark and arched eyebrows, and a barely distinguishable mustache. He gestured often, and had his own particular style of walking. In many senses, he looked and acted like the clowns and fools of the carnival. In fact, Mario Moreno first began his acting career in the "carpa," a popular form of theater that thrived in the lower-class neighborhoods in the 1930's. The carpas consisted of clowns, acrobats and comedians. Carnivalesque in nature, they flouted social conventions, exhibiting or alluding to all that went against "good taste" and "good manners," particularly those involving the body: physical deformities, physiological malfunctions, sexual appetite, and so on.

The Cantinflas films were not nearly so daring as the carpas, and they posed no real threat to the social order. They were, however, inspired by the carpas and the carnivals. Most importantly, by subverting authority, Cantinflas erased social inequalities, accomplishing what Bakhtin described as one of the main functions of the carnival, the "temporary liberation from the prevailing truth and from the established order… the suspension of all hierarchical rank, privileges, norms and prohibitions." (10) Cantinflas provided a relief from the tedium and injustices of everyday life by poking fun at the sources of those unpleasant realities. The laughter he incited was not malicious, and was directed not only at the authorities but at everyone. In other words, it was harmless, temporary and shared by all, like in the carnival. In Monsiváis's words:

> The poor applaud in him what is near and dear and, knowingly or not, they become enthusiastic by... the festive representation and vindication of misery. The rich are thankful for the opportunity to laugh at the demagogues and the poor, and at the near end to the comicity of the small and still rural town. In the mid thirties, the elite celebrate Cantinflas: he's the perfect "puerility" of "los de Abajo" (the underdogs). (*Escenas de pudor y de liviandad* 91)

Cantinflas played roles in four movies in the 1930's: *No te engañes corazón* (1936), *Así es mi Tierra* (1937), *Aguila o Sol* (1937) and *El signo de la muerte* (1939). However, it was in *Ahí está el detalle* (1940), directed by Arcady Boytler, that he gained prominence not only in Mexico but all over Latin America. Interestingly, the film begins with a quote by Rabelais:[8] "laughter belongs to man", alluding to the burlesque atmosphere that pervades the movie. In true carnivalesque form, Cantinflas manages to extricate himself from some seemingly impossible situations: death at the hands of a rich industrialist, Don Cayetano, who thinks he's his wife's lover, marriage to an elderly woman with several rambunctious children for whom she seeks a father, and the death penalty for a murder he did not commit. He does this through a deft and hilarious manipulation of language, which also enables him to undermine the authority of his accusers while enhancing his own. Hence Don Cayetano, who is fooled into thinking Cantinflas is his wife's brother, begins treating him like royalty, and the judges, confused by his language and apparent self-condemnation, end up using "cantinflismos" in their concluding remarks.

In the film, Cantinflas is obliged to assume the identity of Dolores's brother, Leonardo. Dolores is meeting with an old lover who is bribing her when her husband, Don Cayetano, arrives with two policemen. Paranoid that his wife is cheating on him, Don Cayetano is determined to catch her in the act. The man escapes, but Don Cayetano finds a cigarette burning in the ashtray. Cantinflas, who had been meeting furtively with the servant, Pasita, is found hiding in the closet. Since Dolores knows that her husband would not believe her story about being bribed, she pretends that Cantinflas is her brother. Don Cayetano is thrilled because he had been looking long and hard for Leonardo, whose presence is indispensable to the division of Dolores's inheritance, which he desperately needs.

Cantinflas becomes an impostor in this movie, as he does in many others. In this sense, and in the many times he uses language to hide his ignorance, he resembles the gesticulator of Usigli's *El gesticulador* and the pelado of Ramos's and Cuesta's essays. However, Cantinflas's feigning is never depicted negatively in the film. In fact, this quality isn't taken seriously at all. It is merely the source of humor. Furthermore, this and other Cantinflas movies never try to portray Cantinflas as inauthentic. Even while he assumes Leonardo's identity, Cantinflas never acts any differently than he would normally. In fact, it would be hard to find a more genuine person. Cantinflas could care less about what others think of him. He is also completely irreverent. He constantly mocks convention, formality and pretension.

Despite his shortcoming, Cantinflas had many positive qualities. He was unpretentious, good-hearted, and fun loving. He was always trying to help someone at his own expense, such as Dolores. And, in spite of his poverty, he managed to enjoy life. He had time to spend chatting with friends and flirting with women, and he savored food, alcohol, and cigars. Overall, he provided a sympathetic image of the poor. In fact, some Mexicans may have related to aspects of his demeanor and personality. However, he was so obviously stereotyped that it would be erroneous to claim that the Cantinflas films aimed to make their protagonist the embodiment of the national character.

In contrast to Cantinflas, the insecure and pompous Cayetano, and the self-important lawyers and judges, stand out for their pretentiousness. To some extent, by portraying the wealthy in this manner, this and other Cantinflas films provided an emotional outlet for resentments against the rich. However, it is important to emphasize that these figures, like Cantinflas, were caricatures. They were so exaggeratedly stereotypical that they couldn't be taken very seriously by anybody. They simply made for a good laugh. Furthermore, they are flawed but not malicious, and in the end their good sides prevail. Don Cayetano tolerates Cantinflas, who constantly provokes him, is generous to the poor Clotilde with her brood of children, and ultimately apologizes to his wife. The judge metes out justice fairly.

Ahí está el detalle and other Cantinflas films, in other words, took serious matters and made them funny. They neither aimed at fomenting national pride nor at exploring or condemning social injustice. No real criticism of Mexican society emerges. In fact, these films both distracted people from their real problems and made those problems appear less serious. Despite his overwhelming problems, Cantinflas presented the image of a content man. His poverty was never the source of unhappiness, and he never aspired to upward mobility. He was also completely apolitical.

The Mexican government embraced Cantinflas because his films never really challenged Mexican society. Even further, these films helped fortify the status quo in two important ways. First, by allowing the poor and the rich to laugh at each other, they served as containment for social tensions that might have been resolved in otherwise disruptive ways. Second, by portraying both classes as foibled but generally well-meaning, they helped to defuse resentments between the classes. Although the Cantinflas films emphasized the vast differences between the wealthy and the poor, they seemed to point to a lack of communication as the only real problem between social classes. Yet even that problem is not taken very seriously. Cantinflas's incoherency may initially compound his problems, but eventually it endears him to his accusers. In the end, the rich and the poor get along just fine.

Notes

1. Lázaro Cárdenas (1934–1940) was not as eager as the leaders of other Latin American countries (such as Brazil and Argentina) to promote industrialization through import substitution. Instead, he favored the development of an agriculture economy (based on the *ejido*) over industrialization. Nonetheless, "the manufacturing industry continued growing without becoming subservient to agriculture... The incipient domestic bourgeoisie, both industrial and commercial, consolidated itself without great difficulties." (Aguilar Camín and Meier 138) Manufacturing production increased 53% during Cárdenas's presidency. (Aguilar Camín and Meier 134) Beginning in 1940, with Avila Camacho's election to presidency, industrialization and modernization really began to take off. However, the process had begun earlier, prompting increasing numbers of Mexicans to migrate to the city to fulfill the demand for labor.
2. Known popularly as "group without a group" (an expression coined by one of the poets, Xavier Villaurrutia, in reference to the group's diversity), the Contemporáneos' name comes from a review of the same title published between 1928 and 1932. Controversy exists over which writers formed part of this group, but the most commonly cited ones include (besides Ramos and Cuesta) José Gorostiza, Salvador Novo, Carlos Pellicer, Bernardo Ortiz de Montellano, Octavio G. Barreda, Jaime Torres Bodet, Enrique González Rojo and Xavier Villaurrutia.
3. Exceptions include Novo, who satirizes "Mexicanness" in a few of his poems, and Gorostiza, Pellicer and Montellano, who stressed the universal (rather than national) nature of the Mexican.
4. He later became a strong opponent of Caso's philosophy, which he accused of being "francified" and not centered enough on the Mexican experience. His initial contact with this intellectual, however, proved central in his decision to become a philosopher and writer.
5. Ramos was teacher and subsequent Head of Philosophy and Letters at the Universidad Nacional Preparatoria (National Preparatory

University), and coordinator of Humanities at the Universidad Nacional Autónoma de México (National Autonomous University).
6. It seems interesting that while the pelado resides in the city, Ramos treats him as a separate entity, as if he were such an aberration or so inhuman that he didn't even deserve to be included under the classification of "The Mexican of the City".
7. Ramos discards any positive influences the Indians may have had on Mexican culture. In his own words: "Tied to nature, they live in an atmosphere of primitivism that permeates the remainder of the population." (75)
8. See Bakhtin's discussion of the carnivalesque in Rabelais: *Rabelais and his world*.

Chapter Five

The Psyche of the Provincial Mexican

While the novels of the Revolution during the 1930s had focused on the outward manifestations of the Mexican character during the period of armed conflict (*Vámonos con Pancho Villa*, by Rafael Muñoz, and *Cartucho*, by Nellie Campobello) and the caudillismo of the 1920's (*La sombra del caudillo*, by Martín Luis Guzmán), many novels of the 1940's turned inward to examine the Mexican psyche. The shift partly reflected the changing times. When Manuel Ávila Camacho was elected President in 1940, the country's political and economic structures had already taken shape, and a period of marked political stability and economic growth had begun. Accordingly, the main issue of concern in literature shifted from the Revolution's external consequences (social, political, economic and cultural) to its internal or psychological impacts (as could only be assessed at a distance from the Revolution) and their implications for the nation's future. Samuel Ramos had already addressed this issue in his celebrated 1934 essay *El perfil del hombre y la cultura en México* (1934), which also significantly influenced the novel's direction in the 1940's. Novelists were further responding to growing criticisms that the Mexican novel had not gone beyond the purely superficial, picturesque and anecdotal.

Likewise, film turned to the provincial Mexican to define national identity. Seemingly oblivious to the nation's increasing urbanization, the nation's provinces continued to provide the setting for the vast majority of films during the 1940s. An immutable place, the countryside gave a sense of permanence to national identity. In glaring contrast to literature, however, these films altogether avoided a serious critique of the national character. The 1940s continued to churn out "comedias rancheras" and also produced numerous films on the Revolution, all of which glorified the national character. The coexistence of these films is somewhat ironic, given that the former idealized the haciendas of porfirian life and the latter celebrated the movement that put an end to that way of life. Nevertheless, their articulation of national identity was compatible. Although they represented different social classes, both the charro and the revolutionary embodied some of the same qualities of "Mexicanness." For example, they were both usually macho but sensitive, loyal to family, friends and the nation, and devout. The charro and the revolutionary reinforced traditional values such as the importance of family, the church and masculine authority. This was reassuring to audiences during a period of rapid change. Revolutionary melodramas such as *Enamorada* (1947) also promised a new era of equality and alliances between social classes, something they had only hinted at in the 1930s (in films like *El compadre Mendoza*).

The Existential Crisis

Two of the most significant novels of "lo mexicano" in the 1940's sought to capture the essence of the national character through an analysis of the provincial Mexican: José Revueltas's *El luto humano* (*Human Mourning*) (1943) and Agustín Yáñez's *Al filo del agua* (*At the Edge of the Storm*) (1947). However, the authors were much more concerned with the psychological processes at work within their characters than were their predecessors of the 1930's. Reflecting this new focus, they tended to use innovative narrative devices such as interior monologue, stream of consciousness, myth, fragmented time sequences, and so forth. In many respects their analyses converge. According to both, self-destructive forces at work within the national psyche lead Mexicans to be fatalistic, uncommunicative, solitary, and violent. However, their analyses diverge in terms of the historical sources of these psychological tendencies. According to Revueltas, they derive from the alienating and dehumanizing effects of capitalism. Yáñez, on the other hand, attributes them to the repressive influence of the Catholic Church, and views the Revolution as having been psychologically liberating and a true force of modernization.

The two radically different perspectives on the origins of Mexicans' character defects owe themselves to the authors' political orientations. Revueltas, a Marxist, regarded capitalism as the source of Mexicans' (and modern man's) existential crisis. In his view, so long as capitalism rather than socialism remained the dominant economic system,

Mexicans would remain trapped within a psychology marked by solitude and existential longing. He counters the prevailing ideology by consistently demythologizing the nationalistic myths promoted by the state. For example, he views the Revolution not as a source of national pride, but as among the causes of poorer Mexicans' physical and psychological anguish. In stark contrast to Revueltas, Yáñez held a highly distinguished career in public service, and was devoted to the state's nation-building project throughout his entire life. *Al filo del agua* reflects his interest in constructing a modern national subject. Yáñez examines the Mexican character at the onset of the Revolution, uncovering personality traits that persist in post-Revolutionary Mexico. Like Revueltas, he believed that self-reflection would enable Mexicans to begin confronting their character deficiencies rather than continue ignoring them. But while Revueltas looked forward to a day when Mexicans would reject capitalism, and embrace socialism instead, Yáñez hoped that his countrymen would correct their character deficiencies so that the country might progress more rapidly under its current system.

El luto humano

Critics agree that it is impossible to fully understand Revueltas's works without thorough knowledge of his politics, an assertion that the author himself made repeatedly. A review of Revueltas's political life also reveals the sorts of obstacles faced by intellectuals who opposed the state, and sheds light on the Communist Party's failures and shortcomings during this time period.

Revueltas represents one of the few Mexican authors who fought unwaveringly against the Mexican state, both through his political actions and his literary works, and whose actions were thoroughly consistent with his political and social ideals. His struggles both against the Mexican state and the Communist Party were to cost him substantial physical and spiritual hardship throughout his life.

The author's political activity began at the age of 14, when he joined the Socorro Rojo Internacional. At the age of 16 he participated in a demonstration commemorating the 1917 Revolution, for which he was sent to a correctional reform school to serve a one-year sentence. He was paroled after six months. In 1932, at the age of 17, he officially joined Mexico's Communist Party (PCM), as an active participant in the Juventud Comunista de México (JCM). That same year, he was arrested, along with other JCM militants, for attempting to organize a factory strike. After eight days of fasting to protest their detention, the organizers were sent without trial to the Islas Marías penal colony. Revueltas was released after 5 months, when it was discovered that he hadn't yet turned 18. The following year he was once again arrested and sent without trial to Islas Marías, this time for helping to organize a strike for a minimum wage. He was sentenced to ten months of hard labor.

Following Lázaro Cárdenas's election to presidency in 1934, the brutal persecution of striking workers ended, and Revueltas and other political prisoners were granted pardons. As noted in the previous chapter, Cárdenas lent significant support to workers throughout his presidency. He backed labor organizations and strikes, and adopted legislation favorable to workers. For these and other reasons, the PCM openly backed the Cárdenas administration. Revueltas, however, viewed Cárdenas's support of workers as an attempt at government control. He began to criticize the PCM's priority on a popular front, which involved an alliance between the proletariat and the progressive bourgeoisie. As a result, he was eventually expelled from the party in 1943.

In 1949, Revueltas published his third novel, *Los días terrenales*, a critique of the PCM. This novel generated great controversy. Under pressure from his critics, Revueltas withdrew it from circulation, as well as a play, *El cuadrante de la soledad*. He later regretted having succumbed to his critics, saying that he himself was scared by the novel's audacity. (Rabadán 205)

In 1956, Revueltas appealed for readmission into the PCM. Roberto Simón Crespi attributes this action to Revueltas's frustration with trade unionism and bourgeoisie socialism, and the fact that in 1956 the PCM seemed to have broken its "tacit coexistence" with the state. (99) Revueltas was readmitted, but his discontent with the PCM's dogmatism and lack of self-criticism grew again. After various futile attempts to persuade the party to reform itself, he left to join the Partido Obrero Campesino Mexicano (POCM) in 1960. His involvement with the POCM was short-lived. He quit that same year after his efforts to form a Marxist-Leninist party within the POCM failed. He then dedicated himself to creating a new party: La Liga Leninista Espartaco. In 1962 Revueltas published the "Ensayo sobre el proletariado sin cabeza", considered his most important political essay, which denounced the Communist Party and explained the League's objectives. This essay condemned, among other things, the party's support of stalinism and its failure to have created a marxist-leninist program. It also accused the PCM of having facilitated bourgeois control over the proletariat through, for example, political alliances such as the popular front, which subordinated the interests of the working class to those of the democratic bourgeois. He argued that while the Communist Party had alienated the proletariat, the League would represent the proletariat's true interests. It would seek primarily to make this figure aware of his alienation and dehumanization in order that he might revolt as a class.

Revueltas participated in the League until 1964, when he was expelled for refusing to accept a majority position. This represented the end of his involvement in political parties. However, he dramatically returned to the political scene in 1968. In March of that year he traveled to Cuba, against the governments wishes, as a literary judge for the Casa de las Américas. When the government tried to punish him by freezing his salary as an employee of the Secretary of Public Education, he renounced the position. In October of that year government forces attacked supporters of the student movement who were assembled in the Plaza de las Tres Culturas, in Tlatelolco. Hundreds were massacred, and many others were either arrested, fled the country or went into hiding. Revueltas, who had been one of the leaders of the movement, went into hiding, but was discovered ten days later. On November 22 he was formally charged with ten crimes and sent to the Lecumberri Prison to await trial. From September 17 to 18, after a 40 hour uninterrupted trial, he was sentenced to 16 years in prison. During his stay, he endured harsh conditions, including harassment by common prisoners that culminated in a brutal attack on New Years Day of 1970 (allegedly with the knowledge of prison officials) against the participants in the student movement. President Echeverría freed Revueltas and his colleagues in 1971. Revueltas died in 1976.

Revueltas's literary works were the source of much criticism during his lifetime. His most ardent critics were, at times, from the political left, particularly the Communist Party, which accused him (especially following the publication of his third novel, *Los días terrenales*) of embracing the decadence of the European existentialists. Revueltas, they sustained, had failed to show faith in man and in the ultimate triumph of socialism, depicting his characters as morally bankrupt and without salvation. Revueltas, however, flatly denied that he was influenced by Sartrean existentialism. However, he did openly renounce socialist realism, the Marxists' prevailing artistic model. He considered the social realists' portrayal of the human condition to be unrealistic and misleading. In particular, he reacted against its optimism and idealism.

In his literary works, Revueltas attempted to fuse Marxism and existentialism. According to Sam Slick, "there are multiple parallels between Revueltas's philosophical development and the emergence of an existential Marxism in Europe." (20) Revueltas called his approach a "critical", "dialectical" or "analytical" realism. As he put it in a conversation with Antoine Rabadan, "if (the novelist) knows how to use reality in a revolutionary way—that is, realistic, without prejudices—his work will have, even without specifically proposing it, an argumentative, polemical, convincing character, because reality is itself polemical, dialectical." (192) Revueltas argued that his characters appear desperate and without hope because they are unable to liberate themselves through a true, revolutionary consciousness. He didn't consider this a specifically Mexican problem, however, but rather a universal one. Revueltas believed that human beings in capitalist societies experience alienation because they live in "the here and now of the individual." That is, they focus on the individual rather than on the collectivity. He asserted that opposing "the here and now of the individual" required using the "here and now of death". In other words, it meant considering life not as a person, as private property, but rather paying attention to "the generic I." He explains: "When the 'here and now of death' is elaborated, the egotistical, individual 'here and now of life' will end. Death is the dialectics of the natural process of life." (Castro Quiteño 90)

Death constitutes an overwhelming presence in Revueltas's works. By confronting his characters with their mortality, he forces them to reflect upon and acknowledge the meaninglessness of their existence. Referring to one of the characters in *El luto humano*, the novel's narrator states: "Since he was close to death the monstrous sterility of existence was being revealed to him, an existence whose objectives now appeared to him absolutely meaningless. His entire past had been a sad mistake without the slightest moment of victory." (70–71) Death, in other words, reveals the "truth" about humankind's existence in Revueltas's works. This truth centers on capitalism's destructive impact on the human condition and psyche, and entails the ultimate awareness of superiority of socialism. Revueltas asserted that his characters, desperate and tormented, "correspond to unreal beings that, in spite of this, exist in Mexico and will only stop existing when the rationality of an authentic party of the working class makes them disappear, converts them into true communists." (Schneider 101)

While Revueltas stressed Mexicans' universal qualities, he also explored their peculiarities. *El luto humano* (1943), published when he was only twenty-nine, constitutes one of his attempts to probe the national character. Considered among his best works, it won the Premio Nacional de Literatura and was hailed by some of the foremost critics and writers of "lo mexicano" at the time, including Octavio Paz, José Gorostiza and Alí Chumacero.

Despite similarities between his work and those of other writers of "Mexicanness", including Paz's *El laberinto de la soledad*, Revueltas took issue with literature on the Mexican character. For example, in "Posibilidades y limitaciones del Mexicano", he reacts above all against the notion that the national character is isolated from that of universal man, and that it is fixed. Any discussion of a national character, he argues, must begin with "universal absolute Man" (257), and then explore the forces (economic, sociological, historical, etc.) that shaped him into a distinctly national being (whether Mexican or any other). Revueltas, who believed the nation's history (particularly imperialism) damaged the Mexican psyche, calls the national characteristics "limitations." By stressing the changing nature of the national being, he leaves the way open for the transformation of these "limitations" into "possibilities." In his view, this positive transformation will occur with the triumph of socialism: "The revolutionary Mexico of today... will be the same that flourishes without limits, as a national being, with the universal being of man, in the socialist world of tomorrow." (273)

With *El luto humano* Revueltas develops in a fictional format the same ideas on the national character that he outlined in "Posibilidades y limitaciones del Mexicano." His characters, who are desperate, uncommunicative, incapable of love, prone to savage acts of violence, nostalgic, fatalistic, brutally insensitive, and so forth, are products of both the tremendous physical hardships they have had to endure, and an immensely destructive national history. Revueltas penetrates his characters' thoughts and actions to explore the ways in which the nation's history has affected the Mexican psyche, repeatedly employing mythic elements drawn primarily from traditional Western Christianity and pre-Columbian Mexico.

Despite the novel's heavily pessimistic tone, Revueltas provides glimpses of hope. In particular, one character, Natividad, stands out as the socialist hero. Although he is killed, his presence is constantly felt through the thoughts of the other characters, whose admiration for him grows after his death. Natividad is a Christ-like figure: "Natividad was a child of the masses; in them he nourished his tremendous faith. The masses divided up the bread of history and with this bread Natividad was fed. How could he ever die?" (200) Through Natividad, Revueltas expresses his faith in the ultimate triumph of socialism: "Men like Natividad would rise up one morning throughout the land of Mexico; it would be a sunny morning. New men, and smiling. And no one would be able to stop these new men because they would represent enthusiasm and genuine emotion." (199)

Revueltas partially based the novel on a real-life experience. In 1934, under orders from the Mexican Communist Party, he was sent to an area near the town of Anáhuac, in the northern part of the state of Nuevo León, to help organize a farm workers strike (for which he was sent by the government to the Islas Marías penal colony). The strike, which paralyzed the government-sponsored irrigation system, resulted in the shutdown of the project and the evacuation of the town. Revueltas recalled the event in an interview with Adolfo Ortega:

> It's the story under the government of Abelardo Rodríguez, it seems to me, in which the irrigation system had been constructed in an artificial manner and at the cost of millions of pesos. The water was bad. It didn't serve for irrigation. It was a governmental "affair" and as a result they didn't care about salaries... It was a fraud; the populations around there disappeared and (the land) remained hardened. (50)

El luto humano centers on the fate of the ten people who remained in the area following the failure of the irrigation system. At the novel's onset they are assembled in the house of Marcela and Ursulo, whose daughter has just died. At the behest of his wife, Ursulo goes in search of the priest so that he might bless their daughter. Adán helps him along the way. The three make their way back to the house in a heavy storm. During the trip, the priest kills Adán in revenge for the crimes he committed against clergymen in the Cristero War. When Ursulo and the priest reach their destination, the floods have begun to enter the house and they are forced to leave. Their situation is likened to the biblical flood and exodus, only this time the victims are doomed. All but four are killed in the waters during the journey, and the others find themselves in the same spot where they had begun. They climb to the roof of the house, only to await certain death. One by one they perish and are then devoured by the vultures circling above them.

Like the other writers of "lo mexicano", Revueltas turned to one of the most marginalized groups in Mexican society to study the national character—the poor, mostly indigenous Mexican campesino. However, his treatment of them was much different. He did not, as many of the other writers did, attribute negative traits to class or racial inferiority. Rather, he examined much more thoroughly history's role in the shaping of the Mexican psyche. Revueltas likely chose this group because, having experienced the full negative impact of the nation's past, they would best exemplify the national psychoses.

Revueltas traces the origins of the national character all the way to pre-Columbian Mexico. In the descriptions of his characters and in the use of indigenous mythology and symbols (relating to animals, plants and minerals), he repeatedly refers to the nation's Aztec past. He does not idealize pre-Columbian civilization, but rather views it as cruel, mysterious, profoundly religious, prehuman: "Adán was the child of animals, the pre-Columbian animals that had something religious, savage, mysterious, and cruel about them. Even though Ursulo descended from those same animals." (13–14)

Revueltas attributes most of Mexicans' psychoses, however, to their mixed lineage. According to the author, by robbing the Indians of their land, religion, and ultimately identity, the Spaniards caused major psychological traumas that would continue to afflict what would later become the national character. The author identifies a deep nostalgia in the Mexican soul, which he attributes to a yearning for an identity that was lost with the Spaniards' arrival. He stated in an interview, "the Mexican searches blindfolded for all that has been taken away from him. This is precisely what is called nostalgia...The Mexican feels an incredible nostalgia, without knowing himself for whom or for what. He has lost his mother." (Samsel and Rodowska 25) The characters' aimless wandering through the flood waters is symbolic of Mexicans' search for this lost identity. As Helia Sheldon puts it, "pilgrimage is interpreted, psychologically, as a nostalgia for the lost mother and is manifested profusely in the Bible and in some prehispanic codes." (390)

Revueltas opposed the idealistic portrayal of mestizaje that dominated during this period (see chapter six). While such intellectual giants as Manuel Gamio, Andrés Molina Enríquez and José Vasconcelos had vigorously promoted mestizaje, Revueltas depicted it in highly negative terms, as synonymous with the repression and destruction of indigenous identity: "Adán possessed that poisoned *sangre mestiza*, or mixed blood, in which the Indians saw their own fear and discovered their own eternal nostalgia, their retrospective terror, the total shipwreck they could not forget" (18). Revueltas evokes the tragic origins of the mestizo race through Ursulo's memories. Ursulo's mother, a pure Indian, was orphaned at the age of ten. His grandfather was killed in a failed struggle against Porfirio Díaz, and his grandmother died at the hands of the troops sent afterwards to move the community. The grandmother had refused to comply with the orders to move, preferring to die rather than to abandon the land. She therefore killed her one-year old son by striking him against the railway car, which prompted the soldiers to kill her. Ursulo's mother, Antonia, fled through the mountains with a group of Indians, arriving hungry and fatigued at a hacienda. Here she remained, called only by her first name and no other, "like an animal that seems to come from nowhere. Antonia because she was an Indian, something evidently like an animal since she did not even know Spanish" (64–65). Forced by Don Vicente, "Antonia received with resignation the seed with which her gods had died" (67), remembering her forefathers predictions that "'this land was to be possessed by the children of the Sun.'" (64) She died giving birth to Úrsulo, who is referred throughout the novel as "the obsidian dagger." (66)

Ursulo and Adán represent two different but equally destructive types of mestizo. Úrsulo is the mestizo who denies his Spanish inheritance. When at the age of 14 he encounters his father dead and decomposing, hung from a tree by revolutionaries, he says: "'It's all right.'" (67) His heart is like "a dagger incapable of love, he, son of the first knife." (67) Unlike Natividad, whom he admires and respects, Úrsulo is unable to transform his anger into productive energy. He is consumed by selfish, childlike emotions, including the constant desire to sexually possess Natividad's widow, whom he marries. Adán, on the other hand, is the mestizo who denies his indigenous heritage. Paid by government officials, he kills even his own kind. At their request, he murders Natividad, leader of a strike of five thousand farm laborers that, in the officials' opinion, was "a scandal for the Republic and even for the Revolution itself." (130) Violent and totally immoral, Adán represents the mestizo who facilitates the ruling elites' domination of the masses.

The women play an important secondary role in the novel, functioning to elucidate the male characters' thoughts and motives. Most importantly, they stand as symbols of the land that the Spaniards took from them and that the males covet. Ursulo's longing to sexually possess his wife, Cecilia, is driven by his desire to own fertile land. The death of their daughter signifies her infecundity, and the frustration of his desires. Notably, all the other women are also childless, either because they are infertile or because they chose not to have children. Notably, "la Borrada," Adán's wife (given to him as a gift by a cacique) is compared to "la Malinche" but refuses to help perpetuate the mestizo race by having children. Because the women fail to satisfy their desires, the men physically abuse them: La Calixta "had never had children, and her husband used to beat her on her swollen stomach so she would give birth. 'You're pregnant by the devil', he used to tell her." (33) As a result the women become distant and aloof, incapable of love, submissive and resigned to their unhappy fate. Cecilia, for example, has become so demoralized that she reacts indifferently when Calixto makes sexual advances towards her during Ursulo's absence. Similarly, this provokes only a mild response from Calixto's wife, La Calixta, who is present while this is occurring: "She was not jealous. She had not loved him for a long time now and, he, in turn, appeared never to have loved her." (34)

The priest exercises no influence on the characters' behavior, and in fact it is his impotency, and with it that of the Catholic Church (a Spanish imposition), that becomes important in the novel. Despite constant references to Christianity and the bible, the Catholic religion is shown to have made no positive impact on the characters' lives. In fact, while they perform Catholic rituals, the characters have not been spiritually transformed by this religion. Observing Ursulo, the priest "was witness to his open nakedness, and his lack of sorrow and mystery. It was a voice antedating paganism, associated with another mystery: nails of humble, dark flint piercing the feet of the wretched and tender Huizilopochtli. Another non-Catholic mystery of mourning and death." (23) Having witnessed so much violence and suffering, including the torture and deaths of many of his colleagues in the Cristero war, the priest has lost his faith and become totally ineffective. Moreover, he has himself become immoral, succumbing to his basest instincts, including killing a man and sleeping with a prostitute. The priest has lost all sense of life's meaning and purpose, like the two men he accompanies: "The tragedy was the fact that origin and destiny had already been lost and could no longer be found, and the men who were walking, the three men who were walking, two and three religious stones under the storm, were simply vocation and spirit without true purpose." (25) Significantly, he cannot lead the group toward salvation, and ends up drowned.

The Mexican soul, in sum, is depicted in *El luto humano* as morally and spiritually bereft. In this context, the flood does not seem so tragic since, as Revueltas implies, human beings like this do not deserve to go on living. On a symbolic level, the flood is a purging. It offers, with the elimination of this race, the possibility of a new and better one. In Helia Sheldon's words, "the deluge is a ritual death, the destruction of a degenerated humanity, extermination of 'ancient' man as punishment and promise of regeneration." (110–111) To Revueltas, the new man would be modeled after the likes of Natividad, a true socialist.

Although Revueltas was honest about the influence his political convictions had on his literary works, he nevertheless engaged in the same sort of myth-making the state-supported intellectuals engaged in. Like them, he created archetypes of the poor that emphasize the negative qualities of "Mexicanness." His goal was similar to those intellectuals: to provide self-awareness and change. In his own words:

> I increasingly have the feeling that we are all victims of a flood, that we don't know anything about anything, neither about our own selves or anybody else, and that we have vultures flying over our heads. And, well, if that is our reality than it should be recognized. Only by recognizing it can we begin to struggle against it to transform it. (Solares 59)

The only difference was that he depicted the Mexican in a way that was beneficial to the socialist cause rather than the capitalist one. As Noé Angeles puts it: "Revueltas tries to portray the worst and most denigrating aspects of capitalist society, to discover that capitalism is already obsolete and goes against the laws of history." (207) Like the state-supported intellectuals, Revueltas constructed archetypes of the national character (as embodied by the poor masses) for political ends. He stressed the deplorable state of the national psyche in order to convince his readers that socialism should replace capitalism.

Al filo del agua

In stark contrast to Revueltas, Agustín Yáñez held a prominent career in government service. As Roderic Camp points out, his educational and professional backgrounds followed a pattern typical of Mexico's most prestigious writers/intellectuals, although his working class origins were unusual. His political career owes itself primarily to his excellence as a scholar. After receiving his primary and secondary educations in Guadalajara (he was too poor to study in Mexico City), Yáñez dedicated himself to writing, speaking and teaching. In 1929 he founded the literary magazine "Bandera de provincias," in which some of Mexico's most important literary and intellectual figures participated. In 1931, he moved to Mexico City, becoming professor at the National Preparatory School while also enrolled there. Here he came into contact with many of Mexico's future intellectual and political leaders. Until 1952, Yáñez held primarily lower-level government positions: Director of the Radio Extensión Program of the Secretariat of Public Education (SEP) from 1932 to 1934, and Director of Library and Economic Archives from 1934 to 1952. However, he completed most of his major literary works during this period, and held important literary/intellectual posts, including editor of the "Philosophy and Letters Review" of the School of Philosophy and Letters of the National University (1946) and founding director of the literary review *Occidente* (1944). According to Camp, "it was during these years that he developed personal friendships with many intellectuals highly successful in public life." (9) After 1952 he became a speechwriter for Ruiz Cortines, the presidential candidate, and shortly thenceforth governor of his home state of Jalisco. In 1959 he left his post as governor to become professor at the National Preparatory School and the School of Philosophy and Letters at the National University, while also serving as presidential advisor to Adolfo López Mateos. In 1962 he became subsecretary for the Presidency, and in 1964 he obtained the most important post of his entire public career, that of Secretary of Public Education. His last important public position was as President of the National Free Textbook Commission from 1976 to 1979.

Yáñez's allegiance to the state profoundly influenced his literary works. A primary example of this allegiance was his dedication to topics related to the nation. Yáñez wrote repeatedly on the national character. *Al filo del agua* (*At the Edge of the Storn*), considered among Mexico's best novels, constitutes the author's most important attempt to formulate the Mexican psyche.

Yáñez's analysis of Mexicans' character deficiencies shares some similarities with that of Revueltas. For example, they both describe the provincial Mexican in similar terms as fatalistic, melancholic and superstitious. While Revueltas views the Church as impotent and corrupt, Yáñez goes a step further by holding it directly responsible for the national psychoses. However, the authors' proposed solutions for these psychoses are radically different. While for Revueltas socialism—in the form of a Revolution yet to take place—is the answer, Yáñez discovers it in capitalism and the Revolution that already took place.

By far the dominant influence on the provincial characters of *Al filo del agua* is the Church. According to Marta Portal, the novel picks up on "a new aspect of nationalism: anticlericalism is a variant of anti-Spanishness or anticolonialism... It is the denunciation of an evolutionized and degenerated state of colonial dependence, and proposes the definitive independence." (204) Yáñez employs psychoanalysis, and in particular the works of Sigmund Freud, to explore religion's impact on the national subject. Freud maintained that prohibitions are necessary to civilization, as they put a check on human's precivilized, savage selves (which in dreams perform transgressions of all sorts: murder, incest, and diverse sexual behaviors). However, too much repression has a negative effect on the individual, causing anxiety, depression, listlessness, and so on. Freud blamed religion, in particular, for controlling the masses through the excessive use of prohibitions, which lead to child-like neuroses: "If on the one hand religion brings with it obsessional limitations, which can only be compared to an individual obsessional neurosis, it comprises on the other hand a system of wish-illusions, incompatible with reality... a state of blissful hallucinatory confusion." (76) He contends that religion should be replaced by mature, rational, scientific thought: "Man cannot remain a child for ever; he must venture at last into the hostile world. This may be called 'education to reality.'" (86) For Freud, what is at stake is the health of civilization.

In his novel, Yáñez condemns the Church for helping to maintain the status quo of the Porfirian regime, fearing a loss of power and influence that might come with liberal reforms. The Church, he emphasizes, neither denounces an economic and social system that exploits the poor and enriches the already wealthy, nor demands (or provides) the most basic services denied its faithful: a school, health clinic, orphanage, and agricultural cooperative and credit system. More importantly, Yáñez maintains that the Church has caused extensive psychological distress by rigidly controlling behaviors and attitudes. The

Church isolates the villagers from the outside world and employs guilt to oblige them to suppress some of their most natural instincts and emotions. As a consequence, the townspeople cannot live in peace with themselves, as they are constantly plagued by fear and guilt. Additionally, they develop attitudes detrimental to their own health as well as that of the nation, including fatalism, superstitiousness, and passivity.

The Church's pervasive, suffocating presence is felt from the very onset of the novel in the "overture," which sets the atmosphere. It is outwardly apparent in the church bells, which "ring from the towers at definite times... issuing the orders which rule the life of the village" (5), and in the many vigilant "black-robed women" or "Daughters of Mary," designated by the Church to make sure the young women strictly follow the religious codes in "dress, movements, speech, thoughts and feelings." (12–13) It is further evident in the hermetic, convent-like atmosphere, which is devoid of all enjoyment of life. There are no parties or laughter. The taverns are kept far out of sight. And weddings take place while it is still dark, "as though there were something shameful about them, something mysterious." (6)

In its efforts to maintain control over the townspeople, the Church is most concerned with stemming sexual desire. The villagers constantly struggle to repress these urges: "Desires, the very breath of desire, is hidden deep in the heart of the village... One hears it in the prayers and hymns in which it takes refuge: a deep, pulsing vibration, feverish breathing, controlled only with great effort." (5) This battle against "evil" produces deep anxieties and fears. Moreover, it prevents true communication and love between the sexes, and results in loneliness and despair. The characters' inability to forge healthy and satisfying relationships with the opposite sex is a constant throughout the novel.

Despite the Church's iron grip on the village, we soon learn that outside influences are beginning to erode its power. At Retreat House, where the villagers are sent each year in groups (men separate from women) to repent for their sins, the priests begin hearing confessions that indicate a growing opposition to the forces in power. One man passes along love stories and papers speaking ill of God and the clergy. Another confesses to showing pornographic photographs to friends. Another admits to having attended a Masonics meeting. And several others take part in a spiritist meeting. The priests also become aware of a growing interest in socialism: "One man had taken part in a strike in the north; two or three had confessed their hatred of the rich, one confessed working with people from Teocaltiche to found a Juarist Club, and another declared that he was involved in a conspiracy to revolt and attack the rich 'if Don Porfirio was reelected.'" (59) The main priest, Don Dionisio María Martínez, becomes so frightened by these confessions that he falls ill. In the final sermon before the penitents leave the Retreat House, he warns of impending disaster: "The village is surrounded by perils, it is in a state of siege, and the agents of the Enemy are within our gates. Woe unto him through whom comes disaster!" (59–60) He is unable to sleep at night, "beset by worries about the dangers facing his flock: liberalism, laxity in manners, Masonry, Spiritism, socialism, impious books, revolution!... Worst of all is the infiltration of these ideas, these ideas..." (61–62)

The main sources of "these ideas" are the villagers who have returned to the area after working in the United States. With a new awareness of the social and economic injustices perpetrated against their people, and finding the town's atmosphere now oppressive and unbearable, they lash out against both the government and the Church. Most of the townspeople denounce them as lazy, immoral and antipatriotic. However, some of the younger villagers, influenced by the newcomers, begin to openly rebel against tradition. In contrast to the rest of the village, whom the novel depicts as irrational, intolerant and unaccustomed to change, they represent a positive force of change. Micaela, angered by having to return to the "backward" and "hypocritical" village after spending an exhilarating vacation in modern Guadalajara and Mexico City, openly flaunts her sexuality in the hopes of creating a scandal that will compel her parents to send her back. María, who desperately longs to see the world outside the village, furtively reads the travel books forbidden to her by Don Dionisio, her uncle and surrogate father. And Gabriel, who is in charge of the church bells, barricades himself in the church tower after being forbidden to ring the bells because he had begun disturbing the entire rhythm of the town by ringing the wrong tunes at the wrong times. Gabriel's pent up emotions erupt in artistic genius in his bell ringing, which gives expression to the general mood of the entire town. His erratic, restless playing both reflects and heightens the growing discontent felt in the village: "No one could work, let alone pray. No one could bear to be alone. The whole village felt oppressed and confined. The people could hear their own breathing and the beating of their own hearts, and were conscious of sadness, of repressed longings." (167)

The tensions finally explode in a series of incidents that forever alter the town. Notably, all involve frustrated romances. The most shocking incident is a double-murder. In her attempts to provoke scandal, Micaela had begun flirting with the father of a recent suitor, Damián. In a fit of jealous rage, heightened by his father's refusal to grant him his portion of his deceased mother's inheritance, Damián murders his father and Micaela. Afterwards, he blames his irrational act on the priests, whom he accuses of "fostering an atmosphere that makes it impossible to breath." (236) Luis Gonzaga, a promising scholar, goes crazy after an experience of religious ecstasy, and must be interned in an insane asylum. He is obsessed with lewd fantasies involving young women he knew, most of all Victoria, a beautiful urbanite who briefly stayed with Luis's family. Gabriel, unable to consummate his love for either Victoria or María, can no longer bear the town's stifling atmosphere, and leaves. He sends a letter to Don Dionisio, his surrogate father (he was orphaned), asking for María's hand, but to no avail. María, dejected by Gabriel's absence and tormented by her urge to leave the village, courts a man she does not love out of sheer boredom and rebelliousness. She "was now firmly convinced that no one in the village had ever felt the passion of love." (272) Finally, Mercedes Tovar, distraught by feelings of guilt and fear over Micaela's death (she had been jealous of the attentions Micaela had been paying her boyfriend, and had wished her ill), doubts her engagement to Julián and ends up losing him to another woman. She winds up lonely and depressed. When Julián's child is born dead, she again feels guilty because she had envied the couple. Mercedes must be taken away from the village to Guadalajara, where she is sure she will die.

Fears also mount rapidly as the villagers, unaccustomed to change, begin realizing that their town will no longer be able to remain isolated from the rest of the country. A major religious festival is interrupted by the arrival of government troops, determined to make sure the reform laws are kept. The presence of strangers, the report of a comet, and rumors of earthquakes, calamities, revolutions and danger in faraway or nearby places also add to the growing panic which "was now mingled, but not confused, with chronic fear of the end of the world." (285) The end of a former way of life is finally confirmed with the arrival of the revolutionaries, who demand from the rich "a forced loan, restoration of ill-gotten goods and usurious interest collected by force, weapons and horses, saddles, and food." (323) María joins them as they depart, finally attaining her freedom. Don Dionisio, convinced of his failure to guide the faithful in the right direction, has a breakdown, signifying the impending decline of Church power, and its substitution by the more rational state.

Contrary to the vast majority of novels on the Revolution, *Al filo del agua* depicts the war as a positive force for change. Yáñez envisions the Revolution as a potential source of liberation from economic and spiritual repression. From the standpoint of post-Revolutionary Mexico, it provides inspiration for shedding the remaining vestiges of a colonial mentality that manifests itself in behavior and attitudes detrimental to both the individual and the nation: fatalism, passivity, superstitiousness, violence, incommunicativeness, fearfulness, distrust, and so on. Viewed from the Freudian perspective, the Revolution offers the possibility of leaving behind a child-like, repressed, precivilized or backward world for a mature, civilized and modern one. Like the flood in *El luto humano*, the Revolution is the storm (alluded to in the title), which, while destructive, will ultimately lead to healthy change.

Most of all, the Revolution will give birth to a modern national subject by lifting the repressive sexual taboos imposed by the Church. By making sexual repression a major part of his nationalistic, modernist discourse, Yáñez in some senses models the 19th century national romance novelists. As Doris Sommer explains in *Foundational Fictions*, these novelists developed an "erotics of politics" in which "national ideas are all ostensibly grounded in 'natural' heterosexual love and in the marriages that provided a figure for apparently nonviolent consolidation during internecine conflicts at midcentury." (6) However, in contrast to the romance novels of the previous century, "natural" heterosexual love is conspicuously absent in Yáñez's (as well as Revueltas's) novel. Not only are the protagonists unable to experience true love; they cannot procreate. While in Revueltas's novel the national subject symbolically dies, unable to love or reproduce, in Yáñez's he is given new life. The Revolution will allow Mexicans to form healthy bonds with the opposite sex, and consequently to produce offspring unencumbered by pre-colonial attitudes. It is this offspring that Yáñez envisions populating the Mexican nation.

The Exaltation of Machismo and "Mexicanness"

While in the novels the provincial Mexican was afflicted with the most troublesome characteristics of the national soul, in many films he was credited with some of the most admirable ones. The "comedia ranchera" and the revolutionary melodrama exalted "Mexicanness" and reaffirmed traditional values. They further contrasted with the novels by appearing to ignore the social and economic changes that Mexico was undergoing. Both the "comedia ranchera" and the revolutionary melodrama were set prior to the 1940s, and also do not deal in any way with the city. Nonetheless, they were responsive to that time period. As explained in the previous chapter, the "comedia ranchera" fulfilled many Mexicans' desire to evade the perils of modernization by escaping to an idealized past. Furthermore, both genres reaffirmed traditional values that were perceived as being threatened by the modernization process. The revolutionary melodrama, in addition, provided hope for a more egalitarian society by showing alliances between the poor and the rich, and by stressing the importance of class over race.

Los tres García

Most of the "comedias rancheras" did not explore the national character in great depth. They tended to sacrifice detailed character analysis for comedy and intrigue. However, one of the more successful "comedias rancheras" of the 1940's joined literature in its spiritualization of the national subject: *Los tres García* (*The Three García*) (1946), directed by Ismael Rodríguez. The three protagonists of this movie, each very different from the other, form a composite of the national character (symbolized by their relationship as cousins and their sharing of the name "Luis"). José Luis, the poorest of the three, is reserved, melancholic, sensitive, insecure, self-absorbed and self-pitying. He is obsessed with protecting his dignity, refusing either to work ("I prefer to earn little on my own than give away my labor to others") or to accept money from his grandmother ("It isn't pride, it's the dignity of a man.") Luis Antonio (Pedro Infante), by contrast, is boisterous, fun loving, lazy, crude and sentimental. He spends all his time flirting with women and drinking. Luis Manuel, the richest of the three, is elegant, greedy, pompous and arrogant, professing to be unconcerned with anything unrelated to money. Each dislikes the others, and their grandmother must constantly interfere to prevent them from inflicting too much harm on each other. The only thing that disturbs the peace of this idyllic town (ironically named "San Juan de la Paz") are the fights that break out among the three cousins whenever they reunite.

The protagonists reveal their personalities primarily in their attempts to win over the affections of their cousin, Lupe. José Luis tries to attract her by emphasizing his strong sense of dignity and pride. Offended after she and her father offer him money for providing them with directions to town (they didn't recognize who he was at the time), he dreams of Lupe begging him for forgiveness as a crowd of people look on admiringly. Luis Antonio attempts to win her over with his gallantry. He has a dream in which, in front of a large group of admirers who are imploring him not to abandon them, he professes to Lupe that he will sacrifice them for her. Luis Manuel attempts to impress her with his elegance and wealth. In his dream, he dazzles Lupe with a gift of gold jewelry. They all woo her with great romantic skill, resorting to poetry and even more to song (they are excellent singers of traditional Mexican folk music). They also try to impress her with their prowess as "charros" (cowboys), in a scene in which they compete against each other for the final prize, to be awarded by Lupe.

It might appear on the surface that *Los tres García* criticizes the Mexican character, given that many of the protagonists' traits are unpraiseworthy. However, it is clear that the protagonists are caricatures, whose function is mainly comedic. Their boyish fighting is laughable, never dangerous. They insist with a certain amount of machistic pride that "three Garcías are too many," but they never intend to kill each other. Moreover, they unite against a common enemy, the three López's. The three García's are also well liked in the town. Not only are they entertaining, but they also respect and obey moral codes, attending church and heeding family authority (their grandmother). Most of all, they are very manly. The three García's share one outstanding trait: machismo. All demonstrate great expertise with their pistols, with the skills required of the "charro" (horseback riding, roping, bullfighting), and with the pursuit of women. The three López's—murderers and thieves—function to underscore the positive qualities of the three García's, their polar opposites. The three López's are clearly the "bad" guys (a fact that, in a racist gesture, is emphasized by their darker skin color and their slovenly appearance) and the García's the "good" ones.

The two women protagonists are defined by their relationships with the males. The grandmother is more developed and interesting than Lupe. Played by Sara García, the consummate mother figure of Mexican film, she is a burlesque figure. Cloaked in a black dress up to her chin, with her hair in a tidy white bun, and a cigar perpetually hanging out of her mouth, the grandmother "represents the feminine impossibility of becoming a true male." (Ayala Blanco 62) She spends her time fretting over and reprimanding her wayward grandchildren, controlling them through a hilarious and impressive array of verbal insults, and the frequent use of her black cane. But despite her copious criticisms, it is clear that she takes great pride in her grandchildren, particularly their manliness. The film hints that the grandmother played no small role in fomenting the macho behavior of the three García's. When the priest asks her to disarm them, in order to prevent them from killing or being killed by the three López's, she emphatically refuses, declaring: "I prefer to see them dead having defended themselves like men, than alive and cowardly." And when the three cousins get into a particularly ferocious fight, she relishes the scene, taking a seat at the balcony over the patio to watch and cheer. Thus through the grandmother, who represents the ultimate female authority, the film promotes the notion that women support and even enjoy displays of masculinity.

While the grandmother plays the asexual mother figure, Lupe fulfills the other major function of women in Mexican film of the period—that of the coveted sexual object, the male's reward for the hard work of being macho. Lupe lights up the screen with her beauty, charm, and wit, but that is about the extent of her personality. She exists mainly to bring out the qualities of her cousins. Throughout the film, Lupe struggles to decide among the three, all of who impress her. She finally resolves to leave the ranch surreptitiously, avoiding the uncomfortable situation altogether. However, she and her father are obliged to return after finding out that Luis Antonio has been jailed for allegedly killing the three López's (an accusation that proves false). Her cousins trap her in her bedroom as she is preparing to depart for good, obligating her to decide between the three. Ironically, she settles on José Luis, who had most ignored and insulted her. The García's triumph over Lupe, her choice of the most abusive of the three, and in fact her very interest in them at all, play out the male desire, expressed repeatedly in Mexican film, of subjugating the female. Conquering the female is the ultimate expression of machismo. At the same time, it promotes the idea that the female is willingly subservient to the male.

The other main character, Lupe's father and the uncle of the three García, also functions to reinforce the film's nationalistic motive by showing the Mexican to be superior to the North American. He is the stereotype of the rich and stupid gringo, who thinks his wealth gives him the authority to demand and receive whatever he pleases. The uncle is constantly ridiculed in the film. He lacks tact and social refinery, and his pronunciation and usage of the Spanish language are atrocious (which repeatedly causes Lupe embarrassment). His passivity and impotence also contrast with the manliness of his nephews. No one except Lupe respect him. His nephews want nothing to do with him, and even the grandmother (his mother in law) treats him with a measure of scorn.

In the end, none of the characters prove very original or complex, and even their relationships with each other lack profundity. The film, in other words, provides no new insights into the Mexican character. To the contrary, it is like every other "comedia ranchera" in its superficial treatment of its characters. Nevertheless, it (and other films like it) played an important role within nationalism. It provided an escape from worrisome societal developments, reinforced pride in "Mexicanness," and provided a sense of security by emphasizing traditional values and gender roles, including the authority of the male.

Enamorada

Along with the "comedia ranchera", a number of very popular films dealing with the Revolution appeared during the 1940s, including *Flor silvestre* (1943), *Río escondido* (1947), and *Enamorada* (1947). Emilio "El Indio" Fernández, who is widely considered one of the most popular and nationalistic directors of the time period, directed all of these films. Teamed up with the cinematographer, Gabriel Figueroa, the writer, Mauricio Magdaleno, and the actors, Pedro Armendáriz, Dolores del Río and María Félix, Fernández dominated filmmaking during the 1940s, Mexico's so-called "Golden Age" of cinema. According to Julia Tuñón, "his basic concern was to produce a Mexican cinema: 'I dreamt and am still dreaming of a different cinema, of course, but Mexican, pure. Now I have this great desire to mexicanise the Mexicans, for we are becoming americanised.'" (184) Fernández's efforts to express "Mexicanness" were supported and encouraged by the state. At the time, the Banco Cinematográfico was granting more generous credits to those producers who made films that had a nationalistic content. Taking advantage of this incentive, Agustín Fink, president of Films Mundiales, backed Fernández's works. (Mora 62)

The Soviet director, Sergei Eisenstein, who developed an aesthetic of nationalism while working in Mexico (see chapter three), strongly influenced Fernández. The muralist movement also influenced his works. Like Eisenstein and the muralists, Fernández attempted to capture the national essence in his films by paying close attention to particular aspects of the landscape and people. These included, for example, nopals and magueys, the features and clothing of Mexico's native people, and historical and artistic objects such as churches, altars, and monuments, whose beauty and timelessness he wished to capture. According to Julia Tuñón, he wanted his films "to be like paintings, photography or photography in movement... Like the muralists, he tried to unleash profound feelings." (185) John King gives a compelling description of this aesthetic:

> Figueroas' eloquent photography captures, in allegorical fashion, the moment of Adam and Eve in the garden of Mexico, the expressive physiognomies of the main characters which harmonize with the expressive nature of the landscape; its lowering clouds, the emblematic plants, the play of light and dark, the shadows cast by the heat of the sun. Mexico, for Fernández, is elemental, atavistic, the site of primal passions and violence, from which can be forged a new progressive nation. (48)

The majority of Fernández's films are set in the countryside, as he believed it was in this immutable place that the national essence revealed itself. He wished, furthermore, to convey social messages of relevance to the rural poor, such as the need for land reform, education, and the Indians' redemption. Fernández expressed the ideals of the Cárdenas era, even during the 1940s when, under Manuel Ávila Camacho and Miguel Alemán, social concerns were set aside in the interest of economic growth. Because there was no longer any threat of socialism, the Mexican bourgeoisie opened their arms to Fernández, who made it appear as if revolutionary ideals were still alive, even as governmental policies were indicating otherwise.

Fernández also favored rural dramas because through them he could represent the conflicts that emerged when traditional values and ways of life clashed with the new. This conflict is evident, for example, in *Enamorada* (*A Woman in Love*), which portrays the struggle between an older class-conscious society and a new one that values equality. Appearing twenty years after the end of the Revolution, *Enamorada* seems to want to convince audiences that the revolutionary ideal of equality is still central and close to being achieved. While an earlier film on the revolution—*El compadre Mendoza* (1933)—had portrayed equality as an ideal, *Enamorada* views it as a real possibility.

Enamorada focuses on a revolutionary general's love for a young woman, Beatriz, who is from the upper class. Beatriz scorns the general, José Luis, because he is socially inferior to her, and also because he has invaded the town with his troops, demanding cash and goods from the wealthy—including her father—for the revolutionary cause. Beatriz has inherited her father's contempt for the revolutionaries (whom he refers to as "bandits"), and his sense of class superiority. She considers the general a "pelado," or lower-class thug, and mocks him at every chance she gets, even after he frees her father. José Luis continues to pursue Beatriz in spite of her disdain and the fact that she is already engaged to an American. Eventually, however, he comes to realize that his efforts are in vain. He begs for Beatriz's apology and decides to abandon the town without fighting the federal troops, who are fast advancing. As he is retreating, Beatriz is in the middle of a civil wedding ceremony. She is on the verge of signing the wedding certificate when bombs explode in the background. She changes her mind, drops the pen and runs outside. Quickly she returns to say goodbye to her father, then hurries off to join the general. The movie ends as she walks behind the general as a soldadera, her hand on the rump of the horse he is riding.

The last scene is significant for two main reasons. First, through Beatriz's rejection of her American fiancé, the movie emphasizes the importance of patriotism and the repudiation of North American culture. This is significant because the film appeared during a time when some Mexicans (including the film's director, as evident in the aforementioned quote) were worried by the infiltration of North American culture into Mexico. The film does not ridicule or vilify Beatriz's fiancé, as was the case for the North American in *Los tres García*, but rather portrays him as incompatible with her. The fact that they do not understand each other well underscores the differences between North Americans and Mexicans.

More importantly, Beatriz's decision to follow the general symbolizes the beginning of a new era of peace and equality between social classes. Through the exchange of looks that occur at the end, we understand that she has finally forgiven him and is now asking for his acceptance. In other words, the movie stresses forgiveness as a means of resolving class tensions, and symbolically unites the two social classes by joining José Luis and Beatriz in marriage. As Jean Franco explains, Beatriz's decision to leave her hometown to join the General also "signals the change from the old order to the new and the necessary separation of this new family from older rooted communities." (152) These two will give birth to a new revolutionary family (or nation), one that is united across social classes.

The film bids farewell to anachronistic ways of life in other ways as well. Beatriz's father, for example, exemplifies a rigid mentality that will soon die off. In attempting to save the father's life, the foreigner explains to the general that the father "is old and his ideas won't change." He adds that "her father doesn't believe in the Revolution but I do". In other words, a younger generation of wealthy Mexicans support revolutionary ideals and do not consider the lower classes to be socially inferior. Equality is further stressed in a conversation between José Luis and the local priest, in which the general explains that the only difference between the two is that the priest serves God and is concerned about the afterlife, while he serves man and wants to create a heaven on earth.

The movie also attempts to placate the poor by praising the moral attributes of the revolutionaries (symbolic of Mexico's lower classes). José Luis has noble ideals, and is sensitive, upright, and self-sacrificing. He tenderly cares for the daughter of his friends who died in a train derailment, and wishes Beatriz's fiancé well in his marriage to her. The film also exalts the female revolutionaries, or "soldaderas." The introduction explains that these women followed the men into the Revolution, "often fighting and dying alongside them". Furthermore, when Beatriz insults the soldaderas, José Luis promptly comes to their defense in a long speech in which he extols their virtues. Through the soldaderas, the film stresses the importance of women's role as aid to the male.

At the same time that the film prophesizes a new generation of Mexicans, it also reaffirms many traditional values. For example, as Jean Franco has pointed out, it portrays the Church as a moral authority and a fundamental force in the characters' lives. It is the priest who mediates between the revolutionaries and those who oppose the Revolution, and who guides the actions of both Beatriz and José Luis. It is in the church, furthermore, where Beatriz and the general learn to be more tolerant and forgiving of each other. *Enamorada* also stresses the importance of the family unit. All the characters lack either one parent (in the case of Beatriz) or both (in the case of the general and the little girl for whom he cares). By joining together in marriage, Beatriz and the general will form the type of family that they so greatly desire. At the same time, their union symbolizes the sort of family the nation so sorely needs.

Lastly, the film shores up the family and the patriarchal structure by providing gender models. Throughout most of the movie Beatriz behaves in an unfeminine manner. She is extremely outspoken, smokes, and physically abuses the general (in one scene she blows him off his horse with dynamite; in another she slaps him hard on both cheeks for having commented on her figure; and in still another she forcefully strikes a wooden club against the inside of her front door after urging the general to put his face against the outside of that door). Jean Franco attributes her masculine attributes not only to her "proud and independent nature", but also to "the power of her class position." (149) However, the film makes sure to feminize her and to reestablish the traditional male/female hierarchy, as is evident in the concluding scene. We are made to understand that, by her own choice, Beatriz will fulfill her proper role as wife, mother and soldadera. She will be willingly subservient to the male, like the soldaderas.

José Luis, for his part, loses some of his forcefulness and immaturity during the movie as he finally realizes that he can't have Beatriz. By becoming more sensitive to her desires, and by apologizing for his behavior, he ultimately wins her over. By feminizing José Luis, the film to an extent contradicted the prevailing model of machismo. However, it seemed to do this in order to more effectively assure the patriarchal order. As a result of his actions, José Luis gains back his male authority, and also wins Beatriz's loyalty. Furthermore, he guarantees a more solid marriage, one based on love, respect and understanding.

In conclusion, although many films during this period were set in an idyllic rural past, they were actually reacting to the profound societal changes occurring at the time. The "comedia ranchera" and the revolutionary melodramas responded to many Mexicans' fears, insecurities and concerns about the modernization process. They reinforced national identity and pride at a time when the presence of North American culture was being increasingly felt. They reassured Mexicans that certain traditions would survive the transformation to a modern society. And, perhaps most importantly, they attempted to ensure social cohesion and stability. These films enhanced the importance of family, the church and male authority, and provided models of conduct. They also tried to ease tensions between social classes and avert social discontent by stressing equality between the classes and by providing hopes for a better future.

Chapter Six

Indigenism, Mestizaje and National Identity

During the 1940s, the indigenist movement in Mexico gathered momentum as the state stepped up its efforts to integrate the Indian into national life. Signaling indigenism's growing importance (not only in Mexico, but in many other Latin American nations as well), the Mexican state hosted the Primer Congreso Indigenista Interamericano in 1940. This meeting led to the creation of the Instituto Indigenista Interamericano in 1942, which was based in Mexico, and to the foundation of the Instituto Nacional Indigenista in 1947. This decade also marked a period of intense modernization. In 1940, with Manuel Avila Camacho's election to the Mexican presidency (1940–1946), the social reform of the Lázaro Cárdenas years came to an abrupt end. Priority shifted dramatically from social to economic progress, a trend that accelerated during the Miguel Alemán presidency (1946–1952). Indigenism formed an integral part of the state's economic development plans. As Cynthia Steele points out, Indian labor "was considered essential to the nation's economic growth" (70). Braulio Muñoz likewise asserts that integration "translated a desire of the Mexican bourgeoisie...to create an adequate internal market to support its growth" (194). Integration would also strengthen the sense of national unity, which was critical to protecting the nation from internal divisions and foreign intrusions.[1]

Besides paying increased attention to the Indian's integration into mainstream society, the state initiated a new direction in the indigenist movement that would persist into the following decade. In the 1930s, Lázaro Cárdenas had sought to improve the Indian's economic plight in part through agrarian reform, guaranteeing the Indians plots of land from which they could make a living. Avila Camacho and Alemán, on the other hand, instituted a capitalistic model of economic development that favored large-scale agricultural properties over the ejido, and industry over agriculture. They wished to prepare the Indian for entrance into the mainstream working force. Cárdenas and his supporters had also considered Mexico to be "without a doubt indigenous... Indigenous culture...formed the true shape of Mexican society." (Ivie 969) As such, they held the Indian up as symbol of national identity and pride, and attempted to spark interest in native languages and culture.[2] In contrast, Avila Camacho and Alemán were eager to promote the image of Mexico as a modern, mestizo nation and not an indigenous one that, to many, connoted backwardness. They continued to encourage pride in Mexico's indigenous past, but emphasized mestizaje as key to the nation's social and economic welfare.

While anthropologists such as Manuel Gamio and Alfonso Caso took concrete measures to integrate and mesticize the Indian, some of Mexico's most renowned writers, and one if its most nationalistic filmmakers, also aided the state's efforts to promote mestizaje during the 1940s and the 1950s. The essayists, Héctor Pérez Martínez, Agustín Yáñez and Luis Villoro, and the novelist Miguel Angel Menéndez, pointed out the admirable qualities of indigenous culture and psychology, hoping to inspire respect for the Indians and their acceptance by mestizo Mexicans. These writers also probed the mestizo's psyche in order to discover the reasons for his denigration and exploitation of the Indian. They wanted the mestizo to gain self-awareness and an improved self-concept in order that he might appreciate rather than reject his indigenous heritage. They further wished to construct a new type of mestizo Mexican who was emotionally stable, self-confident and secure. Film took a different approach from literature. *María Candelaria* (1943), directed by Emilio Fernández, idealized the Indian in order to inspire sympathy and admiration for Mexico's indigenous groups. Even more importantly, it sought to identify the masses with the Indian by stressing shared experiences and characteristics.

As I will explain in more depth later in this chapter, these artists and intellectuals undermined their own attempts to promote mestizaje by unconsciously fostering negative stereotypes of the Indian. The writers' efforts were further stymied by their inability to reach the masses, the majority of who did not read. The popular arts failed to help them in this task. For example, *María Candelaria* aside, cinema rarely dealt with the topic of the Indian. Moreover, while a few films like *María Candelaria* idealized the Indian, others depicted him in minor roles as the stereotypical dark villain or clown. That is, the Indian was almost always cast in black and white terms in cinema. The problem of racism was also never really addressed in film, and no movies during the period followed the writers' lead by probing the mestizo psyche.

Indigenism as a whole during the 1940s and the 1950s was motivated above all by the desire to unify the nation and to progress economically, although indigenists argued that the Indian would also benefit from his integration into national life. As Héctor Díaz Polanco puts it, "it is only at the moment when capitalism has clearly defined its bases that the contact with other societies generates the appearance of well-formulated theories that try to explain (or justify) the assimilation of all precapitalist or non-capitalist systems." (11) He explains that capitalism tends towards expansionism, and as such sets out to integrate all other social systems into its own by destroying the bases that sustain them. Indigenism, he argues, constitutes one of the strategies to attain such integration. He asserts that in the case of Mexico, all indigenist theories have been based on the idea of progress as defined by Western European capitalism. These theories view indigenous societies as impediments to the nation's development, and advocate the Indian's integration into mainstream society. According to Díaz Polanco, integration requires the destruction of indigenous socioeconomic and political systems, "molding them to fit those systems that liberalism postulated: private property, citizenship, etc...", and the "total dissolution of cultural traits (languages, customs, etc...)." (20–21)

Mestizaje was a much desired by product of integration, as it implied the loss of all racial distinctions, including the physical. By racially homogenizing the nation, it would eliminate internal divisions caused by race, and thereby strengthen the sense of national unity. Seminal works from the beginning of the twentieth century recognized mestizaje's potential. In particular, Andrés Molina Enríquez's *Los grandes problemas nacionales* (1909), and Manuel Gamio's *Forjando Patria* (1916) profoundly influenced indigenist literature and governmental policies of the 1940s and the 1950s.

In *Los grandes problemas nacionales*, which helped to shape the ideology of the Mexican Revolution, Molina Enríquez argues that mestizaje is fundamental to the nation's well being, providing the national unity essential to warding off foreign intrusions into Mexican territory. He proposes the idea that Mexico's different ethnic groups—mestizo, Creole and Indian—have distinct character traits, and that those of the mestizo are superior. The mestizos, he asserts, are the largest, most powerful, and most patriotic of all the Mexicans. Molina Enríquez likens them to a family, saying they share a "community of feelings, acts and ideas that are peculiar to members of a family...mestizos identify with the Indians and together these groups form the true national population." (393) He adds that while the Indians are "passive, unmoved, and taciturn" and the Creoles "audacious, impetuous and frivolous" the mestizos are "energetic, persevering and serious." (419) Molina Enriquez contends that the mestizos' energy comes from their indigenous blood, and is constantly being renewed through mixing with the Indian. Moreover, through this mixing the mestizos are absorbing the Indian population and increasing their own. To Molina Enriquez, mestizaje constitutes a means of ridding the nation of its indigenous and Creole populations. This is necessary in order to form "a true nationality, one that is strong and powerful and has one life and one soul." (424)

Similarly, Manuel Gamio's *Forjando patria* emphasizes the nation's need to unite its diverse ethnic elements in order to become a modern nation. Gamio agrees with Enríquez Molina that the mestizos (a term he makes synonymous with the middle class) represent "national culture, the one of the future, the one that will end up imposing itself when the population, having become ethnically homogeneous, feels it and understands it." (98) He praises this group as the "eternal rebeller, the traditional enemy of the pure-blooded or foreign class, the author and director of revolts and revolutions, the one that has best understood the justified laments of the indigenous class and taken advantage of its powerful latent energies to contain the oppressions of Power." (97) He also contends that it is the only group that has produced intellectually.

During the 1940s and the 1950s, the state struggled to make Enríquez Molina's and Gamio's vision of a unified, mestizo-based society a reality. Anthropologists, including most famously Alfonso Caso and Manuel Gamio,[3] took concrete steps to mesticize the Indian. One of the most important of these was to reformulate the definition of "Indian" so that culture rather than biology held precedent.[4] Peasants of indigenous descent who did not live in or feel a part of a particular indigenous community were reclassified as mestizos. Caso's definition was the most commonly cited:

> An Indian is any individual who feels he belongs to an indigenous community; who conceives of himself as an Indian...; who has the same ethic, aesthetic, social and political ideals of the group; who participates in the sympathies and antipathies of the collectivity and to a large degree collaborates in its actions and reactions. ("Definición del indio..." 215)

This new definition was significant for three main reasons. First, as others have noted, it had the effect of decreasing the number of Mexicans who were previously considered Indian, and increasing those regarded as mestizo. In other words, it made Mexico appear less indigenous and more mestizo. Secondly, it made the process of mestizaje easier by eliminating the need for racial mixing. An Indian could become mestizo simply by adopting Western ways of life. Gamio argued that:

> As the proportion of characteristics of prehispanic origen decrease and those of European origin increase, the groups being studied may be considered as culturally mixed and increasingly less indigenous... When such a proportion is very small and European characteristics are very high, the groups and individuals are no longer culturally indigenous, even when form the racial point of view they are. ("Las características culturales" 16)

Thus according to Gamio, native Mexicans don't even have to be completely westernized in order to be considered mestizo.

A third important result of the new definition was to emphasize the cultural rather than the biological differences between indigenous and non-indigenous Mexicans. Anthropologists were eager to counter the widespread notion that the Indians were biologically inferior to non-indigenous Mexicans. This notion obstructed the process of integration and mestizaje by making it appear as if the Indians were incapable of being civilized. Anthropologists wished to emphasize that the Indians' social, economic and cultural backwardness was not a consequence of biology, but rather of their mistreatment and neglect by the rest of Mexican society. They contended that the Indian would be able to participate in mainstream society at an intellectual level equivalent to the rest of Mexicans were he provided with the same social and economic opportunities. For example, in "¿El indio mexicano es mexicano?" (1956), Caso stresses the Indian's biological equality to non-Indians by contending that culture, not biology, distinguishes the

Indian from the non-Indian. He states: "It's not a racial problem but rather a social or cultural one... Race is a purely biological concept and has nothing to do with the intellectual or cultural capabilities of an individual; the difference between communities in this country is not a racial one." (391) Caso adds that "it's very difficult to find Mexicans who do not have in their veins indigenous blood, and it is also possible that many Indians have mestizo or white ancestors." (393) He sums up the indigenous problem by stating: "there are at least three million Mexicans who do not receive the benefits of the country's progress; that form small islands, incapable of following the rhythm of development in Mexico; that don't feel that they are Mexican." (393) Similarly, in "Consideraciones sobre el problema indígena en América" (1942) Gamio argues that any biological deficiencies on the part of the Indians owed themselves not to heredity but rather to "poor socioeconomic conditions that for so many centuries have weighed down on the aboriginal population." He notes that under the same conditions as non-indigenous Mexicans, the Indians actually possess "better biological defenses against autochthonous diseases and the adverse effects of the geographical environment than those of foreign origin." (20)

By stressing the Indian's likeness to the mestizo, it is probable that anthropologists were attempting not just to encourage racial tolerance, but also to spur racial mixing, the only way to eventually eliminate the physical differences between the Indian and the mestizo and achieve a truly homogeneous population.

The new definition fueled efforts to integrate the Indian into national life. It made mestizaje seem more feasible by eliminating the need for racial mixing, and by verifying that the Indian was capable of being a productive citizen. Many anthropologists further believed that most Indians, and particularly the younger ones, were eager to become a part of mainstream Mexican life. They hence stepped up their efforts to provide indigenous communities with roads, hospitals and schools, modern agricultural and industrial implements and techniques, fertile land, access to reliable water sources, protection for their industries (particularly artesanal), and an education (in part so that the Indian might learn Spanish).

At the same time, however, they seemed to want to avoid the loss of "Indianness" altogether. After all, Mexico's (and indeed Latin America's) indigenous populations had long constituted a source of national identity, helping to distinguish the nation from the rest of the world. They likely wanted to avoid sacrificing this cultural uniqueness. Some anthropologists, including Caso and Gamio, argued for a fusion of the best of indigenous culture with the best of western culture. Caso maintains that "what is needed is to transform the negative aspects of indigenous culture into positive ones, and to conserve what the indigenous communities have that is positive and useful; their sense of community and mutual aid, their popular arts, their folklore." ("¿El indio mexicano es mexicano?" 396) Gamio argues that indigenous culture "distinguishes itself, among other ways, by its beautiful and epic tradition, its high ethical and aesthetic manifestations, its exceptional talents of persistence against all types of obstacles and adversities, and its disinclination towards...egoism." ("Consideraciones..." 22) Yet the qualities of indigenous culture they mention are few, and the anthropologists never discuss in any real detail how the Indian was to retain them once he became a part of mainstream society. They also fail to address the problem of how the Indian was to avoid adopting the negative qualities of Western culture, which Gamio identifies as "artificialism and the exaggerated haste of life, principally in the cities...; political corruption, the exaggerated use of alcohol and drugs, the changing standard of moral values." ("Consideraciones..." 22) They seem to take it for granted that, despite the corrupting influences of western culture, the Indian would be better off integrated than in his current state.

In reality, indigenists were primarily concerned that just one aspect of indigenous culture remains intact: the artwork. Popular art constituted an important source of national identity and pride, and of employment for many Indians and mestizos. As Alfonso Caso put it, "popular arts in Mexico have a special importance, not only because of what they mean in terms of the conservation of a cultural manifestation that is unique to our country, but also because of its economic importance, as it forms the only base of sustenance for a large part of the mestizo and indigenous populations. ("La protección de las artes populares" 25) Caso, Gamio and others conducted numerous studies of indigenous artwork, both prehispanic and contemporary, repeatedly praising its aesthetic qualities. They also vigorously promoted the preservation of indigenous art, and its protection from foreign (especially European) influences. Gamio urged Mexican artists to take inspiration from indigenous art. He also initiated a campaign to breathe life into this art by modernizing its production and distribution, which subsequent governments would continue.

Yet how would the Indians continue to produce indigenous artwork once they were mesticized? Caso resolves this problem by contending that popular art isn't exclusively indigenist but rather "a *Mexican* art because it is the result of a slow intrusion of European ideas into an indigenous background." ("La protección de las artes populares" 25) In other words, he appropriates indigenous art as mestizo or just plain Mexican by arguing both that it was infused with European influences, and also that some mestizo Mexicans produced it. Thus it wasn't necessary to participate in indigenous culture in order to create popular, Mexican art. Caso and Gamio thereby made it seem possible to at once integrate the Indian into mainstream Mexican society and to maintain the production of an authentic indigenous or popular artwork.

Revisions of the Mestizo Self
The Essay

Notwithstanding the general optimism over the Indian's integration, indigenists perceived some major obstacles. Besides scarce resources, these included the Indian's continued exploitation, denigration and neglect by the rest of Mexican society. Hoping to address this problem, some artists and intellectuals in the 1940s took a new approach towards promoting racial harmony, going beyond simply describing the Indians' problems and their solutions. Héctor Pérez Martínez, Agustín Yáñez and Luis Villoro, among others, began to spiritualize the Indian and the mestizo. They aimed to inspire respect and admiration for the Indian by pointing out the positive qualities of both ancient and current indigenous culture. They also wanted the mestizo to understand why he scorns and mistreats the Indian in order that he might refrain from such behavior. They argued that the dual mestizo roots—Spanish and indigenous—were at war within the mestizo soul. The Spanish heritage was dominating, causing the mestizo to deny his indigenous roots and to disparage the Indians. The essayists believed that if the mestizo could understand, appreciate and accept the indigenous component of his own soul, he would begin treating the Indian more humanely.

These writers hoped to induce other behavioral and attitudinal changes in the mestizo as well. For example, they wanted the mestizo to overcome his inferiority complex, a condition that Samuel Ramos had diagnosed in *El perfil del hombre y la cultura en México* (1934). They believed that this sense of inferiority stemmed partly from Mexicans' shame of their indigenous heritage. Yáñez states, "a certain kind of absurd shame has come to be felt for the indigene, a mark of one of our greatest shortcomings and of ignorance with regard to what the indigenous was and is, so far as it subsists within the national soul." (367) Pérez Martínez and Yáñez point out the positive aspects of Mexico's indigenous past in part to counter this sense of shame, and to bolster Mexicans' ego.

Pérez Martínez, Yáñez and Villoro also wished to resolve the contradictions within the mestizo's soul, thereby making him more psychologically stable. They believed the mestizo's European and indigenous selves were at odds with each other. This was causing the mestizo anguish, and prompting him to behave in contradictory ways. The former impelled the mestizo to be rational and objective, while the latter was felt as an instinctual and irrational impulse. Pérez Martínez likens the discord within the mestizo soul to the battle between Cuauhtémoc and Cortés, in which neither side can completely defeat the other. While the Spanish heritage appears to dominate, "suddenly the cry of our indigenous roots rises with its mysterious force of five centuries, and resounds deeply and not strangely, awakening sleeping echoes in our spirit." (209) Yáñez states that "the Mexican of today still feels some kind of mysterious atmosphere, subterranean and familiar", which are vestiges of his indigenous heritage. (126) To Villoro, the indigenous "is felt as a collective and remote power, or as a teluric principle that unites us to earth, to nature". He argues that because it is unrecognizable and hence uncontrollable, it can lead the mestizo to act in bizarre and even dangerous ways. "It is an...occult force that never fully manifests itself but that the mestizo believes he feels deep within his I, latent and terrible, capable of dragging him to commit the strangest acts. What is Indian is tied in this way to unconscious elements..." ("El indio en el alma del mestizo" 2) Yáñez and Pérez Martínez similarly warn that it is detrimental to the mestizo and to the nation to continue ignoring the indigenous heritage. Yáñez states that "the indigenous soul lives on with its heritage, and it has been a vain error to try to ignore it and to deny its force. By such action its vices have become more dangerous, and its virtues are neglected as lost forces, lying stagnant in the history of the nation." (367) Pérez Martínez argues that the Spanish and indigenous heritage must be equally respected. To deny one in favor of the other is "to deny our destiny", he states. (9)

In *Cuauhtemoc: vida y muerte de una cultura* (1948), Pérez

Martínez describes the Aztec culture and mentality, and recounts the battle between the Aztecs and the Spaniards from the indigenous point of view. He wants not just to inform the reader of indigenous history, but also to illuminate aspects of the indigenous culture and character that prevail to his day, in order that the mestizo might better understand the Indian and the indigenous component of his own character. For example, he says that the Aztecs' submission to the sacred caused them to be passive and fatalistic. He contends that contact with the Spaniards constituted another determining factor on the indigenous mentality. He notes that the two worlds that met were contradictory. The Spaniards' was "objective, individualist and direct", while the Aztecs' was "that of a tormented imagination, subjective, and in which the individual disappeared beneath the weight of the tribe." (71) Because of this incompatibility, the Indians were forced to sacrifice practically their whole way of life following the Conquest. This explains their profound sense of loneliness and "that rare mix of extasis and moroseness, love and sorrow, anxiety and fatalism that makes Indians of today deaf to life and filled only with the sound of death." (22–23)

Pérez Martínez makes the point that it is impossible to separate the Spanish and indigenous components of the mestizo soul. Together they form a particular character and sensibility that defines the mestizo but that is also universal. He lists a number of these characteristics, including the capacity for abstraction, stoicism, dissension, the extremes of exaggerated happiness and grim solitude, discretion, sobriety, a love for the grandiose, an extraordinary power of artistic creation, a contempt for life, and a preoccupation with death.

In a similar manner, in "Meditations on the Indigenous Soul" (1942) Yáñez examines pre-Cortesian art, languages, and religious beliefs and practices, discovering in them copious evidence of cultural genius. Yáñez wants to inspire pride in Mexico's indigenous past by redressing the notion that prehispanic Mexicans were uncivilized. He stresses the Indians' cultural refinement, making their civilization appear every bit as great as those coexisting. The ancient indigenous people, he finds, possessed a mastery over the following main areas: abstraction, realism, paradox, poetics, detachment and plastic expression. Plastic expression, he maintains, entailed the command of many other skills: a sense of proportion, mathematical mastery, aesthetic taste, competition, and the "hierarchical ordering of the elements." (365) He adds:

> And if we consider the durability of the materials, the secrets in the coloring of statues, buildings and codices; or if we think of the knowledge of astronomy that produced chronological systems like the Aztec and Mayan, of the devices for carving rock crystal and precious stones, for digging quarries, smelting metals, preserving feathers and making mosaics of them, etc., we shall agree upon the spiritual greatness demonstrated by the plastic art of those races. (366)

Yáñez even takes negative traits like fatalism and passivity and gives them a positive twist by relating them to the Indian's "admirable propensity towards detachment". The quality of detachment, he asserts, is responsible for "states of mind that range from melancholy to deep and heavy sadness; from expectancy to inertia, scorn for life and its vanities, joyous familiarity with death, imperturbality of countenance in the face of sufferings and calamities." (363)

Both Pérez Martínez and Yáñez unwittingly undermined their own efforts to foment respect for the Indian and the mestizo's indigenous roots. First of all, by emphasizing the admirable traits of prehispanic rather than of contemporary indigenous culture, they suggest that the latter lacks laudable qualities. In other words, they seem to imply that contemporary indigenous culture is in such a deplorable state that it is incapable of inspiring respect, but that an appreciation of the Indian could be cultivated by pointing out the commendable aspects of ancient Mexican civilization. Secondly, they actually find very little to redeem the Indians beyond that group's aesthetic prowess. Their attempts to put a positive spin on what they consider to be indigenous character traits (apathy, fatalism, passivity, detachment, etc.) fail. Not only are such traits generally viewed negatively, but they were especially unsuited for a "modern" nation, which many Mexicans wished their country to become. The Indian and the mestizo (by virtue of his indigenous heritage) embodied characteristics that hindered economic progress. The essayists seemed to want the mestizo to understand and appreciate the indigenous part of himself only to later rid himself of many of his indigenous qualities.

Unlike Pérez Martínez and Yáñez, Villoro deals almost exclusively with the mestizo psyche. In *Los grandes momentos del indigenismo* (*The great moments of indigenism*) (1950) he explains a philosophical process by which he believes the mestizo may reconcile himself with his indigenous roots.[5] Villoro argues that the mestizo is now at the point where he wants to understand the Indian in order to mend the split he feels within his soul. He explains that while in the past the mestizo believed the Indian should change his mentality and ways of life to conform with those of the mestizo's own, now he views indigenous culture as part of himself. "It is as if the mestizo were trying to recuperate the Indian, to make indigenous values his own, to recover his arcane spirit." (197) The mestizo thereby begins to reflect upon himself, finding that he is insecure, contradictory, and unstable. "The Mexican sees his being, both personal and social, split and vacillating: the indigenous and the western, historical components of his soul, symbolize perfectly his division." (227)

According to Villoro, reflection fails to illuminate indigenous reality for the mestizo because it is a Western rather than an indigenous principle. Only the Indian can reveal himself to the mestizo. Villoro outlines two ways the mestizo may encourage the Indian to do this. The first is to direct love and action towards him. Through loving action, Indian and mestizo come together as one. They identify with each other on the level of class, realizing that their behavior as part of this social group is one and the same. They now confront the Other, which for the mestizo used to be the Indian himself, but is now the foreigner or the Creole. They distance themselves from this Other racially, culturally and socially. However, at a later stage they reject all such distinctions. Echoing José Vasconcelos's *La raza cósmica* (1925),[6] Villoro envisions future Mexican society as lacking racial distinctions and inequalities altogether: "The moment will come when there are no racial hierarchies no the dominion of one over the other; in which all those who are now diversified will recognize either other reciprocally." (229) He explains that current indigenism affirms the indigenous element of the mestizo soul as of supreme value only to later reject such action in order to allow for "a society where Indian and white recognize each other reciprocally." (229)

According to Villoro, the second way the mestizo may appropriate his indigenous self is through history. Since the mestizo has assumed the Indian as a dimension of his own spirit, the Indian's past becomes his own. He approaches this history in a preliminary state of expectation or perplexity. The historical object or fact is an enigma. Rather than attempting to discern it according to known laws, the mestizo allows it to reveal itself to him. By doing this, he relives past indigenous man as transcendence, one that becomes his own transcendence that has been awakened by the historical sign.

Despite Villoro's contentions, there was little to suggest that mestizo

Mexicans were at the point of wanting to come to terms with their indigenous heritage. In fact, mass culture revealed little interest in the topic of the Indian, much less in any indigenous component to the national character. For example, as we will see later, the only film on this topic that achieved wide success during the 1940s was *María Candelaria* (1943).

Nayar

Several novels during the 1940s also took up the themes of mestizaje and the Indian.[7] They followed the general trend in literature, exemplified in the aforementioned essays, of spiritualizing the Indian and the mestizo. Some focused specifically on the Indian, such as Ricardo Pozas's *Juan Pérez Jolote*, which uses an ethnological approach to examine indigenous society. Others focused on the mestizo psyche, including *Nayar*, by Miguel Angel Menéndez. This novel resembled the essays in showing how the mestizo's mixed heritage leads him not only to mistreat the Indians, but also to act irrationally, violently and dangerously.

Nayar forms part of the repertory of so-called novels of the land that predominated during the first part of the twentieth century, and is particularly reminiscent of one of the more famous of these—*La vorágine*, by José Eustacio Rivera. Like *La vorágine*, it develops a strong identification between the nation and the land by focusing on the tensions and contrasts between domesticated and undomesticated social spaces like the city and the jungle. *Nayar* seeks "Mexicanness" partially in Mexico's hinterland. During the entire novel the two protagonists—Enrique and Ramón—traverse Mexico's most underpopulated areas. Enrique, the narrator, describes in minute detail and with obvious emotion the flora and fauna of these regions, and the human activities that take place within them. He also demonstrates a profound respect for the indigenous populations living within this region. The fondness for the land and the Indian mimics other populist novels of the land, in which civilization sets out to conquer barbarity through love. Doris Sommer explains, "the founding fictions of the last century tend to be about daring political deals that would construct a national territory. By contrast, populism is about a rigid fortification of those now feminized constructions." (265) Works like *La vorágine*, which can be read as allegories of the nation, set out to metaphorically establish alliances with forces outside of the country's control. Frequently this meant falling in love with the object of control, which often took the shape of a female. *Nayar* replaces the female with that of the also feminized (through his relationship to the land) Indian. Enrique, the narrator, and his friend Ramón win over the Indian's trust by allying themselves with the Indian against other non-indigenous Mexicans who attempt to exploit them.

Unlike other novels of the land, however, *Nayar* seeks "Mexicanness" more in the mestizo than in the Indian or the land. Throughout the novel Enrique (who is mostly white) closely observes the behavior of his friend, Ramón, a mestizo. Ramón's racial composition is brought to the reader's attention at the novel's onset, indicating the importance it will have in the story that Enrique is about to tell us: "I am urged to define the color of Ramón: his was the color of the dawn over the estuary just as the night is about to end—half-breed leaven in which the Indian apparently predominated." (5) On a symbolic level, their journey through the forests represents a search for the part of the mestizo's identity that is most unfamiliar to him—the indigenous one. Notably, it is at the point where they meet up with the Indians that they lose their bearings, becoming lost in a regional labyrinth that mimics a psychical one.

Enrique stresses that in nature what becomes important is not reason but instinct, that which is most animalistic. Importantly, of the two characters, it is Ramón who adapts more easily to this difficult environment. Enrique frequently marvels at his friend's instinctual feel for the forest. It is Ramón who leads the way through the dense foliage. The novel infers that Ramón's innate knowledge of the forest is a consequence of his predominantly indigenous blood, for the Indians share this same knowledge. He even sleeps with his eyes open at night, like the Indians, constantly vigilant for unexpected dangers. But while the uncivilized, indigenous part of Ramón is admirable in the forest, it leads him to commit atrocities within civilization. For example, he maims his wife and kills the town judge upon catching them sleeping together. Additionally, he kills an adolescent who had discovered him as he tried to sneak back into town to visit his son.

Ramón's indigenous blood dictates his behavior within white society. Ironically, within indigenous culture his Spanish blood surfaces. At first he shows a natural affinity for the Indians who, for their part, also accept him more readily than Enrique because of his darker skin color: "Toward Ramón he (the Elder) showed more deference than to me because the color of their skin brought them closer." (149)

Ramón not only sympathizes with the Indians' exploitation and suffering, he also easily understands them: "Gervasio was surprised to see that Ramón understood him. He did not know that the half-breed is a pendulum oscillating between two races." (199) Nevertheless, from the very beginning Ramón is critical of the Indians. He questions the myths retold by the Elder, and scorns some of the Indians' customs, particularly those related to superstition and matrimony. After having spent several months in hiding as a result of the Cristero War, which caught the Indians in the middle, Ramón proposes to Enrique that they join up with the government forces. Enrique refuses, saying "we would not like to kill Indians..." He regrets later not having realized at the time that Ramón "was tired of living the life of the Indians" and that "his half-breed clay was urging him", for Ramón winds up turning against the Indians. (246) Outraged by their decision to kill an innocent man for sorcery, he runs to town in search of the federal troops:

> He was not acting of course as a traitor. Something within him, something beyond his will, something sinister which came from afar, compelled him to gallop in the night, over the edge of cliffs and through the labyrinth of gorges. His half-breed leaven had finally conquered the color of his skin, color of early dawn when day is about to break. The light of the Spaniard vanquished over the shadow of the Indian. I visualized him stretched out over the gallop of his horse, maddened by the tempest outside and by the tempest within; his spirit dislocated by the clash of two heritages. (273)

Ramón dies in the battle that ensues, his mixed heritage literally having led to his self-destruction. Pedro Gervasio, his best friend within the tribe, is sent to jail for homicide, where he remains silent and indifferent: "Perhaps he understood at last that his tradition was in conflict with the culture of his conquerors, that it was futile to explain his bitter sorrows because no one would understand them. Deep in his flesh he felt his race conquered once more." (277)

Nayar conforms with the indigenous novels of the 1930's in blaming the mestizo for the indigenous people's isolation and mistrust. It goes farther than those novels, however, by attributing the mestizo's contempt for the Indian to his mixed blood. The war waged within the mestizo between his Spanish and indigenous heritages ultimately results in the victory of the Spanish one, as if history were repeating itself within the mestizo soul. This is something that is out of the mestizo's control. Describing Ramón's betrayal of the Indians, the narrator states:

"It may have been that in his blood rose the two immensities the half-breed has to bear within, and that from this clash issued the thunderbolt which unbalanced his thought." (270) He adds: "Two immensities still struggle against one another, joined confusingly, and now no one knows where the one begins and the other ends; one knows not which is which." (270–271) Notably, the narrator, who as pointed out earlier is mostly white, does not suffer from the same oscillations in character that Ramón does. The novel portrays the whiter Mexican as more emotionally stable and more reasonable. To wit, he is much more civilized. Enrique respects indigenous customs and beliefs even when he may not agree with them, and he tries to persuade the Indians to reconsider their verdict of the man accused of sorcery, rather than turning against them like Ramón. In other words, he recurs to his reason rather than acting purely upon instinctual impulses like his friend.

The novel further stresses the mestizo's barbaric nature in the events that go on outside of the Indian community, such as the Cristero war:

> From Jesús María families arrived fleeing from Juan Pistolas. The Cristeros had entered the town and cleaned up: they had butchered the peasants and abducted the girls. They had cut off the teacher's ears, emptied the granaries. Shortly thereafter the government troops recaptured the town, soaking it with the blood of reprisals. (199)

Enrique portrays the Cristero war as a purely Church and mestizo affair. He notes, for example, that it is led by "*half-breed* (my italics) chiefs, whose authority emanates from their ancestral alliance with the clergy" (195), and that it excites the passion of these "half-breeds", who "ran around frantically, looking for trouble." (197) Ramón, he observes, "vacillated between iconoclastic anger and monastic ecstasy. His mixed blood became confused as a Messianic hysteria swept the sierra, inflaming spirits, destroying bodies, fattening hatred." (197) In contrast to the mestizos, Enrique does not sway between one side or the other, viewing the entire event as barbaric.

The novel doesn't entirely blame the mestizo for the Indians' plight, however. The narrator of *Nayar* also questions civilization as a whole. He does this not only by observing the ignorance, hatred and brutality that characterize the villages of Mexico's interior, but also by becoming aware of his own violent tendencies, which surface when he is hunting. In the forest, his most basic, animal instincts emerge. The narrator struggles to understand why, despite his love of nature, he feels compelled to destroy it. He comes to the conclusion, upon overcoming his initial dismay at the "murderous" act of shooting a heron dead, that man's motive in killing is related to a primitive, virile urge. Enrique, however, is different from Ramón in that he recognizes why he enjoys hunting, and he can limit his aggressive urges to those situations. In other words, he has self-awareness. That Enrique experiences any guilt at all upon killing an animal is evidence of his greater refinement, especially given that Ramón expresses no regret at all at having killed two human beings. While the primitive impulse to kill is still present, it is much more removed than in the case of the darker mestizo.

In *Nayar*, however, nature and the Indian do not distinguish between the color variations of those who attempt to exploit them, opposing them all. This is characteristic of the populist novel of the land in which, as Doris Sommer points out, the objects of control resist their exploiters. Beginning with the protagonists' encounter of the grisly, decomposing body of a man who, mistaken for Ramón, was hung and left to rot deep within the forests, the non-indigenous Mexican only brings death and destruction to this pristine region. Mimicking the forest's resistance to intruders, the Indians initially reject Enrique and Ramón's request to live among them, conditioned by centuries of abuse and betrayal by the mestizo and white man.

Enrique and Ramón, who sympathize with the Indians, feel profoundly guilty for their white blood, as they believe it implicates them in the tribe's suffering. However, the Indians are ultimately correct in mistrusting them. The message is that the white man does not know how to live in harmony with either nature or the Indian, and ends up incurring the wrath of both. Ramón loses his life to that wrath.

Nayar does not idealize the Indian, however. Despite his outward display of respect for the tribe, and his attempt to appear non-judgmental, it is obvious that Enrique considers the Indians uncivilized. First of all, he observes that the Indians live in abject poverty, as they are forced to endure a nomadic lifestyle that permits them to escape from those who claim ownership to the land. Second of all, he repeatedly notes their dependence on superstition to achieve what only science and nature can accomplish: good weather, abundant harvests, the curing of the ill, and so forth. Thirdly, he stresses the Indian's rigid adherence to absurd customs. The main example is the death (by hanging and incineration) of the man accused of sorcery. Many other deal with the treatment of women, particularly as related to sex and matrimony. The female is repeatedly depicted as being controlled and abused by the male. The most salient example involves a married woman who, caught cheating on her husband, is forced to parade naked through the village. Enrique notes the rigidity of indigenous tradition in his description of the Elder as he commands her to undress:

> I saw the idol's eyes: they were cold, opaque; his lips tightly shut were more than ever a terrible scar. Neither emotion, nor blinking of the eyes. He was a stone, a hard stone overlaid with the patina of time; he was the tradition that cannot change, that has to remain always the same: inflexible, blind, deaf, dumb, brutal. (191)

Ironically, although considered an "indigenist" novel, *Nayar* sheds very little light on the Indians' culture and psychology. It explores the mestizo character in much greater depth. The protagonists do not even meet up with the Indians until nearly half way through the novel, and they are excluded from participation in all the important meetings and ceremonies. Since there is no omniscient point of view, and Enrique is the only narrator, the reader never penetrates the Indians' thoughts. We only learn a few of their more exotic customs, those a non-Indian would most likely be interested in (i.e. related to sex, superstition and the use of peyote). The indigenous traits the novel observes have repeatedly been ascribed to the Indians—melancholy, impassiveness, ignorance, superstitiousness, brutality, etc...—, and the Indians' exploitation by a local tyrant is also a recurrent theme in indigenist literature.

The novel, furthermore, fails to offer fresh insights into the Indians' continued marginalization. Like many other indigenist novels, it emphasizes the Indians' mistrust of mestizo/white society, on the one hand, and the mestizo's repression of the Indian, on the other, as the main challenges to integration. Since the mestizo cannot control his urge to brutalize the Indian—a result of his mixed heritage—, and since the Indian, already resistant to change, clings more fiercely to his traditions the more he is exploited, the novel expresses little hope for a reconciliation or harmonious relationship between the mestizos and the Indians. However, the novel seems to consider integration the only solution to ridding the nation of conflicting forces (both external and internal) that impinge upon unity and progress. Perhaps Menéndez, like the essayists, wished to provide the mestizo with self-awareness in order that he might begin to reconcile his indigenous and Spanish selves. This offers the only hope for integration, since the Indians are unlikely to engage as social actors and propose a solution for their own integration so long as the mestizo continues to exploit and disparage them.

The Indian as One of Us: *María Candelaria*

As was the case during the 1930s, the Indian did not enjoy a major presence in Mexican film during the 1940s. However, one film centering on this group achieved enormous success: *María Candelaria*, directed by Emilio "El Indio" Fernández, one of the most popular and nationalistic directors of the time period.[8] It won several important prizes at two major film festivals—Cannes, in 1946, and Locarno, in 1947—, more for its technical merits than its treatment of the Indian.[9] Yet, as I will show, even *María Candelaria* fails to address the real problems confronting the Indian, and subverts its intention of promoting racial harmony.

Throughout his career, Fernández demonstrated a strong interest in dignifying the Indian through his films. It is likely this was at least partially due to his own indigenous origins (his mother was a Kikapú Indian), which apparently made him feel excluded from society on both a personal and professional level. (Tuñón 180–181) *María Candelaria*, which is loosely based on *Janitzio* (1935), portrays the native Mexican as a noble savage whose idyllic life is shattered by the intolerance of his community and exploitation by outsiders. The film attempts to generate admiration and sympathy for the Indian, who embodies what is "authentically" Mexican. It also attempts to identify the popular classes with the Indian by stressing shared experiences and characteristics. The masses could relate to the protagonists' woes—their struggle to earn a living, their exploitation by the powerful and corrupt, and their marginalization from society. The audiences could also recognize in the two protagonists traits that film had repeatedly ascribed to them: dignity, honesty, stoicism, self-respect, sensitivity, loyalty, and so forth. Lorenzo was the ideal image of the male—strong, protective, and honorable— and María Candelaria of the female—beautiful, innocent, and self-sacrificing. In other words, the film attempts to identify the masses with the Indian by making them both symbolic of the national spirit.

María Candelaria focuses on the tribulations of a young Indian woman and her fiancé. María Candelaria and Lorenzo are simple people whose only wish is to marry and live peacefully. They are waiting until María's pig is older so that they can sell it and purchase a wedding dress. However, Don Damián, who fancies María Candelaria, wants to confiscate the pig to pay off a debt she owes him. To avoid losing the animal—her only hope of marrying Lorenzo—she tries to sell flowers in the village, but the residents there block her way and force her to turn back. They refuse to let her step foot in the village because her mother was allegedly a prostitute. Lorenzo also tries to reason with Don Damián, but only succeeds in fueling his anger. In a turn for the worse, Don Damián kills the pig behind the couple's backs. Then, María Candelaria falls ill from malaria. To cure her, Lorenzo tries to obtain quinine from Don Damián, who is in charge of distributing it to the community, but the storeowner refuses it to him. Desperate, he breaks into the store at night and steals both the quinine and a dress for María Candelaria. She recovers and they go to get married, but just before they are about to say the vows, Don Damián arrives to take Lorenzo away. María Candelaria turns for help to a local artist, who had seen her once at a marketplace and had wanted to paint her (the couple had refused and fled). In return for his help, she agrees to let him paint her face, but when he asks her to pose nude, she flees. Another model agrees to pose in her place. A local woman sees the portrait of the naked María Candelaria, and spreads the gossip. Outraged, the townspeople hunt her down and, in front of Lorenzo who is staring helplessly from the prison, they stone her to death. Lorenzo manages to escape from the jail, and the movie ends as he is impassively carrying her body away.

The film's popularity within Mexico may be partially attributed to the fact that it never confronts the problem of racism. *María Candelaria* circumvents the issue of collective guilt for the Indians' suffering by blaming others. María Candelaria and Lorenzo are not victims of the average Mexican, but rather of the Indian community, a villainous mestizo storeowner, and an artist. The community shuns her because her mother allegedly prostituted herself. Don Damián persecutes her for her refusal to yield to his advances. And the artist exploits her for her beauty—to paint a portrait that will eventually cause her death. But mainstream society is never condemned for its real involvement in the marginalization and impoverishment of the indigenous people.

The movie also allows the audiences to actually maintain their stereotypes by very clearly indicating that the two protagonists are atypical. Not only do they behave differently from the rest of the community, but they also have European features and light skin. These characters were played by two of Mexico's most famous actors—Dolores del Río and Pedro Armendáriz—, who were non-indigenous.

The star system was critical to marketing films during this period, and famous indigenous actors were scarce. Thus Fernández employed non-indigenous actors to play the key characters.

Fernández presents an ambiguous view of the indigenous people in this film. On the one hand, he idealizes the protagonists.[10] María Candelaria and Lorenzo are models of conduct. On the other hand, not all the Indians in this movie are depicted positively. In fact, the indigenous community as a whole is portrayed as petty, cruel, and intolerant, as evident in its treatment of María Candelaria. Not one person from the community takes her side, although she is very clearly innocent of any of the so-called crimes her mother committed.

The movie is further ambiguous regarding the Indian's integration. On the one hand, this group's isolation is considered to be undesirable. The community has not benefited in any way from its seclusion. Its traditions (at least those shown on the film) are rigid and unfair, and ignorance, poverty and disease are rampant. Clearly, the indigenous community cannot survive well on its own, as evidenced by its dependence on the government's distribution of quinine to fend off malaria. Through María Candelaria and Lorenzo's example, the film further suggests that the Indian is capable of exemplary conduct if he is separated from his community. In other words, the movie suggests that the indigenous community has a negative impact on the Indians' morality. On the other hand, the movie also reacts against the "modern" world (in the form of don Damián and the artist) that tries to exploit the Indians.[11] Importantly, however, the artist is deeply repentant for his part in María Candelaria's death. Moreover, Don Damián does not represent mainstream Mexicans as a whole, and in fact the movie attempts to generate anger at him for having caused the Indian's mistrust of mestizo/white Mexicans. Whereas much of indigenous literature had blamed mestizo society as a whole for the Indians' marginalization, *María Candelaria* points the finger at just a few individuals. Thus in the end the movie seems to favor the Indian's integration.

As Laura Podalsky observes, *María Candelaria* is further contradictory in its questioning of the tradition whereby the "essence" of the nation is extracted from the Indian, a tradition the movie itself exploits. On the one hand, the opening shots, consisting of pre-Cortesian sculptures and the artist's paintings, "plug into an already familiar canon—the legitimate, naturalized, or 'authentic' representation of the Indian as established by Diego Rivera. The model in the film is actually the one that Rivera himself used." (Podalsky 67) On the other hand, we learn from the artist that his painting of María Candelaria caused a tragedy. Determined to paint this woman, in whom he had found the "rare, delicate features, the essence of Mexican beauty", the artist ignored her (and Lorenzo's) initial refusal to be painted, and took advantage of María Candelaria when she had nowhere else to turn.

It is possible that this contradiction is a result of the movie's attempt to portray the film genre as more true-to-life than other artistic genres. It suggests that the types of hardships that plague María Candelaria and Lorenzo are nowhere to be seen in Diego Rivera's paintings. The movie, in other words, supports the portrayal of the Indian as the embodiment of the national essence, but makes the case that the film genre is more suitable than other artistic mediums for this task.

In *María Candelaria* Fernández strives to capture and promote "Mexicanness" through his indigenous characters. He does this by stressing their physical beauty, their peaceful coexistence with nature, and their moral and spiritual purity. It is significant that Fernández chose an Indian woman to embody the authentic national essence. Joanne Hershfield argues that *María Candelaria* reconstructs allegorically the myth of La Malinche, the Indian woman who allegedly betrayed the nation by serving as the mistress, guide and translator for Hernán Cortés. She explains that María Candelaria, like La Malinche, serves as an intermediary between the Indians and their oppressors (embodied by Don Damián and the artist). María Candelaria also betrays her people (by modeling for the artist), as did La Malinche. Hershfield concludes that the film can be read "as a narrative attempt to absolve the criollo's guilt for his part in the destruction of Mexico's indigenous cultures by reminding Mexico that it was an Indian woman, La Malinche, who betrayed the Mexicans." (60–61) I would argue that the movie actually tries to counter the negative connotations associated with La Malinche. María Candelaria never willingly aids her oppressors, as La Malinche did. As previously noted, she rejects Don Damián's advances, and she only turns to the painter when she has no other options for freeing Lorenzo. Even then, she refuses to model nude for the artist. María Candelaria betrays no one. To the contrary, Don Damián and the painter take advantage of her, and the indigenous community falsely accuses her. Unlike them, her actions are always noble. María Candelaria's chastity liken her to the Virgin of Guadalupe, the polar opposite of La Malinche and one of the major role models for women during the period.

To a degree *María Candelaria* thwarts its very objectives of inspiring pride in and identification with the Indian. Because the protagonists are exceptional in character, experience and even appearance, it must have been difficult for the audiences to consider the Indian in general as embodying the best and most authentic qualities of "Mexicanness", as Fernández would have liked them to do. It is even more difficult given the film's negative characterization of the larger indigenous community, as discussed previously. Moreover, while the audience may have sympathized and identified with the protagonists, they would likely have distanced themselves from the indigenous community, which lacks admirable qualities. Thus it is unlikely that the film did much to bridge the gap between the mestizo and the Indian. Finally, the film's ability to help combat racism and thus speed the Indian's integration into mainstream Mexican life is impeded by its complete avoidance of a serious treatment of the real problems confronting the native Mexicans.

Not only did indigenist writers and filmmakers subvert their own efforts to promote "mestizaje", but film also undermined the writers' efforts. The writers' goals were incompatible with those of the filmmakers. Pérez Martínez, Yáñez, Villoro and Menéndez sought to improve the mestizo's understanding of the Indian, and to induce self-awareness so that he might begin to appreciate and accept the indigenous part of his heritage. In contrast, films—which could reach a large audience—rarely dealt with the Indian, and never with the indigenous component of the mestizo character. Furthermore, the indigenous characters tended to lack psychological complexity. More importantly, film was hesitant to criticize its mostly mestizo, lower class audience. *María Candelaria* may have helped to cultivate a sense of national identity, unity and pride, but it did little to help combat racism. Not surprisingly, by the end of the 1950s, the goal of an integrated, mestizo-based population was far from being realized.

Notes

1. The task of integrating the Indian was formidable. According to Mexico's 1940 census, the Indians comprised between 20% and 25% of the nation's population, or some three million people. (Labastida 1) Around one third of all the indigenous peoples of North and South America combined resided in Mexico. Most of the Indians lived in abject poverty, isolated from the rest of Mexican society. About 15% of them spoke one of some 50 languages other than Spanish. (Aguirre Beltrán 3)
2. As Stanley Ivie further notes, the "rural school" also educated the Indian differently from the rest of the population. They taught subjects that would be of practical use to the Indian, such as farming and hygiene. They also attempted to foster a sense of self-worth in the Indian by teaching him prehispanic history and allowing him to begin his education speaking his own language. In contrast, during the 1940s and the 1950s the Indians were educated no differently from the rest of the population. (968–969)
3. Caso, also an archaeologist and historian, published extensively on the Indians and held numerous high governmental posts. In 1939 he founded the Instituto Nacional de Antropología e Historia, and he founded and became director of the Instituto Nacional Indigenista in 1947. He was known as one of the celebrated "Grupo de Siete" sages. Manuel Gamio also published widely and held many governmental positions. He served as director of the Interamerican Indian Institute from 1942 to 1960.
4. Besides Caso's "Definición del indio y lo indio" (1948), see "Consideraciones sobre el problema indígena en México" (1942), "Las características culturales y los censos indígenas" (1942), and "Calificación de características culturales de los grupos indígenas" (1942), by Manuel Gamio; "Base para una nueva definición práctica del Indio" (1945), by Oscar Lewis and Ernest E. Maes; and "Definición, pase y desparición del Indio en México" (1948), by J. de la Fuente.
5. Villoro was a member of the Hiperión group of writers/intellectuals, which regarded philosophy as central to the understanding of the

Mexican. Other members of this group included Emilio Uranga, Leopoldo Zea, Ricardo Guerra, Joaquín McGregor, Jorge Portilla and Salvador Reyes Nevárez. See chapter six for an explanation of this group's philosophy of the Mexican being.

6. In *La raza cósmica*, José Vasconcelos suggests that mestizaje throughout the world is leading to a new type of race (which he calls the fifth race), superior to any of those existing. He argues that Latin America is best suited to forge this new race because it demonstrates greater sympathy towards foreigners than other nations and also has a long history of mestizaje.

7. In addition to *Nayar* and *Juan Pérez Jolote*, indigenist novels published in the 1940's and the early 1950's included *Los peregrinos inmóviles* (1944), by Gregorio López y Fuentes, *Lola Casanova* (1947), by Francisco Rojas González, *Donde crecen los tepozanes* (1947), by Miguel N. Lira and *El callado dolor de los tzotziles* (1949), by Ramón Rubín. *Lola Casanova*, like *Nayar*, deals with the topic of mestizaje. It does not examine the mestizo psyche, but rather serves as an allegory for the birth of mestizaje. It envisions a new type of mestizo—one who values his indigenous and European heritages equally, rather than privileging the European.

8. Fernández also directed the highly popular films *Flor silvestre* (1943), *Río escondido* (1947), and *Enamorada* (1947).

9. Like many of the 1930s indigenist films, *María Candelaria* idealizes the Indian. However, Julia Tuñón maintains that in the aftermath of the war, European audiences were attracted to the image of the Indian as naturally benevolent. (182) This may account for the international popularity of this film.

10. Many critics denounced the film for this reason, arguing that the Indians are nothing more than noble savages. Carl Mora, however, sustains that "false idealization or not, Fernández presented a positive view of Indians—a group that more often than not had been the butt of music-hall jokes." (65–66)

11. By showing the obstacles to the Indian's integration, the film is similar to indigenist literature, and in fact was written by one such author—Mauricio Magdaleno, who wrote *El resplandor* (1937), which is analyzed in chapter three of this work.

Chapter Seven

The Construction of the Modern Mexican

Under Miguel Alemán (1946–1952), economic growth became even more of a priority than it had under Ávila Camacho. Responding to the nation's rapid urbanization and industrialization, many writers and filmmakers of the late 1940's and the early 1950's began to focus even greater attention on the construction of a modern national subject. Both were concerned with preparing Mexicans for participation in the emerging economy, but went about this task in different ways. On the one hand, many writers, and in particular essayists, pointed out Mexicans' character flaws, in the hopes of inducing self-awareness and change. They were eager to assert Mexico as a modern nation that could compete with and defend itself against the more developed nations. They were particularly concerned about encroachments from the United States. At the same time, they wished to maintain the status quo, which promoted the interests of the newly emerging middle classes and valued the work of intellectuals like themselves. Many films, on the other hand, attempted to forge a modern national subject by providing Mexicans with models and codes of behavior. At the same time, they sought to reinforce many traditional, middle class values. They wished to help stem the social disintegration that can result from immigrants' sudden contact with modern lifestyles and values. They also sought to defuse class tensions resulting from the poor distribution of income and other social and economic inequalities. They attempted to accomplish this by idealizing the popular classes (as they had done in the past) as morally superior to the wealthy and content with their lot in life.

The essayists, Emilio Uranga, Leopoldo Zea and Octavio Paz, stressed inauthenticity as the major problem confronting the Mexican, just as Samuel Ramos, Jorge Cuesta and Rodolfo Usigli had done in the 1930s. However, in contrast to their predecessors, they viewed the national character and its possibilities more optimistically. Reacting to fears of North American penetration into Mexican culture, Uranga, Zea and Paz compared the Mexican culture and character favorably to those of the United States. They argued that in an age of rapid modernization and greater reliance on technology, certain qualities of the Mexican, including his introspective, sensitive nature, could serve as a model for humanity.

At the same time, a variety of movies dealing with the city ended cinema's nearly exclusive focus on the provincial Mexican (primarily through the "comedia ranchera"). The Cantinflas movies continued to enjoy tremendous success, while a new figure also emerged: that of the pachuco[1] "Tin Tan." While the Cantinflas and Tin Tan films were comedies, a number of other movies dramatized the plight of the urban poor, including the cabaretera (cabaret) films that featured the prostitute and city nightlife. One of the most popular of these urban melodramas, *Nosotros los Pobres* (*We the Poor*), focused on the travails of "Pepe el Toro," a working class character. While essayists employed the "pelado" to identify Mexicans' worst psychoses, film idealized this figure.[2] "Pepe el Toro" struggles against impossible hardships but always maintains his integrity. Through him, *Nosotros los pobres* sought to build a sense of pride and identity among the most disadvantaged Mexicans, and to establish models of conduct important to maintaining social harmony and to preparing Mexicans for participation in a modern economy. It stressed such characteristics as devotion to family and community, honesty, hard-work, ingenuity and determination, which would help to stave off social decay and create an effective labor force. It also attempted to provide an outlet for discontent over social inequalities by portraying the poor as morally superior to the wealthy and content with their lives.

Most films, like *Nosotros los Pobres*, never aspired to promote social change, but rather to suggest changes and reforms while preserving the status quo. They therefore evaded taking a hard look at the impact of social and economic policies on the poor, or even at the realities of poverty itself. However, there was one outstanding exception: *Los olvidados* (*The Forgotten Ones*), by Luis Buñuel. This film viewed modernization as having a devastating effect on the poorest Mexicans. Buñuel's characters suffer not only from severe economic hardships, but also from moral and spiritual degradation. While this film won several awards abroad, it was sparsely attended in Mexico during its time, as film viewers preferred melodramas like *Nosotros los pobres*.

Unmasking the Mexican
Emilio Uranga and Leopoldo Zea

Emilio Uranga and especially Leopoldo Zea[3] are considered the most influential members of Hiperión, which comprised a group of young writer/philosophers who were associated with the Faculty of Letters and Philosophy at the UNAM (The Autonomous National University of Mexico). The Spanish philosopher and immigrant to Mexico, José Gaos, influenced the members (who also included Ricardo Guerra, Joaquín McGregor, Jorge Portilla, Salvador Reyes Nevárez and Luis Villoro). The Hiperión writers regarded philosophy as central to the understanding of the Mexican. By offering self-awareness, they believed it would lead Mexicans to abandon their imitation of imported doctrines and overcome their self-denigration—a by-product of cultural dependency. However, they stressed that the process of self-awareness should ultimately lead to the discovery of universal man rather than a strictly national one. As was the case for Ramos and Cuesta, their desire to create a universal philosophy reflected an interest in asserting Mexico as a world leader, although they also believed that any genuine philosophy reflected universal values. They believed that to compete culturally with Europe and the United States, Mexico must create a philosophy that could extend beyond national borders to reach all of mankind, as the European philosophies had done. Uranga and Zea believed it was a prime moment to formulate such a philosophy. In their opinion, in the wake of World War II, Europe lacked ideas and values and could no longer be considered a moral leader. On the other hand, they sustained that Mexico, and Latin America as a whole, was ripe for the creation of a new humanism.

In their analyses of the Mexican character, Uranga and Zea target inauthenticity as the major problem afflicting the national character. Zea, who wrote on both the Mexican and the Latin American character, explains in *En torno a una filosofía americana* (*On an American Philosophy*) that Latin American man has tried to adapt his own circumstances to the ideas and beliefs of European culture. That is, he has tried to copy or imitate Europe in order to be what the European wanted him to be. Zea likens this situation to that of a child attempting to become like his father instead of developing his own personality. Since the Latin American could never live up to Europe's expectations of what Latin America should be, he has suffered from an inferiority complex. This inferiority complex, in turn, has prevented him from creating and realizing his own projects and plans. Afraid of appearing ridiculous, he has opted to remain safe by imitating Europe. Zea argues that were Latin Americans to become aware of their true relationship with European culture, they would be able to shed their inferiority complex and begin to take responsibility for solving their own problems.

Like their predecessors, Uranga and Zea considered cultural nationalism an obstacle to their goal of bringing about self-awareness and change, and they hence warn against it. In their opinion, it provided the Mexican with a prop he could use to avoid coming to terms with his real self. In *Análisis del ser del Mexicano* (*Analysis of the Mexican Being*), Uranga maintains that nationalism's gravest danger consists of "the separation or secession that it operates within the Mexican, cutting him off from what is human." (40) He asserts that if the Mexican were to forget his nationality he would find that "his life itself is a form of being that reaches the source from which emerges all humanism." (41) Similarly, in "Dialéctica de la conciencia en México" ("The Dialectics of Consciousness") (1951), Zea argues that nationalism is only a step in the process of self-awareness, and that Mexicans are now at the point where they should go beyond it to seek "concrete man." (102) He believed that any genuine philosophy should seek not just to solve national problems, but also those of humankind. That is, it should be universal.

Ironically, Uranga and Zea use similar tactics as the cultural nationalists in order to gain support for their ideas. Much like the cultural nationalists, who exalted the poor as morally and spiritually superior to the wealthy, Uranga and Zea portray the Mexicans as morally and spiritually superior to the Europeans. They propose the Mexican character as a source for the elaboration of a new and more humane philosophy of man.

Because of their new focus, Uranga and Zea are careful to note the differences between their group and previous writers of "Mexicanness," including Ramos, Yáñez and Usigli. They fault those writers for their dependence on psychoanalysis and their use of the European as a measure against which to judge the Mexican. Uranga maintains that neither Ramos nor Yáñez succeeded in plummeting the very depths of the national being like the Hiperión group because of their failure to employ the philosophy of ontology (existence), which he regarded as "the only direction of thought and action that can do full justice, even though radical, to this secular tradition of self-diagnosis of the Mexican." (65) Arguing against Ramos's psychoanalytical approach, he states that "through psychology the Mexican not only obtains a provisional knowledge of himself that is insuperable, but also faces the danger of 'reifying' his own person and thereby freeing himself of all responsibility." (66) He further contends that Ramos's diagnosis of an inferiority complex could lead to resignation, indifference, and the unquestioning acceptance of the norms of the "superior" culture. In its place, he offered the Heideggerian notion of "insufficiency," which denotes a need. According to Uranga, because "insufficiency" implies the capacity of the individual to provide for himself the "sufficiency" he lacks, it provokes action rather than paralysis. Furthermore, it confers greater dignity on the Mexican by interpreting his/her reaction to Spain's superiority as one of admiration rather than an "inferiority complex." He states: "recognizing an hierarchy of values doesn't mean manifesting an 'inferiority complex,' and knowing how to 'admire', far from being a symptom of inferiority, speaks rather of a generous and 'sufficient' disposition as far as moral health." (53)

Likewise, in *Conciencia y posibilidad del Mexicano* (*The Consciousness and Possibility of the Mexican*), Zea argues that Ramos, Yáñez and Usigli failed to understand the Mexican character because they reacted defensively to a reality that seemed to go in other directions than those they wished: "They intuited an 'authentic reality' but could only see its negative aspects, since it was presented to them as an obstacle in the realization of what they wished were a better Mexico." (76) Zea argued for an inversion of values. That is, he maintained that by discerning the positive possibilities those negative traits offer, healthy change could be effected. For example, in *En torno a una filosofía Americana* he suggests that the clue to the Latin American identity might lie in the Latin American's very sense of inferiority with respect to Europe. He explains: "Recognizing that we are a bad copy doesn't mean that we are inferior but rather, simply, that we are different...that we have personality." (66)

In *Análisis del ser del Mexicano*, Uranga applies the theory of ontology (as developed by the German philosopher Martin Heidegger), in addition to historical analysis, to study the Mexican character. He argues that Mexicans are melancholic, sentimental, fragile, overly sensitive and pessimistic because they suffer from a deep ontological wound: "At the deepest part of the Mexican character is a melancholy. The ontological wound... illuminates, nourishes and communicates the most primary character." (84) He continues:

> Our character is sentimental... Because of our emotivity we are fragile and sensitive, everything reaches and harms us. Reluctance makes us see the world with meek disdain and melancholy causes us to relive the past, with a painful memory. This character constitutes a base over which anxiety, like a pendulum swings back and forth. (94)

Like Ramos, Uranga sustains that a fundamental cause of this ontological wound is Mexico's historical dependence on Spain, which the national subject attempts to deny. According to Uranga, the denial of the Spanish heritage manifests itself in an oscillation between the "pelado" and the "decente". These were archetypes that Yáñez also employed in his introduction to Joaquín Fernández de Lizardi's *Periquillo Sarniento*. In Yáñez's essay, the "decente" is the affected, upper class Mexican, who denigrates the "pelado" as belonging to an inferior social class. He is "the man of formulas, of habits, who can't live without a mask and is inspired in a climate of dissimulation, of hypocrisy." (xxxiv) In Uranga's scheme, the "decente" is not separate from the "pelado" but rather coexists in the interior of every Mexican. In fact, he argues that the Mexican character is determined by "the incessant struggle between the two." (60) On the one hand, the "pelado" reacts to the superiority of the Spaniard by inverting values. That is, he not only denies that the "superior" values are "superior", but replaces the "superior" values with the "inferior" ones. He tries to defy the "superior" culture by substituting what is noble for what is contemptible. This inversion of values, "sustained with a rude, hard, gross and brutal hand" (59), is cynical and leads to disillusionment, detachment and resignation. On the other hand, the "decente," feeling impotent in the face of the "superior" culture, renounces his independence and submissively accepts his inferiority. Contrary to the "pelado," he puts on an act of appearing refined, delicate, and courteous, but he is just as cynical. Moreover, the "decente" is hypocritical, for behind his apparent scrupulousness he is waiting for the moment to invert values, becoming a "pelado". Inside, the "decente" is desperate and discouraged.

Zea agrees with Uranga that the Mexican has never discovered who he truly is because, throughout his history, he has adopted foreign points of view. In "Dialéctica de la conciencia en México", he argues that since the Conquest, the Mexican has struggled with the feeling that "he has stopped being European but he hasn't decided to be fully Mexican." (92) Zea maintains that the only authentic moment in Mexican history was the Revolution. This movement, he says, was "rooted in the innermost part of Mexican man" and gave the Mexican "a clearer awareness of what is human." (101) "Before the Revolution, this man had remained hidden behind the false, imported images with which he had tried to justify himself." (102)

Zea, whose approach to the study of the Mexican character is more historical than Uranga's (although he was influenced as well by phenomenology), discovers in the Revolution the source of many of the Mexican's most salient traits. However, he tempers his praise of the Revolution by blaming it for leading to a political system that is based on the immediate and practical. He explains in "Dialéctica de la conciencia en México" that after the Revolution political relations became personal rather than abstract, so that the Mexican was inclined to fight for a caudillo rather than an ideal. Furthermore, personal loyalty led to abuses and deceptions, which in turn caused resentment, suspicion, timidity and unreliability. Long-term projects were met with cynicism because of disappointments in the past, so that everything became directed towards the satisfaction of the "here and now". The Mexican, he generalizes, is tentative, mistrustful and lacks a sense of responsibility.

Despite their criticisms of the Mexican, Uranga and Zea compare him favorably to the European. Uranga argues that the Mexican is in closer contact than the European with the "accidentality" that characterizes human existence. This "accidentality" is felt as a pain or anguish:

> The Mexican continuously listens to the voice of his being, in the form of that daily feeling in our life that is the 'grief'... In the Mexican there is a sensation that is almost never dominated of the oppression of being... The 'distrust' and reluctance with which the Mexican approaches everything are demonstrations of his closeness to the accident. (25)

Because he is in touch with the "accidentality" of existence, he represents an excellent means through which to probe man's universal nature: "Our character enjoys a special ontological peculiarity, an exceptionality, as Heidegger would say. More tenuous, more transparent than others, our way of being is an excellent model through which to discern the constitution of man." (36) European man fails to deal with the question of his own being, Uranga concludes, because he identifies being European with being human. The Mexicans, on the other hand, feel they have to constantly justify themselves. It is thus from Mexicans that "the authentic meaning of man must emerge." (50) "From the ontology of the Mexican a Mexican humanism will be extracted, and from there the meaning of man in general and of being in general." (50)

Zea agrees that European man has never considered it necessary to justify himself. "All that he was, his culture, his history and his existence were... the highest expression of what is human, and what wasn't like him was relegated to the lowest category, to barbarity." ("Dialéctica..." 90) However, he argues that the post-War crisis has put this assumption into question, and that the European is now becoming aware of other forms of culture besides his own. In addition, he notes that the colonies are also beginning to gain self-awareness and are rejecting the Europeans' point of view. He points to this as the reason why European philosophy, including existentialism and historicism, is flourishing: "Now they are searching within their own beings for the only worthy justification for their being men." ('Dialéctica..." 91) In *Conciencia y posibilidad del Mexicano* Zea argues further that Mexican man is a model for all of humankind. He says that the Mexican's constant anxiety has made him creative. He adds that, despite contrary beliefs, the Mexican has made good use of technology since the Revolution. In contrast to the Europeans, he has managed to put this technology to the use of man, avoiding becoming a slave to the machine. He has also managed to maintain close personal relations with his fellow men, despite the rapid spread of technology. Thus, unlike other modern countries, the Mexican has avoided the dehumanization caused by machines, while at the same time he has learned to take advantage of the positive aspects of technology.

Lending urgency to Hiperión's work, both Zea and Uranga maintain that the Mexican is in a crucial stage in the process of self-awareness, and that it is time to reject what is inauthentic. Uranga urges Mexicans to take on the responsibility of self-awareness, which he emphasizes is not an easy or comforting task. The philosophers can aid the process, he says, but change ultimately rests on the shoulders of the individual:

> We can't, we shouldn't, remain the same before and after having carried out our self-diagnosis. Let us not convert our reflections on the Mexican into a new formula for imitation, as before we imitated the European, but rather let us understand, once and for all, that being Mexican requires a moral task of purification and responsibility. (10–11)

In the same vein, Zea argues in *Conciencia y posibilidad del Mexicano* that Mexicans are leaving behind a period of irrationality to enter into a rational one, and that this transition will require making readjustments. Thus whereas Ramos likened the Mexican's stage of growth to that of a child or adolescent, in Zea and Uranga's opinion the Mexican is now on the verge of becoming an adult.

Despite their more philosophical and historical approach to studying the national character, Uranga and Zea come to basically the same conclusions as their predecessors concerning the need for self-awareness. However, they go beyond previous writers/philosophers by making the case that Mexicans can form the base for the construction of a universal character and not a strictly national one. This idea was attractive to wealthier and educated Mexicans who were fearful of U.S. cultural invasions and the potential loss of culture and identity this could incur. Uranga and Zea's works also appealed to this group because they pointed out some of the positive aspects of the Mexican character, rather than focusing exclusively on the negative. Their audience could relate to the virtues of the national character while distancing themselves from the defects, which were attributed to the poor (in Uranga's analysis it is the "pelado" who exemplifies the "insufficiencies" from which the Mexican suffers). Octavio Paz would also express this articulation of national identity in his renowned work, *El laberinto de la soledad*.

El laberinto de la soledad

The Hiperión experienced a short life span—1948 to 1952—, and the philosophy of "Mexicanness" went into sharp decline thereafter. Monsiváis attributes this to the banality and semiacademicism into which studies of "Mexicanness" fell. (*Historia general de México* 401) While this is true, it is also important to point out that nationalism as an ideology also waned after 1950. By that time Mexico's most important institutions had been established, political stability was assured, and economic development (in the classical capitalist framework) was underway. The economy was also booming. Nationalism, which included the promotion of "Mexicanness" in film and literature, had served its purpose and was no longer as important. However, one book of essays published during this period was to achieve long-lasting acclaim—*El laberinto de la soledad* (*The Labyrinth of Solitude*) (1952), by Octavio Paz. Along with Ramos's *El perfil del hombre y la cultura en México*, this work constitutes by far one of the most significant studies on the Mexican character.

From the very beginning of his career, in the 1930's, Paz struggled against cultural nationalism and sought to modernize the arts. These efforts were reflected, above all, in his co-founding of literary reviews ("Taller", published from 1938 to 1941, and "El Hijo Pródigo", from 1943 to 1945), and in his poetry and essays. His earlier works expressed a fervent belief in the revolutionary function of art. In his view, art's mission was to oppose rigid ideologies and systems, and to transform man by providing the means by which he could transcend his alienation and solitude. Like the Contemporáneos, Paz believed in aesthetic experimentation and the rejection of art as a nationalistic tool, but he repudiated that group's indifference towards social concerns. His work sought to modify man and society. Of the Taller poets (which besides Paz included Efraín Huerta, Alberto Quintero Álvarez and Neftalí Beltrán), he says:

> For us... poetic and revolutionary activity confused themselves with each other and were the same. To change man demanded the previous changing of society... it was about the urgent need, poetic and moral, to destroy bourgeois society so that total man, poetic man, finally owner of himself, might appear. (Monsiváis *Poesía del Siglo XX. Antología* 55–56)

Paz's works reacted not only against cultural nationalism in Mexico, but also the international threat of dehumanization caused by the increasing spread of technology. Paz was strongly influenced by pessimistic existentialism, which was in vogue in intellectual circles at the time. The themes of authenticity, anguished solitude or incommunication, and the confrontational relationships between individuals—all of which predominate in Paz's writings—owe themselves to the existentialist school. (Katra 5) Ironically, at the same time that Paz sought to free literature and man from repressive ideologies, he himself helped to promote state control. This was reflected in his career as foreign diplomat and in his literary works. As I will attempt to show, *El laberinto de la soledad* reinforces the dominant Mexican ideology of his times, constituting what Jorge Aguilar Mora has called "a civilized form of cultural repression." (58)

In *El laberinto de la soledad* Paz pretends to offer a socially-removed, objective analysis of the Mexican character, but as I will demonstrate, he actually expresses the viewpoints of the middle and elite social classes. The work is motivated largely by the identity crisis experienced by those groups as a result of the increasing Americanisation of Mexican life. According to Gordon Wing, "there exists a curious parallel between the new middle class and the intellectuals of the fifties—in a word, the more Mexican society became Americanised, the more both groups came to stress Mexican uniqueness." (45) He adds: "*El laberinto de la soledad*, and indeed much of Paz's other work of the fifties, represents a sophisticated response to the identity crisis of the new middle classes which they themselves were unable to articulate." (45)

Paz rationalizes this identity crisis by contending that self-contemplation is necessary during certain periods of a nation's growth. To more effectively make his point, he compares Mexico to an adolescent, just as Ramos and Uranga had done:

> The adolescent cannot forget himself... and we cannot escape the necessity of questioning and contemplating ourselves... It is natural that the Mexican should withdraw into himself after the explosive phase of the Revolution, to spend a few moments in self-contemplation. (11)

According to Paz, some Mexicans have already begun the process of self-awareness. While he never specifically names these groups, it is fairly clear that he is referring to the new middle classes, as Aguilar Mora has noted:

> Those he labels "Mexicans who are aware of themselves" turn out to be, although he never explicitly says so, the bourgeoisie who emerged from the Mexican Revolution and the incipient middle class that began to create itself as a result of the emphasis Ávila Camacho and Miguel Alemán (1940–1952) placed on the country's industrialization. If not, what other classes could be those who each day "model the country more to their image?" (44)

Paz praises these Mexicans, who constitute, in his opinion "the only active group in comparison with the Indian-Spanish inertia of the rest." (12) This somewhat condescending reference to other Mexicans is one of many subtle indications throughout the work of Paz's commitment to certain social classes above others. A more obvious one is his portrayal of the pachuco.

Paz employs the pachuco, like Ramos and others did the pelado, as an archetype or point of departure from which to probe the Mexican character. It seems likely he chose to begin the book with this figure for two main reasons. First, because the pachuco lived in the United States without ever having become integrated into that culture, he provided the author with a convincing means by which to contrast the Mexican with the North American. This contrast was important because, as mentioned earlier, the Mexican middle classes wished to differentiate their national identity from that of the North American. Paz admits that the majority of the ideas in the work occurred to him while he was living in the United States. Second, the pachuco is an extreme (the title of the essay is "The *Pachuco* and Other Extremes"), which meant that he was plagued by the most troublesome aspects of the Mexican character (although Paz does not explicitly say so). This is evident in his description of this figure: "The pachuco is an impassive and sinister clown whose purpose is to cause terror instead of laughter…he seeks and attracts persecution and scandal…He is someone who ought to be destroyed." (16–17) The pachuco is the rebellious adolescent who needs to grow up, or rather the Mexican who has no self-awareness (the same image of the pelado found in Ramos's and Uranga's works).

Besides questioning the use of the pachuco archetype, critics have pointed out some major problems with Paz's description of this figure. First of all, the author fails to put the pachuco's behavior within a proper social perspective. For example, he makes no mention of such factors as unemployment, poor working conditions, cultural discrimination, and persecution by the police, all of which helped to define the pachuco's reality. Secondly, his description of the pachuco is overly simplistic and negative. Paz chooses only those characteristics that will aid his study. Since his readership was primarily the Mexican middle-class, they would not relate to the more extreme or pathological aspects of the pachuco, and hence would not react negatively towards this unfavorable description. As William Katra puts it: "Their warm reception of the work suggests their belief that Paz was not speaking about themselves in his pages, but only about their less acceptable, marginalized compatriots, or perhaps the hidden or repressed demons in their own psychology." (7) In fact, some critics have suggested that Paz's negative portrayal of the pachuco captures the resentment felt by the middle classes towards the campesinos who were migrating in large numbers to Mexico City. Like the pachuco, these campesinos were considered a threat to mainstream society. (Katra 11–12)

There was a certain romantic aspect to the pachuco, however, to which Paz and his audience were probably attracted: his solitude. Indeed, this characteristic provides the link between the pachuco and the mainstream Mexican in this work. To Paz, Ramos's inferiority complex was not the underlying determinant of the Mexican character. Rather, the Mexican's sense of orphandom and aloneness was. He explains: "when you sense that you are alone, it does not mean that you feel inferior, but rather that you feel you are different. Also, a sense of inferiority may sometimes be an illusion, but solitude is a hard fact. We are truly different. And we are truly alone." (19) According to Paz, the Mexican's profound sense of solitude causes him to hide behind masks. The Mexican is reserved, defensive, sensitive, suspicious and violent. He doesn't know himself, and won't open up to others. He doesn't tell the truth, for the mere pleasure of it and also to hide himself. And he experiences extreme swings in emotions and behaviors: "melancholy and rejoicing, silence and sheer noise, gratuitous crimes and religious fervor." (19–20) The only time the Mexican will open up, Paz explains, is during the fiestas. It is then that "society communes with itself" and "its members return to original chaos and freedom." (52)

Paz considers the Mexican character to be "a product of social circumstances and history." (70) For example, he says that the colonial period led to Mexicans' closed, unstable attitude, and that the independence period contributed to the perpetuation and strengthening of the servant psychology. He says that Mexicans struggle with "imaginary entities, with vestiges of the past or self-engendered phantasms." These phantasms are supported by a "fear of being." "Everything that makes up the present-day Mexican, as we have seen, can be reduced to this: the Mexican does not want or does not dare to be himself." (73) Like many of the other writers of "lo mexicano", Paz urges the Mexican to confront these phantasms. History can clarify their origins, but it cannot dissipate them, he says. "We must confront them ourselves... We are the only persons who can answer the questions asked us by reality and our own being." (73)

Paz does not privilege one historical moment above another insofar as its impact on the formation of the national character. However, like Zea, he views the Revolution as the only authentic moment in Mexico's history, the one time that Mexicans "refuse all outside help, every imported scheme, every idea lacking some profound relationship to their intimate feelings, and... turn to themselves." (147) To Paz, the Revolution was like a fiesta: "The revolutionary explosion is a prodigious fiesta in which the Mexican, drunk with his own self, is aware at last, in a mortal embrace, of his fellow Mexican." (148) However, he concludes that the lessons of the Revolution have been lost: "The Revolution has not been capable of organizing its explosive values into a world view, and the Mexican intelligentsia has not been able to resolve the conflict between the insufficiencies of our tradition and our need and desire for universality." (168)

Although Paz favors the Mexican male as representative of the national character, he also describes what national identity has meant for the female. His analysis is accurate. However, as critics have pointed out, he actually helps to perpetuate oppressive myths about Mexican women by failing to question their validity. For example, he says that the woman is virtually a creation of the male: "The Mexican woman quite simply has no will of her own. Her body is asleep and only comes really alive when someone awakens her. She is... a vibrant and easily worked material that is shaped by the imagination and sensuality of the male." (37) Furthermore, he reinforces the predominant stereotypes of the female as weak, submissive, and self-sacrificing. Paz explains that women are considered inferior beings in Mexican society because they are submissive and emotional—the antithesis of the ideal of manliness. She is "a dark, secret and passive being... her instincts are not her own but those of the species, because she is an incarnation of the life force, which is essentially impersonal." (36–37) The male takes advantage of the female's "natural" weakness by using her as an instrument to fulfill his needs, which are both sexual and moral. The female thus takes on a dual nature. On the one hand, she is "La Malinche" or "La Chingada", the violated mother, symbol of sexuality and betrayal. On the other hand, she is the long-suffering mother or "Virgin of Guadalupe", who upholds the ideals of family and society.

Paz offsets his largely unflattering portrayal of the Mexican character—both male and female—by comparing him favorably to the North American. To a certain extent Paz romanticizes the Mexican by making him appear in some ways superior to his northern neighbor. For example, he says that while the Mexicans reflect upon their reality, the North American wants to use it. In matters like death, for instance, the North Americans not only have no desire to understand it, but actually avoid the idea. In contrast, the Mexican "is familiar with death, jokes about it, caresses it, sleeps with it, celebrates it; it is one of his favorite toys and his most steadfast love." (57) The North Americans are hygienic, sterile and work oriented, he continues. And they haven't experienced true joy like the Mexicans: "In the hubbub of a fiesta night our voices explode into brilliant lights, and life and death mingle together, while their vitality becomes a fixed smile that denies old age and death but that changes life to motionless stone." (24)

Paz criticizes not only the United States, but advanced capitalism as well. He says that the modern worker "lacks individuality" and is deprived of his human nature by being reduced "to an element in the work process, i.e., to an object. And like any object in the business world, he can be bought and sold. Because of his social condition he quickly loses a concrete and human relationship to the world." (67) Paz finds the Mexican to be unsuited for capitalism. In contrast to the modern worker, the Mexican "works slowly and carefully; he loves the completed work and each of the details that make it up; and his innate good taste is an ancient heritage." (70) Paz adds, however, that "this does not mean that the Mexican is incapable of being converted into what is called a 'good worker.' It is only a question of time." (70) "When this moment arrives," he continues, "it will resolve all our contradictions by annihilating them." (70) In other words, despite his romanticization of the Mexican worker, Paz considers the country's modernization to be necessary and inevitable. As Aguilar Camín puts it: "Paz respects and celebrates revolutionary and popular traditions in Mexico, but favors in the end the material process that denies or dilutes them in order to make way for capitalism." (232).

Paz argues that "Mexicanism" has failed to express the Mexican's individuality. He maintains that it is inauthentic, "a way of not being ourselves, a way of life that is not our own." (169) Although he doesn't explicitly say so, Paz is referring to the "Mexicanism" of the cultural nationalists. This is clear by his criticisms of Vasconcelos, whose philosophy he says "does not contain the essentials of our being or our culture" (155), and in his denunciation of the Marxists. It is evident most of all in his praise of the "anti-nationalistic" writers of "Mexicanism." For example, he says that while "a part of the intelligentsia embraced Marxism (almost always in its official, bureaucratic form)... other men took up the task of revision and criticism." (160) These men included Samuel Ramos, whose book *El perfil del hombre y la cultura en México* constitutes, in Paz's opinion, the "point of departure" for studies on "lo mexicano." Paz contends that, despite the book's limitations, "the majority of its observations are still valid, and the central idea—that the Mexican hides himself when he expresses himself, that its words and gestures are almost always masks—are as true as ever." (160) Paz praises, above all, the work of the young philosophers of his time, including Leopoldo Zea, Edmundo O'Gorman, and Emilio Uranga, whom he says understand the need to find a universal solution to Mexico's problems. They "have realized that the theme of Mexicanism can only be a part of a larger meditation on a much vaster theme: the historical alienation of dependent peoples and of mankind in general." (171) Like this group, Paz believes Mexicans should take off the mask of "Mexicanism" to discover the "genuine human being it disguised." (171) Since "the modern world no longer possesses any ideas", it is up to the Mexicans to "think out for ourselves certain problems which are no longer exclusively ours but pertain to all men." (171) In other words, he envisions a philosophy of man that would emanate from Mexico.

Curiously, in his criticisms of the Mexican intelligentsia, Paz distances himself, speaking of a "they" rather than a "we." He laments that following the Revolution the intellectuals began to work for the state, losing their independence: "They have made compromise both an art and a way of life... they have lost their independence and their criticism has become excessively diluted." (158) As Steven Bell has pointed out, much of what Paz writes about intellectuals could easily be applied to him, yet his "judiciously critical tone in these sections never raises as an issue his own potential implication in the problem." (111) Paz makes it appear as if he were one of the few uncompromised and critical intellectuals. The reader is to believe that Paz is courageously speaking the truth, in contrast to the majority of Mexico's other intellectuals, in particular the cultural nationalists.

Throughout *El laberinto de la soledad* Paz pretends to maintain a critical distance, all the while reinforcing the dominant discourse on national identity. This work contains many of the same elements of former studies on "lo mexicano," although it differs somewhat in its consideration of Mexicans' sense of orphandom and solitude as the main determinants of their character, in its positioning vis a vis the United States rather than Europe, in its treatment of the female character, in its much more complex study of various aspects of the Mexican's behavior and history, and in its far superior prose. His argument also reached a much larger audience, both nationally and internationally. *El laberinto de la soledad* was a great triumph for writers/intellectuals of "Mexicanness."

The Urban Melodrama

At the same time that Uranga, Zea, Paz, and others were underscoring Mexicans' inauthenticity, and calling for self-awareness, film was idealizing "Mexicanness" like never before. To an extent, film even borrowed from literature, only to reformulate literature's articulation of the national character in order to emphasize the positive. For example, *Campeón sin corona* (1945) championed the pelado and the Mexican's so-called inferiority complex. Despite his nagging sense of inferiority, and in fact because of it, the pelado who is featured in this film—a boxer whose lower class status prevents him from succeeding in the sport—is depicted as a lower class hero. The protagonist may not get ahead, but he (and the audience) could take comfort in his inherent goodness. Many other films from the period also seemed intent on countering the Mexican's inferiority complex by emphasizing the many laudable qualities of the national character. These included machismo and authenticity. In contrast, many authors had condemned the Mexican's machismo, and stressed his inauthenticity. Cinema, unlike most literary works, repeatedly portrayed the lower-class urban type, whether it be the pelado, the pachuco or the prostitute, as an exemplary Mexican. In film, this figure suffered from adverse socioeconomic conditions, but always maintained his integrity. One of the few exceptions to this unrestrained romanticization was *Los olvidados* (*The Forgotten Ones*) (1950), by the highly acclaimed director Luis Buñuel. Given its unsparing look at the hard realities of poverty, and its lack of melodrama, it comes as no surprise that this movie was unpopular in Mexico during its time. However, it later achieved wide recognition as one of Buñuel's best films.

Nosotros los Pobres

It is unlikely that any film from the 1940's or early 1950's illustrates cinema's romanticization of poverty, and the huge success that the urban melodrama enjoyed, better than *Nosotros los pobres* (1947), directed by Ismael Rodríguez. This movie was immensely popular during its time. According to Jorge Ayala Blanco, "it has been the biggest and most long-lasting box office success in the history of Mexican cinema. Even today it continues to be exploited commercially in the third and fourth class movie theatres of the capital." (97) It is still shown on television as well. It was this film that thrust Pedro Infante—one of Mexico's most famous actors and singers—into stardom.

Ayala Blanco explains that this film constituted a response to the demands of a growing urban audience for "the elaboration of a mythology that corresponded to its daily life." This public "was anxious to recognize its sensibility and hardships in sympathetic images." (98) The director, Ismael Rodríguez, confirms this assessment in the film's introduction. In this part, two poor children who are digging around in the trash come upon a book that has the same title as the film. In the book's dedication, signed by Rodríguez, the director apologizes for the movie's "crude phrases" and "audacious situations". He explains that his intention has been "to present a faithful portrayal of our poor neighborhoods—which exist in every large city—in which, along with the seven capital sins flourish all the virtues and nobilities, and the greatest of all the heroisms—that of poverty!" He concludes by dedicating the film "to all those simple and good people, whose only sin is to have been born poor."

In the film, the "pelado" Pepe el Toro works contentedly as a carpenter, providing both for his mother and his niece, Chachita, whom his sister abandoned. His problems begin when his girlfriend's stepfather robs him of a large sum of money that was to be used to build a bed for a client. He is then falsely accused of murdering and robbing a moneylender, and sent to jail. Chachita and his mother must stay with his girlfriend's (Celia's) family. While he is in jail, the client ("Licenciado Montes") orders his henchmen to confiscate all of Pepe's belongings, including the chair his mother rested in and the presents he had recently given Chachita for her birthday. Moreover, Celia's stepfather tries to force Chachita to become his servant, and he also attacks the grandmother, whose accusatory gaze (she witnessed him steal the money) he can no longer endure. The grandmother must be hospitalized. When Pepe finds out she is dying, he manages to escape from prison. He discovers that his sister Yolanda is also perishing in the same hospital. Pepe returns to jail only to stumble upon the moneylender's real assassins. He single-handedly fights all three, forcing one of them to confess Pepe's innocence. The movie ends on a happy note as Pepe and Celia (now married and with a newborn child) visit the tombs of Pepe's mother and sister.

Besides satisfying the demands of many lower-class urban Mexicans for flattering images of themselves, *Nosotros los pobres* also benefited the state by attempting to contain social tensions. It did this by instilling a sense of pride in the poor, by providing models of conduct through the hero, Pepe el Toro, by providing catharsis for social discontent, and by offering compensations to the poor for their hardships. This film at once pleased its audience and promoted nationalistic goals.

Pepe represents the state and wealthier Mexicans' ideal image of the poor, urban Mexican. He is devoted to family and community, honest, hard working, pacific, reliable, and content with his lot in life. Likewise, the community in which he resides is cohesive, and while the inhabitants suffer, they make the most of their situation. This is reinforced in the opening scene, in which the community is happily singing, whistling and working together. It is further reinforced through the inhabitants' use of nicknames to refer to each other (the flirt, the tattered drunkard women, the newspaper delivery boy who wants to immigrate to the United States, etc.), and by their constant use of humor, which includes putting catchy phrases on the bumpers of their vehicles. This humor is what Rodríguez tells us provides "the salt that is lacking on their tables."

In stark contrast to Ramos's pelado and Paz's pachuco, Pepe is an exemplary Mexican in whom poor Mexicans could take pride. For example, he is a devoted family man. Although he earns little money as a carpenter, he provides unselfishly for both his mother (who is paralyzed and mute) and his niece, Chachita, whom he treats like a daughter. He is tender and caring as well towards his fiance, Celia. Despite having little contact with his sister, whom he had never forgiven for causing his mother's paralysis and abandoning her daughter, he defends her when she is insulted by a former lover, and comforts her in the hospital as she is dying. Pepe has a strong sense of honor and self-respect. He refuses to accept charity or to join in a potentially lucrative robbery scheme when he is desperate for money. He also demonstrates amazing courage and perseverance in the face of unremitting misfortune. Pepe never complains and always tries to make the best of his situation.

Another outstanding trait of Pepe el Toro is his authenticity. Part of his attractiveness as a person is that he neither attempts to hide his poverty nor to pretend to be something he is not. To the contrary, he is very proud. Furthermore, all of his actions seem to spring straight from his heart. At times, this gets him into trouble. For example, when Chachita chastises him for giving her incorrect information regarding the whereabouts of her mother's tomb, he slaps her. The viewer is inclined to forgive him (as Chachita does) because it is clear that he reacted out of a profound anger and regret at not being able to tell her the truth about her mother, and because he immediately repents by pounding his hand against the door until it bleeds. This incident, and the many times he fights to defend his honor, only further ingratiate him with the audience, who applaud his sincerity.

The female characters are defined by their relationship to Pepe, and lack psychological depth. Through their examples, the film reinforces women's role as caretaker. Chachita, who is only a child, acts as a sort of protective mother to both Pepe and her grandmother. She is constantly crying over others—her mother, Pepe, her grandmother. She is only content when, at the end of the movie, she finally discovers who her real mother was and has "a tomb to cry over." Celia is as devoted to Pepe as Chachita. In her own words, she is "willing to do anything" to be near him and help him. This includes putting up with her abusive stepfather, and offering to become the secretary of licenciado Montes—who has made advances towards her—in return for money to help Pepe get out of jail. Her devotion reaches absurd proportions when she tells her mother that she doesn't care if Pepe murdered his own sister (as rumor has it), and also that she understands why her mother refuses to leave her physically and morally abusive husband. Finally, Pepe's mother, who can neither move nor talk, has little function in the film other than to underscore her son's devotion to his family.

Nosotros los pobres further warns women against sexual promiscuity. It is the "good girl" Celia who wins Pepe's love, not the prostitute who repeatedly flirts with him. More tellingly, Pepe's sister Yolanda serves as an example of the unfortunate fate to which promiscuous women may fall. Yolanda is repeatedly abused by the male, and also loses her family as a result of her philandering. She longs to be welcomed back into the family, but Pepe's honor prevents him from doing this. The movie urges the audience to commiserate with this woman, but at the same time it stresses that her mistakes are too grave to be forgiven. Yolanda ends up dying alone in the hospital, never having been reunited with her family.

Nosotros los pobres aspired to shape the behaviors and attitudes of the poor through the females' and Pepe's example. It emphasized traits such as devotion to family, community and work, integrity, valor, stoicism, and perseverance that would be important in avoiding the social disintegration that could result from immigrants' sudden contact with so-called "modern" society. Pepe and the community in which he lives form a reassuring image of the poor to the privileged classes. They are non-threatening to the status quo, and represent dependable and cheap sources of labor.

Nosotros los pobres further strived to contain social tensions through catharsis. It invites the audience to weep over its woes rather than fight against the injustices perpetrated against them. Because Pepe's machismo prevents him from shedding tears, the sentimentality of the women, particularly Chachita, provides an emotional outlet for the audience.

A final way the film sought to achieve social containment was by offering a number of compensations for the financial hardships suffered by the poor. By casting Pepe as a real macho—tough (never allows himself to be humiliated), popular with the women, and always in charge—, and by defining the women in relationship to him, the film reassured males of their gender superiority. It further attempted to compensate poor Mexicans of both genders by emphasizing their moral and spiritual superiority. It not only idealized the poor, but also portrayed the rich as unhappy and unscrupulous. It sent the message that the poor are better off than the rich because they understand and experience true love. This is verbally expressed by one of the wealthy characters in the film, "Licenciado Montes," who unsuccessfully attempts to woo Pepe's fiance: "I've always had to pay for everything... You the poor are happy because you have love."

Los olvidados

No film of this period could have been more diametrically opposed to *Nosotros los pobres* than *Los olvidados* (*The Forgotten Ones*) (1950), directed by Luis Buñuel. Completely stripped of any romanticization of the poor, this film offered a dismal picture of urban life for Mexico's impoverished masses. Rather than being morally uplifted by their poverty, as in *Nosotros los pobres*, the poor are physically and spiritually degraded by it. Families and communities are broken up and loveless, kids are abandoned, and delinquency abounds. The lower classes do not serve as models of conduct for successfully dealing with modernization, but rather as examples of modernization's catastrophic effects on the human condition. They are also powerless to change their situation. This film perceives little hope for the poor, as clearly stated in the film's introduction: "This film, based on real life, is not optimistic but leaves the solution of this problem to the progressive forces of our time."

Buñuel, who was born in Spain in 1900, came to Mexico in 1944 and lived there until his death in 1983. He made a total of 18 Mexican films during his lifetime. (Wood 41) During his early years in Mexico in the late 1940s he traveled throughout the country and was struck by the miserable living conditions of many Mexicans. This led him to direct *Los olvidados*, an attempt to realistically portray the life of Mexico City's slum children. (Mora 91) The film's merit was immediately recognized. It was exhibited at the 1951 Cannes festival, where Buñuel also received the best director award. (Pérez Turrent 203) However, *Los olvidados* failed to be a box-office hit in Mexico, and Buñuel also had very few followers in Mexico at the time. According to John King, "Buñuel was a radical presence, both inside and outside the industry, but he remained eccentric to the dominant modes of filming and left very few traces in terms of influence or disciples in Mexico." (130)

The film's stark portrayal of the urban poor did not appeal to most Mexican film viewers, who were accustomed to melodramas like *Nosotros los pobres*. It also apparently "bothered certain sectors of the Mexican government and bourgeoisie." (Pérez Turrent 203) By idealizing the poor and the nation, the nationalistic films largely won the approval of both the audience and the state. *Los olvidados*, on the other hand, idealized neither, and was consequently unpopular with the audience and the state. The film portrays the poor as morally depraved, even those who fall victim to crime. For example, a blind man who begs for a living is beaten and robbed by a gang of delinquents, but he in turn practically enslaves an abandoned peasant boy and fondles a young woman against her wishes.

Buñuel attributes the morally abhorrent actions of the poor to poverty itself. Although he is careful to note that Mexico City is like any other large metropolis, Buñuel implicitly blames the state for this situation. As Jean Franco observes, he does this on a symbolic level by making practically all of his characters fatherless, precisely at a moment when the Mexican state is consolidating its paternal authority over its citizens. (154) As Jean Franco adds, he also does this by showing the failure of a modern reform school to help the most problematic youngsters. (156–157) Pedro, resentful that he was sent to the school, angrily kills some of the chickens being raised there. In an attempt to gain the child's trust, the paternalistic director of the school lends him 50 pesos to buy him a pack of cigarettes, and shows the youngster the open door where he can leave. On the way out, Pedro's "friend" Jaibo robs him of the money. Pedro goes after Jaibo to retrieve the money, only to be eventually killed.

In contrast to *Nosotros los pobres*, in which the action takes place primarily indoors, Buñuel makes a point to show his characters' environment. He wants to emphasize that they are living on the fringes of a society undergoing rapid modernization. The new therefore coexists with the old. The frames of high-rise buildings about to be erected stand next to dilapidated constructions and lifeless, empty lots. Ironically, Buñuel used the photographer Gabriel Figueroa, known for his nationalistic esthetic. Figueroa worked on many highly nationalistic films, including *Allá en el rancho grande* (1936), *Flor silvestre* (1943), *María Candelaria* (1943), and *Río escondido* (1947). In *Los olvidados*, his photography is radically different. He romanticizes neither the landscape nor of the people. To the contrary, the surroundings are cold and desolate, and he shows children who are exploited for their labor, and living conditions that are substandard.

The film's action centers on Jaibo, an adolescent who has escaped from reform school. Jaibo is a sort of anti-hero—completely the opposite from "Pepe el Toro." He is a juvenile delinquent and the leader of a gang of adolescents that robs and physically attacks innocent people. There are absolutely no redeeming qualities about him. In fact, Jaibo's brutality is so severe that he winds up killing two adolescents without suffering the least remorse. He beats Julián to death for his alleged responsibility in getting Jaibo sent to reform school, and he does the same to a member of his gang (Pedro) who witnessed the murder and informs on him. Jaibo himself is eventually shot to death by a policeman.

Some of Jaibo's more salient traits fit Ramos and Uranga's description of the pelado, and Paz's description of the pachuco; he is hostile, violent, aggressive, easily provoked, defiant and uneducated. Where Buñuel diverges from those writers' articulation is in his allocation of blame for these anti-social behaviors. In his view, poverty and a lack of opportunities are the main culprits. The writers never mention the impact of socioeconomic factors on the formation of the pelado's character.

As Buñuel sees it, modernization has not brought economic benefits to the slum people. In fact, it has had an adverse effect on them. Poverty has become so intense that everything has been reduced to a commodity. Jean Franco has observed that even milk loses its original status as a gift between mother and child, to be turned into an object of desire that is for sale. (155) More importantly, the characters' lives themselves become objectified. All love has been lost between parent and child, and between neighbors and friends, as each exploits the other in the struggle to survive. Symbolically, at the end of the movie Pedro's dead body is dumped into a trash heap, behind the modern buildings, like any other unwanted object.

Along with the myth of the heroic poor, Buñuel destroys the myth of the woman as willing caretaker of the family. Only two mothers are shown in the film. One is a hypochondriac who lies in bed all day and leaves the domestic chores to her daughter. The other—Pedro's mother—plays a more important role in the movie. She is so beaten down by having to work to provide for her family that she has lost the capacity to love. This has devastating effects on her son. Rejected by his mother, Pedro has turned to street life and membership in a gang. Periodically, he returns home to plea for forgiveness and acceptance. However, his mother remains indifferent, even to his requests for food. As she explains to a police officer, she rejects him because he is the child of a rape and because "I'm tired of working so hard to feed other people." He becomes so desperate for any kind of attention from her that he begs her to hit him for his poor behavior. He also cedes to her demand that he be taken to the authorities for a crime he did not commit—stealing a knife from the store where he finally gets a job (Jaibo is the actual culprit). There, she agrees to have him sent off to a reform school. The mother says goodbye to her son only at the request of the officer in charge, and coldly walks away as he screams to her not to leave him. He has trusted his mother, only to be abandoned. Only at the end of the movie does she show an interest in Pedro, but then it is too late. As she wanders around the neighborhood asking if anyone had seen him, his dead body is being hauled off in a sack strapped over a mule.

The articulation of women in this film radically departs from that of the vast majority of Mexican movies of the time. Buñuel destroys the myth of self-abnegation, and also makes the woman a primary participant rather than a spectator in the male's quest for identity. Pedro's actions, as pointed out earlier, are largely shaped by his desire to win his mother's love. Likewise, Jaibo, who was orphaned at a very young age, yearns for his mother. He has vivid memories of her hovering over him when he was just a baby. Also, an abandoned peasant boy's thirst for motherly love is depicted symbolically when he drinks milk directly from a cow's udder. Despite these differences, however, Buñuel to some extent promoted the standard articulation of the female by linking her with nature and nurture, and by centering the film on the male's rather than the female's search for selfhood.

Buñuel's film offered a marked contrast to the prevailing images of the male, the female, poverty and modernization. It thoroughly destroyed the nationalistic myths being promoted in cinema and other artistic mediums. Viewed in contrast to urban melodramas like *Nosotros los pobres*, it points up the high degree to which those films promoted nationalistic goals. That it was unpopular among the audiences provides further proof of an implicit pact between many filmmakers, the state and film viewers. In this pact, filmmakers gained the approval of the audience by portraying the poor as heroes, at the same time that it promoted nationalistic goals. *Los olvidados*, in contrast, aimed to draw attention to the real problems afflicting the poor. It ended up being a lone voice in the wilderness.

Notes

1. The pachuco was the urban lower class Mexican who migrated to the large cities of the southwestern United States. He was featured not only in the "Tin Tan" movies but also in Octavio Paz's *El laberinto de la soledad*.
2. The term "pelado" referred to the poor Mexican immigrant to the city, who was of mostly indigenous descent.
3. Besides writing extensively on the topic of "Mexicanness" and the possibilities of creating a Latin American philosophy, Zea established a Center of Studies on the Mexican in 1952, which published a collection of investigations titled "México y 'lo Mexicano.'"

Conclusion

Consistently throughout the 1930s and the 1940s many authors constructed images of national identity that were markedly different from those portrayed in the majority of films. Critics like Roger Bartra failed to take into account these differences, viewing articulations of the national consciousness during this period as uniform. As a result, they neglected to see the disparate purposes these constructions served within the nationalist project. As I have attempted to show, through their constructions of national identity, authors and filmmakers appealed to and shaped the interests, desires, and fears of two distinct audiences.

Many authors were writing for the middle class and the educated elite. They expressed a strong interest in the nation's modernization, and viewed themselves as key players in that process. At the same time, however, they were concerned with the loss of cultural identity that might result from modernization and the imitation of North American culture. They therefore analyzed the national character in order to reveal its defects, and exhorted Mexicans to renounce the imitation of foreign cultural models as well as the "false" nationalism being promoted by the cultural nationalists. By discovering the most troublesome character traits in the most disadvantaged Mexicans, they privileged their particular audience and provided an emotional outlet for fears and resentments of the growing number of poor urban immigrants.

Cinema was run primarily by businessmen, and also tended to promote the values and interests of the middle class. However, it needed to take into account a huge popular class audience as well. Articulations of national identity in film sought to address the needs of Mexico's lower classes, and to shape their attitudes and behaviors. Partially subsidized by the government, it attempted to accomplish numerous nationalistic goals; it promoted national unity, identity and pride; it enabled Mexicans to temporarily escape from disturbing societal changes (particularly with the "comedia ranchera"); it provided models of conduct necessary to help maintain social stability and prepare

Mexicans for socioeconomic change; and it defused class antagonisms. Films gained audience approval by portraying the poor as the most authentic and upright Mexicans, an articulation of this group that contradicted that in the novels and essays.

In both the case of the authors and the filmmakers, the challenges facing the country's modernization were viewed as involving primarily the lower classes. It is for this reason that both used archetypes representing the most marginalized Mexicans—the peasant, the Indian and the urban poor. These archetypes reinforced images of the underprivileged that promoted the interests and desires of the middle and elite classes. They were instrumental in preserving the status quo, which privileged wealthier Mexicans and strengthened the state.

Despite their common goals, archetypes of the poor in much of literature were quite different from those in many films. On the one hand, literature tended to construct archetypes that exemplified the problems with the national consciousness. On the other hand, film tended to construct archetypes that exalted the Mexican character. This caused considerable tension between artists and intellectuals, many of whom joined one of two camps: that of the "universalists" or that of the "cultural nationalists." Many authors denounced the "cultural nationalists" for advocating a "false" notion of national identity. They were frustrated by their adversaries' idealization of the national character, which they believed obstructed the process of critical self-analysis and change. This same frustration was not evident in film, which generally supported the cultural nationalists' articulation of national identity. This was probably because filmmakers did not view literature's construction of national identity as a threat to its own. During a period when most Mexicans were illiterate, it was not literature but rather film—which reached the largest audience of any other artistic medium—, that was to construct the predominant image of national identity.

To the state, the polemic between the "cultural nationalists" and the "universalists" was probably of little consequence. First, it did not reach a broad audience, but rather was confined to a group of intellectuals. Secondly, it did not negatively impact the state's nationalistic goals. To the contrary, each group fulfilled its roles within nationalism quite nicely. The authors satisfied wealthy and educated Mexicans through their articulations of national identity, and the filmmakers did the same for the lower classes. Contradictory in and of themselves, constructions of national identity in much of literature and film were complementary within the framework of nationalism.

Glossary

campesino: peasant; poor farmworker

caudillo: strongman; political boss, leader

charro: horseman, cowboy; hacendado (wealthy landowner)

comedia ranchera: a film genre that idealized life on the landed estates, or haciendas, during the porfiriato. It became extremely popular in Mexico and all over Latin America from the mid 1930s to the end of the 1940s.

creole: a person born in Latin America, but of Spanish extraction

ejido: an indigenous form of organization in which land is owned by the entire village and farmed either communally or individually

hacienda: a large privately owned estate, traditionally organized to function as a self-contained unit; it paid its workers minimally and often maintained them through a system of debt peonage

mestizaje: crossbreeding; miscegenation

mestizo: of mixed Spanish and indigenous descent; half-breed, mixed race

modernity: the experience of living in a society characterized by rapid change. It is brought about by "modernization", the process which includes the industrialization of production, technological and scientific discoveries and urbanization.

pachuco: the lower class Mexican migrant to the large cities of the southwestern United States. He was featured not only in the "Tin Tan" movies but also in Octavio Paz's *El laberinto de la soledad*.

pelado: the poor immigrant to Mexico City, who was of partial indigenous descent

porfiriato: the regime under Porfirio Díaz

pueblo: people; country; nation

soldadera: female revolutionary; she fulfilled the domestic needs of the male revolutionaries, and also sometimes fought in battles alongside the men

Works Cited

Primary Sources
Literature

Campobello, Nellie. *Cartucho/My Mother's Hands* Trans. Doris Meyer and Irene Matthews. Introd. Elena Poniatowska. Austin: University of Texas Press, 1988.

—."My Mother's Hands." *Rereading the Spanish American Essay: Translations of 19th and 20th Century Women's Essays.* Ed. Doris Meyer. Austin: University of Texas Press, 1995.

Caso, Alfonso. "Definición del indio y lo indio." *América Indígena* 8.4 (1948): 239–247.

—. "¿El indio mexicano es mexicano?" *El Ensayo Mexicano Moderno.* Ed. José Luis Martínez. Mexico City: Fondo de Cultura Económica, 1958.

—. "La protección de las artes populares." *América Indígena* 2.3 (1942): 25–29.

Cuesta, Jorge. "French culture in Mexico". *The Modern Mexican Essay.* Ed. José Luis Martínez. Trans. H.W. Hilborn. Toronto: University of Toronto Press, 1965. 339–343.

—. *Ensayos políticos.* México, D.F.: Universidad Nacional Autónoma de México, 1990.

—. *Poemas y ensayos.* México, D.F.: Universidad Nacional Autónoma de México, 1964.

Gamio, Manuel. "Las características culturales y los censos indígenas." *América Indígena* 2.3 (1942): 15–19.

—. "Consideraciones sobre el problema indígena en América". *América Indígena* 2.2 (1942): 17–23.

—. "Dialogue on Indian Questions". *Boletín indigenista*. 14.4 (1954): 233–239.

—. *Forjando patria*. Mexico City: Editorial Porrúa, S.A., 1960.

Guzmán, Martín Luis. *La querella de México, A orillas del Hudson, otras páginas*. Mexico City: Compañía General de Ediciones, S.A., 1958.

—. *Obras completas*. Mexico City: Compañía General de Ediciones, S.A., 1961.

López y Fuentes, Gregorio. *El Indio*. Trans. Anita Brenner. New York: Bobbs-Merrill Company, 1937.

Magdaleno, Mauricio. *Sunburst*. Trans. Anita Brenner. New York: The Viking Press, 1944.

Menéndez, Miguel Angel. *Nayar*. Trans. Angel Flores. New York: Farrar & Rinehart, Inc., 1942.

Molina Enríquez, Andrés. *Los grandes problemas nacionales*. Mexico City: Ediciones Era, 1978.

Muñoz, Rafael. *Vámonos con Pancho Villa. La novela de la Revolución Mexicana*. Ed. Antonio Castro Leal. Vol. 2. Mexico City: Aguilar, 1960. 2 vols.

Paz, Octavio. *The Labyrinth of Solitude: Life and Thought in Mexico*. Trans. Lysander Kemp. New York: Grove Press, Inc., 1961.

Pérez Martínez, Héctor. *Cuauhtémoc: vida y muerte de una cultura*. Buenos Aires: Espasa-Calpe, S.A., 1948.

Ramos, Samuel. *The Profile of Man and Culture in Mexico.* Trans. Peter G. Earle. Austin: University of Texas Press, 1962.

Revueltas, José. *Human Mourning.* Trans. Roberto Crespi. Minneapolis: University of Minnesota Press, 1990.

—. "Posibilidades y limitaciones del Mexicano." *Filosofía y Letras* 40 (1950): 255–273.

Uranga, Emilio. *Análisis del ser del Mexicano.* México, D.F.: Porrúa y Obregón, 1952.

Usigli, Rodolfo. *El gesticulador.* Englewood Cliffs, New Jersey: Prentice-Hall, Inc., 1963.

Villoro, Luis. *Los grandes momentos del indigenismo en México.* México, D.F.: Ediciones de la Casa Chata, 1979.

—. "El indio en el alma del mestizo." *Novedades: México en la cultura* 21 Aug. 1949: 1–2.

Yáñez, Agustín. *The Edge of the Storm.* Trans. Ethel Brinton. Austin: University of Texas Press, 1965.

—. "El pensador y la crítica." Introduction. *El pensador mexicano.* By Joaquín Fernández de Lizardi. México, D.F.: Ediciones de la Universidad Nacional Autónoma, 1940.

—. "Meditaciones sobre el alma indígena." *El Ensayo Mexicano Moderno.* Ed. José Luis Martínez. Mexico City: Fondo de Cultura Económica, 1958.

Zea, Leopoldo. *Conciencia y posibilidad del mexicano.* México, D.F.: Porrúa y Obregón, 1952.

—. "Dialéctica de la Conciencia en México." *Cuadernos americanos* 57 (1951): 87–103.

—. *En torno a una filosofía americana*. México, D.F.: El Colegio de México, 1945.

Film

Ahí está el detalle. Dir. Arcady Boytler. Mexico City, 1937.

Allá en el rancho grande. Dir. Fernando de Fuentes. Mexico City, 1936.

Campeón sin corona. Dir. Alejandro Galindo. Mexico City, 1945.

El compadre Mendoza. Dir. Fernando de Fuentes. Mexico City, 1933.

El indio . Dir. Armando Vargas de la Maza. Mexico City, 1938.

Enamorada. Dir. Emilio Fernández. Mexico City, 1947.

Janitzio . Dir. Carlos Navarro. Mexico City, 1934

Los olvidados. Dir. Luis Buñuel. Mexico City, 1950.

Los tres García. Dir. Ismael Rodríguez. Mexico City, 1946.

María Candelaria. Dir. Emilio Fernández. Mexico City, 1942.

Nosotros los pobres. Dir. Ismael Rodríguez. Mexico City, 1947.

Vámonos con Pancho Villa. Dir. Fernando de Fuentes. Mexico City, 1935.

Secondary Sources

Aguilar Camín, Hector. *Saldos de la Revolución: cultura y política de México, 1910– 1980*. México, D.F.: Editorial Nueva Imagen, S.A., 1982.

Aguilar Mora, Jorge. *La divina pareja: historia y mito en Octavio Paz*. México, D.F.: Ediciones Era, S.A., 1978.

Aguirre Beltrán, Gonzalo. "La acción indigenista y sus problemas." *Novedades: México en la cultura* 2 Nov. 1952: 1, 3.

Anderson, Benedict. *Imagined Communities: Reflections on the Origin and Spread of Nationalism*. New York: Verso, 1995.

Ángeles, Noé. "Para comprender a Revueltas: Apuntes." *Revista mexicana de ciencias políticas y sociales*. 34.134 (1988): 203–209.

Aub, Max. "De algunos aspectos de la novela de la Revolución mexicana." *Diálogos* 7.1 (1971): 4–11.

Ayala Blanco, Jorge. *La aventura del cine mexicano en la época de oro y después*. México, D.F.: Editorial Grijalbo, S.A. de C.V., 1993.

Bakhtin, Mikhail. *Rabelais and His World*. Trans. Helene Iswolsky. Cambridge, Massachusetts: M.I.T. Press, 1968.

Barthes, Roland. *Mythologies*. Trans. Annette Lavers. New York: Hill and Wang, 1976.

Bartra, Roger. *The Cage of Melancholy: Identity and Metamorphosis in the Mexican Character*. Trans. Christopher J. Hall. New Brunswick: Rutgers University Press, 1992.

Bell, Steven M. "Contexts of Critical Reception in *El Laberinto de la Soledad* : The Contingencies of Value and the Discourse of Power." *Siglo XX/20th Century* (1992): 101–124.

Berman, Marshall. *All That is Solid Melts into Air: the Experience of Modernity*. New York: Simon and Schuster, 1982.

Blanco, José Joaquín. *Se llamaba Vasconcelos*. Mexico City: Fondo de Cultura Económica, 1977.

Camp, Roderic. "An Intellectual in Mexican Politics, The Case of Agustín Yáñez." *Mester*. 11.2 (1983): 3–17.

—. *Intellectuals and the State in 20th Century Mexico*. Austin: University of Texas Press, 1985.

Carballo, Emmanuel. *Protagonistas de la literatura mexicana.* Mexico City: Editorial Porrúa, S.A., 1994.

Castro Leal, Antonio. Introd. *La novela de la Revolución Mexicana.* México, D.F., 1958.

Castro Quiteño, Norma. "Oponer el ahora y aquí de la vida, el ahora y aquí de la muerte." *Conversaciones con José Revueltas.* Introd. Jorge Ruffinelli. Veracruz, Mexico: Centro de Investigaciones Linguístico-Literarias, Universidad Veracruzana, 1977. 87–92.

Cornejo Polar, Antonio. *Literatura y sociedad en el Perú: La novela indigenista.* Lima: Editora Lasontay, 1980.

Cosío Villegas, Daniel. "L'intellectuel mexicain et la politique." *Intellectuels et état au mexique au xxe siecle.* Paris: Editions de C.N.R.S., 1979. 9–17.

Crespi, Roberto Simón. "José Revueltas (1914–1976): A political biography." *Latin America Perspectives* 6.3 (1979): 93–113.

De la Vega Alfaro, Eduardo. "Origins, Development and Crisis of the Sound Cinema." *Mexican Cinema.* Ed. Paulo Antonio Paranaguá. London: British Film Institute, 1995. 79–93.

De los Reyes, Aurelio. "The Silent Cinema." *Mexican Cinema.* Ed. Paulo Antonio Paranaguá. London: British Film Institute, 1995. 63–78.

Dessau, Adalbert. *La novela de la Revolución Mexicana.* México, D.F.: Fondo de Cultura Económica, 1986.

Díaz Polanco, Héctor. "La teoría indigenista y la integración." *Indigenismo, modernización y marginalidad: una revisión crítica.* Mexico City: Juan Pablos Editor, 1979. 9–47.

Espinsoa, Paul. "Ideology in the Works of Octabio Paz and José Carlos Mariátegui: The Pre-Columbian Case." *Atisbos* (1976–1977): 71–96.

Franco, Jean. *Plotting Women: Gender and Representation in Mexico.* New York: Columbia University Press, 1989.

Freud, Sigmund. *The Future of an Illusion.* Trans. W.D. Robson-Scott. New York: Liveright Publishing Corporation, 1953.

García Riera, Emilio. *Historia documental del cine mexicano.* México, D.F.: Ediciones Era, S.A., 1969.

Hansen, Roger D. *The Politics of Mexican Development.* Baltimore: The Johns Hopkins Press, 1971.

Hernández Luna, Juan. "Biografía de Samuel Ramos." *Obras completas II: hacia un Nuevo Humanismo. Veinte años de educación en México. Historia de la filosofía en México.* By Samuel Ramos. México, D.F.: Universidad Nacional Autónoma de México, 1976. v–xix.

Herrera Sobek, María. *The Mexican Corrido: A Feminist Analysis.* Bloomington: Indiana University Press, 1990.

Hershfield, Joanne. *Mexican Cinema/Mexican Woman: 1940–1950.* Tucson: The University of Arizona Press, 1996.

Ivie, Stanley D. "Política nacional y educación indígena: una comparación entre los Estados Unidos y México". *América Indígena* 31.4 (1971): 955–975.

Katra, William. "Ideology and Society in *El laberinto de la soledad,* by Octavio Paz." *Chasqui* 15.2–3, 1986.

King, John. *Magical Reels: A History of Cinema in Latin America.* London: Verso, 1991.

Labastida, Horacio. "La economía indígena: ¿un límite de la Revolución?" *Novedades: México en la cultura* 23 Nov. 1952: 1–2.

Lempériere, Annick. *Intellectuels, etat et société au Mexico XXe siécle: Les clercs de la Nation.* Paris: Editions L'Harmattan, 1992.

López, Ana M. "Tears and Desire: Women and Melodrama in the 'Old' Mexican Cinema." *Mediating Two Worlds: Cinematic Encounters in the Americas*. Ed. King, John, Ana M. López and Manuel Alvarado. London: BFI Publishing, 1993.

Malmstrom, Dan. *Introduction to Twentieth Century Mexican Music*. Uppsala, Sweden: The Institute of Musicology, Uppsala University, 1974.

Mayer-Serra, Otto. *Panorama de la música mexicana: desde la Independencia hasta la actualidad*. Mexico City: El Colegio de México, 1941.

Medin, Tzvi. *Ideología y praxis política de Lázaro Cárdenas*. Mexico City: Siglo XXI Editores, 1976.

Meyer, Jean. "Mexico: Revolution and Reconstruction in the 1920's." *The Cambridge History of Latin America*. Ed. Leslie Bethell. Vol. 5 New York: Cambridge University Press, 1986. 11 vols.

Meyer, Lorenzo. "El primer tramo del camino." *Historia general de México*. Vol. 4. México, D.F.: El Colegio de México, 1976. 111–201. 4 Vols.

Mistron, Deborah. "The Role of Pancho Villa in the Mexican and the American Cinema." *Studies in Latin American Popular Culture* 2 (1983): 1–13.

Monsiváis, Carlos. "De las relaciones entre 'alta cultura' y 'cultura popular.'" *Texto Crítico* 11.33 (1985): 46–61.

—. *Escenas de pudor y de liviandad*. México, D.F.: Editorial Grijalbo, S.A., 1981.

—. "Landscape, I've got the drop on you!" (On the fiftieth anniversary of sound film in Mexico". *Studies in Latin American Popular Culture* 4 (1985): 236–246.

—. "Mexican Cinema: Of Myths and Demystifications'. *Mediating Two Worlds: Cinematic Encounters in the Americas*. Ed. King, John, Ana M. López and Manuel Alvarado. London: British Film Institute, 1993. 139–146.

—. "No con un sollozo, sino entre disparos (Notas sobre la cultura mexicana 1910–1968)." *Revista Iberoamericana* 55 (1989): 715–735.

—. "Notas Sobre la Cultura Mexicana en el Siglo XX." *Historia general de México* (4): 303–476.

—. *La poesía mexicana del siglo XX. Antología*. México, D.F.: Empresas Editoriales, S.A., 1966.

—. "Pop Culture and Literature in Latin America." *Review: Latin American Literature and Arts* 34 (1985): 9–13.

Mora, Carl. *Mexican Cinema: Reflections of a Society: 1896–1988*. Los Angeles: University of California Press, 1982.

Moraña, Mabel. "Historicismo y Legitimación del Poder en *El gesticulador* de Rodolfo Usigli." *Revista iberoamericana* 55 (1989): 1261–1275.

Morton, Rand. *Los novelistas de la Revolución Mexicana*. Mexico City: Editorial Cultura, T.G., S.A., 1949.

Mraz, John. "How Real is Reel? Fernando de Fuentes's Revolutionary Trilogy." *Framing Latin American Cinema: Contemporary Critical Perspectives*. Ed. Anne Marie Stock. Minneapolis: University of Minnesota Press, 1997. 92-119.

Muñoz, Braulio. *Sons of the Wind: The Search for Identity in Spanish American Indian Literature*. New Jersey: Rutgers University Press, 1982.

Mussacci, Daniele. "Une lecture de *El Resplandor* de Mauricio Magdaleno." *Revista canadiense de estudios hispánicos*. 7.2 (1983): 375–386.

Nickel, Catherine. "Nellie Campobello (b. 1900) Mexico." *Spanish American Women Writers: A bio-Bibliographical Sourcebook*. Ed. Diane E. Marting. New York: Greenwood Press, 1990.

O'Malley, Irene. *The Myth of the Revolution: Hero Cults and the Institutionalization of the Mexican State: 1920–1940*. New York: Greenwood Press, 1986.

Ortega, Adolfo A. "El realismo y el progreso de la literatura mexicana." *Conversaciones con José Revueltas*. Introd. Jorge Ruffinelli. Veracruz, Mexico: Centro de Investigaciones Lingüístico-Literarias, Universidad Veracruzana, 1977. 45–51.

Oviedo, José Miguel. *Breve historia del ensayo hispanoamericano*. Madrid: Alianza Editorial, S.A., 1991.

Parle, Dennis J. "Las Funciones del Tiempo en la Estructura de *El resplandor* de Magdaleno." *Hispania* 63 (1980): 58–68.

—. "Narrative Style and Technique in Nellie Campobello's *Cartucho*. *Kentucky Romance Quarterly* 32 (1985): 201–211.

Parra, Manuel Germán and Wigberto Jiménez Moreno. *Bibliografía indigenista de México y Centroamérica*. Mexico City: Instituto Nacional Indigesta, 1954.

Parra, Max. "Memoria y Guerra en *Cartucho* de Nellie Campobello." *Revista de Crítica Literaria Latinoamericana*. 24.47 (1998): 167-186.

Pérez-Turrent, Tomás. "Luis Buñuel in Mexico." *Mexican Cinema*. Ed. Paulo Antonio Paranagua. London: British Film Institute, 1995. (202–208)

Podalsky, Laura. "Disjointed Frames: Melodrama, Nationalism, and Representation in 1940s Mexico. *Studies in Latin American Popular Culture* 12 (1993): 57–73.

Portal, Marta. *Proceso narrativo de la Revolución Mexicana.* Madrid: Espasa-Calpe, 1980.

Pye, Lucien W. *Crises and Sequences in Political Development.* Princeton: Princeton University Press, 1971.

Rabadan, Antoine. *El luto humano de José Revueltas o la tragedia de un comunista.* México, D.F.: Editorial Domés, S.A., 1985.

Ramírez-Berg, Charles. *Cinema of Solitude: A Critical Study of Mexican Film, 1967–1983.* Austin: University of Texas Press, 1992.

Ruanova, Díaz. "No he conocido ángeles." *Conversaciones con José Revueltas.* Introd. Jorge Ruffinelli. Veracruz, Mexico: Centro de Investigaciones Linguístico-Literarias, Universidad Veracruzana, 1977. 111–114.

Samsel, Roman and Krystna Rodowska. "Charla con José Revueltas." *Plural* 15–12.180 (1986): 22–27.

Schmidt, Donald L. "The Indigenista Novel and the Mexican Revolution." *The Americas* 33 (1977): 652–660.

Schmidt, Henry. *The Roots of Lo Mexicano: Self and Society in Mexican Thought, 1900–1934.* College Station: Texas A&M University Press, 1978.

Schneider, Luis Mario. "Revive la polémica sobre José Revueltas."*Conversaciones con José Revueltas.* Introd. Jorge Ruffinelli. Veracruz, Mexico: Centro de Investigaciones Linguístico-Literarias, Universidad Veracruzana, 1977. 93–105.

Sefkovich, Sara. *México: país de ideas, país de novelas.* Mexico City: Editorial Grijalbo, S.A., 1987.

Sheldon, Helia A. "El arquetipo femenino en 'El Luto Humano' de José Revueltas." *Comunidad* 9.49 (1974): 389–395.

—. *Mito y desmitificación en dos novelas de José Revueltas.* México, D.F.: Editorial Oasis, 1985.

Sheridan, Guillermo. *Los contemporáneos ayer.* Mexico City: Fondo de Cultura Económica, S.A. de C.V., 1985.

Slick, Sam. *José Revueltas.* Boston: G.K. Hall & Co., Twayne Publishers, 1983.

Smith, Anthony D. *National Identity.* Reno: University of Nevada Press, 1991.

Solares, Ignacio. "La verdad es siempre revolucionaria." *Conversaciones con José Revueltas.* Introd. Jorge Ruffinelli. Veracruz, Mexico: Centro de Investigaciones Linguístico-Literarias, Universidad Veracruzana, 1977. 53–59.

Sommers, Doris. *Foundational Fictions: The National Romances of Latin America.* Berkeley: University of California Press, 1991.

Sommers, Joseph. "Literatura e historia: Las contradicciones ideológicas de la ficción indigenista." *Revista de crítica literaria latinoamericana* 5.10 (1979): 9–39.

Stavans, Ilan. *The Riddle of Cantinflas: Essays on Hispanic Popular Culture.* Albuquerque: University of New Mexico Press, 1998.

Steele, Cynthia. "Ideology and the *Indigenista* Novel in the Nineteenth-Century United States and in Twentieth-Century Mexico." *Proceedings of the Xth Congress of the International Comparative Literature Association.* Ed. Anna Balakian and James J. Wilhelm. New York: Garland Publishing Inc., 1985. 76–81.

Tuñón, Julia. "Emilio Fernández: A Look Behind the Bars." *Mexican Cinema.* Ed. Paulo Antonio Paranaguá. Trans. Ana M. López. London: British Film Institute, 1995. 179–192.

Verlinger, Dale E. "Nellie Campobello: Romantic Revolutionary and Mexican Realist." *Latin American Women Writers: Yesterday and Today*. Eds. Yvette E. Miller and Charles M. Tatum. Pittsburgh: Latin American Review, 1975.

Von Ziegler, Jorge. "Novelistas o novela de la Revolución Mexicana." *La palabra y el hombre* Jan.-June 1985: 128–132.

Wing, Gordon. "Octavio Paz, or the Revolution in Search of an Actor." *Books Abroad* 47.1 (1973): 41–48.

Wood, Michael. "Buñuel in Mexico." *Mediating Two Worlds: Cinematic Encounters in the Americas*. Ed. John King, Ana M. López and Manuel Alvarado. London: British Film Institute, 1993. 41–51.

Index

A

A orillas del Hudson, 34–35
agrarian reform, 49, 58–59, 77
Al filo del agua, See *At the Edge of the Storm*
Alemán, Miguel, 12, 131–132, 156
Allá en el Rancho Grande, 47, 97
Allí está el detalle, 11–12, 97–100. *See also* Cantinflas
Análisis del ser del mexicano, 159–164
Anderson, Benedict, 2, 17
archetypes, 7, 10
Armendáriz, Pedro, 125, 150
At the Edge of the Storm, 13, 105–106, 115–121
Ateneo de la Juventud, 35
authenticity, 11, 80–101, 156–157, 158, 165, 172, 174
Avila Camacho, Manuel, 12, 55, 77, 102, 104, 131–132
Azuela, Mariano, *Los de abajo*, 30, 31

B

Barthes, Roland, 2–3
Bartra, Roger, 8–9
Bermann, Marshall, 6, 17, 96
Boytler, Arcady, *Allí está el detalle*, 11–12, 97–100
Buñuel, Luis, *Los olvidados*, 14–15, 157–158, 172, 176–180

C

Campeón sin corona, 172
Campobello, Nellie, *Cartucho*, 10, 30, 42–46
Cantinflas, 6, 12, 13, 27–28, 80, 81–82, 97–101, 157
capitalism, 1–2, 23–24; and indigenism, 133; and Lázaro Cárdenas, 58, 77; and writers, 105–106, 109–110, 115, 117–119, 121, 170
Cárdenas, Lázaro, 54, 58–59, 77, 78, 80, 97, 102, 107, 126
carpas, 27–28, 98
Cartucho, 10, 30, 42–46
Caso, Alfonso, 14, 132, 134–138, 154
Caso, Antonio, 18, 25–26, 28, 35
caudillismo, 1, 36, 42
censorship, 27, 46
charro, 81, 96–97, 105, 122–125
Chávez, Carlos, 20
church, and film, 13–14, 97; and the novel, 11, 70, 72, 105, 114, 117–121
cinema, and the female, 7–8, 123–124, 128–129, 175, 179–180; and the Golden Age, 9; and the Indian, 10, 11, 14, 57, 73–76, 78–79, 132–133, 149–153, 155;

and the revolutionary, 10, 13, 14, 30–31, 46–54, 104–105, 121–122, 125–129; and social control, 4–8; and the urban poor, 11, 12, 14, 15, 80–81, 97–101, 156–158, 172–180; and the 1920's, 18–19, 26–28. *See also* comedia ranchera, melodrama, and comedy
comedia ranchera, 6, 12–13, 47, 81, 96–97, 104–105, 121–125
comedy, 4–6, 27–28, 97–101
communism, 61, 85. *See also* Revueltas, José, and Mexican Communist Party
Conciencia y posibilidad del mexicano, 160, 163–164
Contemporáneos, los, 21–23, 29, 83–84, 102, 165
Cornejo Polar, Antonio, 70–71
cosmopolitanism, *See* universalism
Creoles, and Martín Luis Guzmán, 34; and Samuel Ramos, 83, 84; and Andrés Molina Enríquez, 134
Crisol, 61, 83–84
Cuauhtémoc: vida y muerte de una cultura, 13, 132, 138–141, 153
Cuesta, Jorge, 11–12, 80–81, 82–85, 89–92, 157, 158
cultural nationalism, 9, 12, 18–23, 61; and cinema, 26, 46–47; and women, 43; and writers, 81, 82–85, 88–89, 90–92, 159, 165

D

De Fuentes, Fernando, 47; *Allá en el Rancho Grande*, 47, 97; *El compadre Mendoza*, 10, 30–31, 47–52; *Vámonos con Pancho Villa*, 10, 30–31, 47–48, 52–54
Del Río, Dolores, 125, 150
"Dialéctica de la conciencia en México", 159, 162, 163
Díaz, Polanco, Héctor, 133
Díaz, Porfirio, 2, 23

E

Eisenstein, Sergei, 73–74, 125–126
El compadre Mendoza, 10, 30–31, 47–52
El gesticulador, 11–12, 92–96
El indio (film), 10–11, 73, 75
El indio (novel), 10–11, 56–57, 59–73
El laberinto de la soledad, See *Labyrinth of Solitude, The*
El luto humano, See *Human Mourning*
"El pensador y la crítica," 161
El perfil del hombre y la cultura en México, See *Profile of Man and Culture in Mexico, The*
El resplandor, See *Sunburst*
En torno a una filosofía Americana, 158–160
Enamorada, 13–14, 125–129
Ensayos politicos, 91–92
essay, the, 25, 82

existentialism, 12, 108–109, 163, 165

F

Fanon, Frantz, 23–24
Fernández, Emilio "El Indio," *Enamorada*, 13–14, 125–129; *María Candelaria*, 14, 57, 73, 75, 78, 79, 132–133, 149–153, 155
Figueroa, Gabriel, 125, 178
Forjando Patria, 57–58, 133–134
"French Culture in Mexico," 90

G

Galindo, Alejandro, *Campeón sin corona*, 172
Gamio, Manuel, 14, 132, 134–138, 154; *Forjando Patria*, 57–58, 133–134
Guzmán, Martín Luis, *A orillas del Hudson*, 34–35; *La querella de México*, 34; *La sombra del caudillo*, 10, 30, 33–39

H

Herrera Sobek, María, 7
Hiperión, 155, 158, 164
Hollywood, 9, 19, 27, 46
Human Mourning, 13, 105–115

I

inauthenticity, *See* authenticity

Indian, and archetypes, 7, 10; and the essay, 34, 39, 103; and film, 10–11, 14, 56, 73–76, 126, 132, 149–153; and muralism, 2; and novel, 10–11, 14, 56–57, 59–73, 132, 143–148. *See also* indigenism and integration
indigenism, 11, 14, 57–59, 70–74, 131–155
Infante, Pedro, 15, 122, 173
inferiority complex, 11, 26, 86, 87, 94, 138–139, 159, 160, 168, 172
integration, and Indian, 11, 59, 71, 56–57, 131–155
intellectuals, 3–4, 10, 30, 33, 35, 46, 55, 60–61, 83–85, 106, 115, 155, 166, 171

J

Janitzio, 10–11, 73, 74–75, 149

L

La querella de México, 34
La raza cósmica, 26, 86, 142, 155
La sombra del caudillo, 10, 30, 33–39
Labyrinth of Solitude, The, 14–15, 156–157, 164–172, 178, 181
Liga de Escritores y Artistas Revolucionarios (LEAR), 61
Lola Casanova, 155
López y Fuentes, Gregorio, *El*

indio, 10–11, 56–57, 59–73
Los de abajo, 30, 31
Los grandes momentos del indigenismo, 132, 138–139, 141–143, 153, 155
Los grandes problemas nacionales, 133–134
Los olvidados, 14–15, 157–158, 172, 176–180
Los tres García, 13, 122–125

M

machismo, and film, 8, 12, 52–54, 81, 97, 121–129; and literature, 40, 172
Magdaleno, Mauricio, *Sunburst*, 10–11, 56–57, 59–73; and film, 47–48, 125
Malinche, la, 7–8, 152, 169
marxism, 61. *See also* Revueltas, José
María Candelaria, 14, 57, 73, 75, 78, 79, 132–133, 149–153, 155
"Meditations on the Indigenous Soul," 132, 138–141, 153
melodrama, 4–5, 12–13, 15, 27, 74; revolutionary melodrama, 121–122, 125–129; urban melodrama, 157, 172–176, 177
Menéndez, Miguel Angel, *Nayar*, 14, 132, 143–148
mestizaje, 14, 26, 112–114, 131–155
mestizo, 14, 34, 60, 63–64, 69–70, 75, 78, 131–155
Mexican Communist Party, 61; and José Revueltas, 106–108, 11
Mexican Revolution, The, 1–3, 5, 9; and the essay, 162, 168–169; and film, 10, 13–14, 27, 30–31, 46–54, 75, 97, 104–105, 122, 125–129; and the Indian, 56; and intellectuals, 23–24, 85; and the novel, 10–11, 13, 30, 31–46, 60, 62–63, 69, 104, 105, 106, 117, 121
modernity, 1, 4, 6, 9, 11, 16, 17, 96
modernization, 17, 80, 102, 131; and film, 5–7, 13, 15, 96, 122; and literature, 81, 89, 96; and national identity, 3
Molina Enríquez, Andrés, *Los grandes problemas nacionales*, 133–134
Muñoz, Rafael, *Vámonos con Pancho Villa*, 10, 30–31, 39–42
muralism, 2, 19–20, 48, 56; and film, 125–126
myth, 2–3

N

nation, 2, 6, 17
national identity, 1–4, 6–10, 15–16, 23, 182–184; and archetypes, 7; and female, 7–8, 10, 42–46, 113–114, 123–124, 128–129, 169, 175, 179–180; and the Indian, 10–11, 14, 56–79, 131–155; and machismo, 8,

12, 40, 52–54, 81, 97, 121–129, 172; and the mestizo, 60, 131–155; and 1930s and 1940s, 12–13; and 1920s, 25–26; and the peasant, 10, 13–14, 30–55, 104–122, 125–129; and the urban poor, 11–12, 15, 80–82, 83, 86–87, 97–101, 103, 156–158, 161, 164, 166–168, 172–180
nationalism, 1–4, 23–24, 40, 56–59, 73, 117, 164. *See also* cultural nationalism
Nayar, 14, 132, 143–148
Navarro, Carlos, *Janitzio*, 10–11, 73, 74–75, 149
Nosotros los pobres, 14–15, 157–158, 172–176
novel, and the Indian, 11, 56–73, 132, 143–148; and the Revolution, 10, 13, 30–42, 47–48, 52–54, 105–106, 115–121

O

O'Malley, Irene, 3, 40
Orquesta Sinfónica de México (OSM), 20
Ortega y Gasset, José, 85

P

pachuco, 181; and film, 6, 13, 157, 172; and literature, 166–168
Partido Comunista Mexicano, See Mexican Communist Party
Paz, Octavio, *The Labyrinth of Solitude*, 14–15, 156–157, 164–172, 174, 178, 181
pelado, 6, 10, 11, 12, 12; and film, 80, 81–82, 97–101, 157, 172–176; and literature, 80–81, 82, 86–87, 157, 161, 164
Pérez Martínez, Héctor, *Cuauhtémoc: vida y muerte de una cultura*, 13, 132, 138–141, 153
Profile of Man and Culture in Mexico, The, 11–12, 80–81, 82–89, 93, 95–96, 102, 104, 138, 157, 158, 159–160, 161, 164, 165, 166, 167, 170–171, 174, 178

R

Ramos, Samuel, *Profile of Man and Culture in Mexico, The*, 11–12, 80–81, 82–89, 93, 95–96, 102, 104, 138, 157, 158, 159–160, 161, 164, 165, 166, 167, 170–171, 174, 178
Revolution, See Mexican Revolution, The
revolutionary fighter, and film, 30–31, 46–54, 125–129; and novel, 10, 30–46
Revueltas, José, *Human Mourning*, 13, 105–115
Revueltas, Silvestre, 20
Reyes, Alfonso, 18, 25–26, 28
Rivera, Diego, 19, 151–152

Rodríguez, Ismael, *Los tres García*, 13, 122–125; *Nosotros los pobres*, 14–15, 157–158, 172–176
Rojas González, *Lola Casanova*, 155

S

Santa, 27
Smith, Anthony, 2
socialism, and José Revueltas, 13, 105–11, 115; and Lázaro Cárdenas, 77
soldadera, 128, 129
state, the, and film, 4–5, 26, 46, 48, 125; and intellectuals, 18, 21–25, 33, 39, 55, 106–108, 116; and the male, 97; and national identity, 1–3, 7, 28; and the 1920s, 36; *See also* indigenism
Sunburst, 10–11, 56–57, 59–73

T

Taller, 165
Tamayo, Rufino, 20
Tin Tan, 6, 13, 157, 181

U

universalism, 20–23, 83, 158, 171
Uranga, Emilio, 14–15, 156–157, 158; *Análisis del ser del mexicano*, 159–164
Usigli, Rodolfo, 80–81, 89–90, 157, 159, 160; *El gesticulador*, 11–12, 92–96

V

Vámonos con Pancho Villa (film), 10, 30–31, 47–48, 52–54
Vámonos con Pancho Villa (novel), 10, 30–31, 39–42
Vargas de la Maza, Armando, *El indio*, 10–11, 73, 75
Vasconcelos, José, and Ateneo de la Juventud, 35; and cultural nationalism, 18–22, 23, 43, 83; and film, 26; and *La raza cósmica*, 26, 86, 142, 155; and political campaign, 24–25
Villa, Francisco ("Pancho"), and film, 40, 52–54; and novel, 39–41, 43–44
Villoro, Luis, *Los grandes momentos del indigenismo*, 13, 132, 138–139, 141–143, 153, 155

Y

Yáñez, Agustín, *At the Edge of the Storm*, 13, 105–106, 115–121; "El pensador y la crítica," 161; "Meditations on the Indigenous Soul," 132, 138–141, 153

Z

Zapata, Emiliano, 40, 48, 49
Zea, Leopoldo, 14–15, 156–

157; *Conciencia y posibilidad del mexicano*, 160, 163–164; "Dialéctica de la conciencia en México", 159, 162, 163; *En torno a una filosofía Americana*, 158–160

Currents in Comparative Romance Languages and Literatures

This series was founded in 198, and actively solicits book-length manuscripts (approximately 200–400 pages) that treat aspects of Romance languages and literatures. Originally established for works dealing with two or more Romance literatures, the series has broadened its horizons and now includes studies on themes within a single literature or between different literatures, civilizations, art, music, film and social movements, as well as comparative linguistics. Studies on individual writers with an influence on other literatures/civilizations are also welcome. We entertain a variety of approaches and formats, provided the scholarship and methodology are appropriate.

For additional information about the series or for the submission of manuscripts, please contact:

> Tamara Alvarez-Detrell and Michael G. Paulson
> c/o Dr. Heidi Burns
> Peter Lang Publishing, Inc.
> 516 N. Charles St., 2nd Floor
> Baltimore, MD 21201

To order other books in this series, please contact our Customer Service Department:

> 800-770-LANG (within the U.S.)
> 212-647-7706 (outside the U.S.)
> 212-647-7707 FAX

or browse online by series at:

> www.peterlang.com